ENDORSEME[

"Charles Schmitt's new book, *Are These* [
buster! As a field missionary and missions professor, I am always
eager to find books on eschatology that are aligned with finishing the
Great Commission. Charles' book does a superb job in this area. This
is a 'must read' for clarity on the end times. Any leader will find it to
be an outstanding resource of both exposition and exegesis of all the
scriptural passages on the last days. I highly recommend this book."

—DR. HOWARD FOLTZ
FOUNDER AND PRESIDENT OF
ACCELERATING INTERNATIONAL MISSION STRATEGIES

"Charles Schmitt provides a comprehensive overview of the eschatological prophecies of the Hebrew Bible and the New Covenant Scriptures, interpreting historic and current events in their light, in a
search to answer whether we are living in the end times. While this
overview is thorough and this analysis compelling, perhaps the most
important aspect of this work is its challenge to all believers to ask
themselves, in the words of Peter, *"What kind of people ought we to
be?"* And the answer is clear: we must be ready and on guard, living
lives consecrated to God, making ourselves ready for the return of
Messiah Yeshua."

—AVI MIZRACHI,
DIRECTOR OF DUGIT MESSIANIC OUTREACH CENTRE IN
TEL AVIV, ISRAEL

"Charles Schmitt has written an exceptional book answering the
question that so many are presently asking, 'Are these the last days'
Reading this book is truly a revelation, a genuine 'Road to Emmaus'
experience—a very enjoyable, readable and easy to follow survey of
'that which all of the prophets have spoken'. I so appreciate Charles
Schmitt's thoroughly grounded, Scripturally rooted, and Israel-cen-
tered view of the story of God's unfolding prophetic plan of the ages!"

—JOEL RICHARDSON,
NEW YORK TIMES BESTSELLING AUTHOR OF
Islamic Antichrist AND *Mideast Beast*

"If you think that everything has been written that can be written on Bible prophecy, think again. Charles Schmitt's *Are These The Last Days* bring a fresh and fascinating perspective to a debate that grows louder with every new war, natural disaster or Middle East crisis: namely, are we nearing the end of history as we know it and the triumphant return of Jesus Christ? Exhaustively researched, Scripturally sound and wonderfully written, Charles' latest work is a guidepost for Christian and non-Christian alike as we navigate through these perilous, challenging but exciting times."

—**ERICK STAKELBECK,**
CBN NEWS HOST AND AUTHOR OF
The Brotherhood: America's Next Great Enemy

ARE THESE THE LAST DAYS?

CHARLES P. SCHMITT

CREATION
HOUSE

ARE THESE THE LAST DAYS? by Charles Schmitt
Published by Creation House
A Charisma Media Company
600 Rinehart Road
Lake Mary, Florida 32746
www.charismamedia.com

Design Director: Bill Johnson
Cover design by Lisa Cox
Copyright © 2014 by Charles Schmitt
All rights reserved.

Visit the author's website: www.immanuels.org.

Library of Congress Cataloging-in-Publication Data: 2013952189
International Standard Book Number: 978-1-62136-716-1
E-book International Standard Book Number: 978-1-62136-717-8

First edition

14 15 16 17 18 — 987654321
Printed in Canada

DEDICATIONS

Dedicated to the generation that Jesus declared "will certainly not pass away until all these things have happened" (Matt. 24:34).

And dedicated to my five much loved grandchildren: Chase Patrick, Kai Francis, Dylan Charles, Brooke Morgan, and Hunter Scott. You are called to be a part of "the generation of those who seek him" (Ps. 24:6). May you seek the Lord with your whole heart and find Him in this momentous hour!

My thanks to Dotty, my wife of fifty years. You are an inspiration in all that I set my hand to do!

My thanks to Carol Wilkinson, my faithful secretary for many years. Even after you retired, you patiently worked on this manuscript. This is really your book as well as mine!

And my thanks to Pirkko O'Clock, who patiently proofread every line; and to Undine George, who picked up the torch from Carol to type and retype the many corrections; and to Hayley Johnson, Tom McClay and others for creating the maps and the illustrations. Thank you all so very much!

CONTENTS

Introduction
OPENING THOUGHTS

IN ECCLESIASTES 12:11 SOLOMON wrote, "The words of the wise are like...firmly embedded nails—given by one shepherd." It is the desire of my heart that this prophetic study will be a revelation of our Shepherd's heart. Solomon also wrote: "Of making many books there is no end" (v. 12). There *are* many books outlining dispensational theology and also covenant theology. There are also books on amillennialism and more on premillennialism and a few on postmillennialism. There are studies in abundance on the pre-Tribulation rapture, some on the mid-Tribulation rapture, and now an increasing number on the post-Tribulation rapture.[i] Authors have also come and gone, identifying the Antichrist kingdom—all the way from the Roman Empire to Hitler's Nazi Socialism to communism—all viable candidates in their day. And then there is the lawless one himself—from Nero to Hitler to Stalin to Gorbachev (with the interesting birthmark on his forehead), just to name a few.

So what hope do we have in publishing *yet another book* on such an overwritten subject? Perhaps our hope lies in a further insight given by Solomon in Proverbs 4:18: "The way of the righteous is like the first gleam of dawn, which shines ever brighter until the full light of day" (NLT). The wording of the New King James Version speaks of the "shining sun, That shines ever brighter unto the perfect day." That "perfect day" is undoubtedly eschatological in its nature, describing the end of all things, the last days. So, according to Solomon, we can reasonably expect an *increase* in enlightenment and an *expansion* of our understanding as we approach the last

---

i. Appendix 1 gives a brief description of these different theological understandings.

days. Was not Daniel himself told that his prophecies were "closed up and sealed until the time of the end" (Dan. 12:9, NIV)? And that may give us the needed boldness to add yet one more volume to the many volumes that have already been written on the end times, each book meaningful in its own way in its own day.

Paul also describes that perfect day in his words to the Corinthians: "We know in part and we prophesy in part, but when perfection [literally, 'the perfect'] comes, the imperfect disappears" (1 Cor. 13:9–10). Paul then gives us a good idea on how we can wisely and humbly conduct ourselves in our end-time study: "Now I know in part; then I shall know fully, even as I am fully known" (v. 12). Humility confesses that we only "know in part" as we look forward to the coming of "the perfect." And we will want that humility to be ours as we explore together perhaps different ways of looking at certain end-time truths. I like the way Eugene H. Peterson translates 1 Corinthians 13:12–13 in *The Message:*

> We don't yet see things clearly. We're squinting in a fog, peering through a mist. But it won't be long before the weather clears and the sun shines bright! *We'll see it all then,* see it all as clearly as God sees us…But for right now, until that completeness, we have three things to do to lead us toward that consummation: Trust steadily in God, hope unswervingly, love extravagantly. And the best of the three is love.

And so, in that Christlike spirit of love let us venture together into our inquiry: Are these the last days?

PART ONE: A PROPHETIC HANDBOOK OF END-TIME PROPHECIES FROM THE OLD TESTAMENT IN LIGHT OF TODAY'S EVENTS

Chapter 1

THE CONFLICT OF ALL AGES

THE SCRIPTURES ARE the story of the final outcome of a great conflict—a conflict that began in the Garden of Eden with the fall of humankind. Yet in the face of this horrendous fall, it is clear that our omniscient (all-knowing) and omnipotent (all-powerful) God was not caught unawares! In the face of sin and devastation and death, God *already had a plan*. But God's plan, in the words of Peter, could not come to pass without the shedding of "the precious blood of Christ, a lamb without blemish or defect. He was chosen before the creation of the world, but was revealed in these last times" (1 Pet. 1:19–20). And this holy plan was clearly announced by God in the very beginning in the Garden of Eden in the face of man's sin and fallenness.

In the Garden of Eden Jehovah God actually had a prophetic word over the serpent, the form in which Satan disguised himself as he came into the Garden to tempt Eve.

> The LORD[ii] God said to the serpent…"I will put enmity Between you and the woman, And between your seed and her Seed; He shall bruise your head, And you shall bruise His heel."
> —GENESIS 3:14–15, NKJV

This is a striking prophecy! First of all, a conflict began that would be ongoing in every generation between the seed of the serpent (those who carry Satan's DNA) and the Seed of the woman. That Seed of the woman, the Messiah, the Christ, had already been

---

ii. In biblical text, whenever God's name appears as LORD, that usage signifies that the holy tetragram, the four holy consonants (YHVH), appears in the Hebrew text. Translated with vowel sounds, "YHVH" becomes *Jehovah* or *Yahweh*, God's memorial name forever, used over 7,000 times in the Old Testament.

in the plan of God, chosen before the creation of the world. In the words of Jehovah God to Satan, the Promised One would crush the head of the serpent but in the process would receive from the serpent a fatal wound—"You [Satan] will strike His heel" (NIV). What an accurate picture of Calvary! On Skull Hill, Jesus "disarmed the powers and authorities, [and] made a public spectacle of them, triumphing over them by the cross" (Col. 2:15); but that crushing blow to Satan and his demonic hosts would dearly cost the Promised One. Hanging on the cross, He was wounded by venomous fangs with a fatal strike that would cost Him His very own life. Yes, the Promised One "shall crush your head [Satan], and you shall bruise his heel"! And from that time forward, the Book of Genesis, covering some 2,300 years, would be devoted to tracking that holy Promised Seed and tracking the emerging conflict of the ages.

Tracking this Promised Seed, we note that out of the immediate sons of Adam, the family of Seth was chosen. And from the family of Seth, Enosh was chosen. And after him his son Kenan was chosen and then Mahalalel and then Jared, who was the father of the godly Enoch who "walked with God" (just as his great forebearer, Adam, had done in the Garden before the Fall). Enoch's great grandson, Noah, was likewise a God-walker—"he walked faithfully with God"—"a righteous man, blameless among the people of his time" (Gen. 6:9). Of Noah's three sons, God chose Noah's middle son, Shem (which means in Hebrew, "the name," and from which we derive the word *Semite*). God had chosen the Semitic people out of all the other peoples on the earth as the people through whom the Promised Seed would come. Consequently, from the line of Shem came Arphaxad, followed by his son Shelah and then his son Eber (from which we get the word *Hebrew*). Eber brought forth a son named Peleg, who then had a son, Reu, who had a son Serug, who had a son Nahor, who had a son Terah. And Terah was the father of Abram. This Abram would occupy the next quarter of the whole Book of Genesis.

The God of glory miraculously appeared to this Abram while he was living in Mesopotamia (Acts 7:12), and the God of glory promised Abram, "I will make you into a great nation, and I will bless you…and you will be a blessing…and all peoples on earth will be blessed through you" (Gen. 12:2–3). But to this promise of blessing was added a sober note: "And whoever curses you I will curse," referring to this ongoing conflict of all ages. From that day on, time and time again Jehovah God would promise Abram as he journeyed through Canaan:

> All *the land* that you see I will give to you and your offspring ['your seed,' literally] forever.
> —GENESIS 13:15, EMPHASIS ADDED

> The LORD made a covenant with Abram and said, "To your descendants I give *this land,* from the river of Egypt to the great river, the Euphrates."
> —GENESIS 15:18, EMPHASIS ADDED

> The whole land of Canaan, where you are now an alien, I will give as *an everlasting possession* to you and your descendants after you; and I will be their God.
> —GENESIS 17:8, EMPHASIS ADDED

The direct inheritor of these promises of God to Abram (now renamed Abraham) was his son Isaac. Consequently, to Isaac the LORD then promised, "To you and your descendants I will give all these lands and will confirm the oath I swore to your father Abraham. I will make your descendants as numerous as the stars in the sky and will give them all these lands, and through your offspring ["your seed"] all nations on earth will be blessed" (Gen. 26:3–4).

Of Isaac's two sons, Jacob, the younger, would carry this promised seed in his loins (the birthright) and would receive the father's inheritance (the blessing). The Lord consequently promised Jacob, "I will give you and your descendants [this] land...[and] All peoples on earth will be blessed through you and your offspring ['your seed']" (Gen. 28:13–14).

The land would always be of great importance because in it God would build a nation, Israel, and from that nation would come *the Promised Seed,* the Promised One of Genesis 3:15. So throughout Genesis we notice the continual references to "the land" and to "the seed"—two important and everlasting promises. However, because of these promises, the land would also become part of the conflict of the ages, as we shall see.

At this juncture in our overview we need to acknowledge that Abraham had other sons besides Isaac—Ishmael by Hagar and six other sons by Keturah, Abraham's second wife. Isaac also had another son besides Jacob: Esau. All of these sons would be sons of destiny—but in a way different from Isaac and Jacob and in a different land, a land east of the Promised Land. And all of them would have an end-time place in the purposes of God, though in the process they would initially be caught up by the enemy of our souls and contribute to the conflict of the ages by their antagonism and hate. But that is the subject of the next chapter. At this point in time as Genesis closes we see that God has revealed Himself to be "the God of Abraham, Isaac and Jacob."

In Genesis 32 Jacob is renamed "Israel" by God, and Jacob's (Israel's) twelve sons will become the twelve tribal leaders of the twelve clans of Israel as they take possession of the land of Canaan. And so, by the end of Genesis God is well on His way to fulfilling His promise of a Holy Seed who would become the Savior of the world and the Deliverer of His people, for Genesis concludes, as it begins, with a wonderful messianic promise. Of the twelve sons of Jacob, the fourth son is singled out, Judah (from whose name we get the word *Jew*). To Judah this grand promise is given, "Judah, your brothers will praise you; your hand will be on the neck of your enemies; your father's sons will bow down to you. You are a lion's cub, O Judah" (Gen. 49:8–9), hence, the significance of the messianic name "the Lion of the tribe of Judah" in Revelation 5:5. Out of Judah will come that Promised Seed, of whom Jacob continued to prophesy, "The scepter shall not depart from Judah, Nor a lawgiver from between his feet, Until Shiloh [the Man of Peace] comes; And to Him shall be the obedience of the people" (Gen. 49:10).

At the end of Genesis and the beginning of Exodus we trace the history of these twelve clans of Israel—how they migrated from Canaan where they were strangers, down to Egypt where they became slaves, then to their amazing exodus from Egypt under Moses and on to their possession of the Promised Land of Canaan under Joshua. Then after the dismal failure of the Judges, who tried to lead Israel, the monarchy was birthed, and its greatest king, King David, appeared. And so, when we read the genealogy of our Lord Jesus Christ, we are impressed that Jesus is "the son of David, the son of Abraham" (Matt. 1:1), that One promised by Jehovah God in the Garden of Eden, the tragic site of the fall of humankind.

But, according to that original prophecy, the history of humanity was destined to be a history of conflict—the seed with the DNA of the serpent in constant conflict with the Promised Seed—but we are well assured of the end of the matter.

> The end *will* come, when he [the Promised One] hands over the kingdom to God the Father after he has destroyed all dominion, authority and power. For he must reign until he has put all his enemies under his feet....so that God may be all in all.
>
> —1 CORINTHIANS 15:24–25, 28, EMPHASIS ADDED

Chapter 2

THE OTHER SONS OF ABRAHAM

AN ORPHAN SPIRIT hangs over the Arab world. One can see it reflected in the faces of Arab youth as, filled with hatred, they throw their stones and their fire bombs in the streets of cities across the Middle East. That orphan spirit can also be seen reflected in the faces of young Arab suicide bombers, strapped with explosives, as they give their final testimonials before going to their horrific and destructive deaths. This orphan spirit fanned flames of rage in the lives of the two jihadist brothers, Tamerlan and Dzhokhar Tsarnaev, responsible for the massacre in Boston in April 2013, and ignited the suicide bombings threatening the 2014 Olympics in Sochi, Russia. This orphan spirit, the spirit of hopeless abandonment, can be traced back to the very birth of the Arab world.

None of us is free from making mistakes, even big mistakes. But Abram and Sarai's lapse of faith in the promises of God has generated a present-day nightmare of international proportions. Genesis 16:1–4 tells us, "Now Sarai, Abram's wife, had borne him no children. But she had an Egyptian maidservant named Hagar; so she said to Abram…'Go, sleep with my maidservant; perhaps I can build a family through her.'" Hagar's son, Ishmael, was Abraham's firstborn, one of the very few men in Scripture to be directly named by heaven itself. The future prophecy that accompanied Ishmael's naming, however, carried some ominous overtones with it: "You shall name him Ishmael, for the LORD has heard of your misery. He will be a wild donkey of a man; his hand will be against everyone and everyone's hand against him, and he will live in hostility toward all his brothers ['live to the east of all his brothers,' NIV margin]" (Gen. 16:11–12).

I recently pondered Ishmael's circumcision celebration. Here stood a father and his teenage firstborn son, now becoming sons of the covenant together.

> This is my covenant with you and your descendants after you....Abraham was ninety-nine years old when he was circumcised, and his son Ishmael was thirteen; Abraham and his son Ishmael were both circumcised on that same day.
>   —GENESIS 17:10, 24–26

What a happy day that must have been! And then there were the words of that awesome prophecy: "As for Ishmael...I will surely bless him; I will make him fruitful and will greatly increase his numbers. He will be the father of twelve rulers, and I will make him into a great nation" (Gen. 17:20)! What joy that must have brought to young Ishmael's heart! But how short lived was that joy. With the passing of time it became clear that things simply were not working out in that little desert household, and Abraham felt deeply distressed over the boy Ishmael in his mocking attitude toward Isaac, his brother. It seemed best for Abraham and Sarah and Isaac to send Ishmael and Hagar, his mother, away. And so in one day Ishmael's whole life was shattered as he went from being a covenant firstborn son of the household to a wandering, homeless boy. From the rights and inheritance of a son, Ishmael went to being a distraught teenager with only a small bag lunch and a canteen of water strapped to his back. Mother and son wandered in the hot desert of Beersheba and almost died there (Gen. 21:8–16). And that sense of orphan abandonment and fatherlessness has followed the sons of Ishmael to this very day. It is as if it became coded into their very DNA as it passed from generation to generation.

"God heard the boy crying" (Gen. 21:17), and He still hears the boy crying. We are told that half the present population of the Palestinian Authority, for example, are children and teens—all of them spiritual orphans, crying out in pain of heart in the desert. You can see it on their angry faces; you can hear it in their bitter rage. But God is still listening—"Do not be afraid; God has heard the boy crying" (Gen. 21:17). And God is still *speaking*—"Lift the boy up and take him by the hand, for I will make him into a great nation" (Gen. 21:18). I can scarcely read these Scriptures without breaking down; I can scarcely watch current news reports of teenage Arabs rioting in the streets without crying. In the mornings as my wife, Dotty, and I pray at our breakfast table, we seek to "lift the boy up" in prayer that God will harvest millions from the orphaned Arab world for His kingdom! "Take him by the hand, for I will make him into a great nation." Ishmael has a yet unfulfilled destiny, and the need of the hour is for men and women of compassion to "take him by the hand" and patiently lead him out of the labyrinth of deception and hate into the path of peace and healing love! And so we are told "God was with the boy as he grew up. He lived in the desert and became an archer. While he was living in the Desert of Paran, his mother got a wife for him from Egypt" (Gen. 21:20–21). So it was in this region that Ishmael multiplied and increased and lives right up to this very day.

In Genesis 25:12–18 we are given some genealogical thoughts about Ishmael. Nebaioth was Ishmael's firstborn. Kedar was his second born and is claimed to be the ancestor of Muhammad the prophet of Islam. Muhammad himself was an orphan, raised by his uncle. His father, Abdullah, died before his birth; his mother, Aminah, died when he was about six years old. The Quran references his orphanhood: "Did He not find thee an orphan and protect thee?" (93:6). Little wonder that Muhammad, in his own orphan pain, could not understand how God could ever be *a Father* or how Jesus could ever be God's *Son*.

And so overlaying the orphan spirit of Ishmael has come the orphan spirit of Islam, leaving a whole race of people without true sonship but rather with the spirit of slavery that toils ceaselessly to find some way to earn merit with God. But, thank God for those millions of Muslims who *have* received the free gift of God, that they "might receive the full rights of sons" (Gal. 4:5). The Scriptures declare over these: "Because you are sons, God sent the Spirit of his Son into our hearts, the Spirit who calls out, 'Abba [Daddy], Father.' So you are no longer a slave, but a son; and since you are a son, God has made you also an heir" (vv. 6–7)!

The concluding history of Ishmael in Genesis 25:18 tells us that

"His descendants settled in the area from Havilah to Shur, near the border of Egypt, as you go toward Asshur [in the northwestern Arabian wilderness]. And they lived in hostility toward all their brothers ['they lived to the east of all their brothers,' NIV margin]."

THE FAMILY OF ABRAHAM
"SENT AWAY...TO THE LAND OF THE EAST"

Apart from Ishmael, Abraham also had six other sons by Keturah, his second wife. The names of several of these also stand out, for instance, Midian, from whom came the Midianites or Arabs dwelling in the deserts of Arabia, and Sheba, the grandson of Abraham. Sheba was the founder of the Kingdom of Sheba (or Yemen) on the southern end of the Arabian peninsula, from where the Queen of Sheba came.

In conclusion we are told that "Abraham left everything he owned to Isaac. But while he was still living, he gave gifts to the sons of his concubines and sent them away from his son Isaac to the land of the east" (Gen. 25:5–6). And their descendants live in that very geography to this day, carrying in their hearts that same orphan spirit of rejection as their forbearers. But as millions are now coming to Jesus, we can praise God that He has given them that sonship freedom for which Christ has set us free (Gal. 5:1).

Esau, the Grandson of Abraham

Esau, Abraham's grandson, is yet another orphaned firstborn. To his understanding, he had been taken advantage of and cheated by his brother Jacob:

> Esau held a grudge against Jacob…He said to himself, "The days of mourning for my father are near; then I will kill my brother Jacob."
>
> —Genesis 27:41

In this rage of Esau can be found the seeds of what has become that spirit of terrorism today—a hatred passed on from generation to generation among the people who yet live "in the hill country of Seir" (Gen. 36:1), east of the Promised Land, in what is now the northwestern Arabian Peninsula.

One further note about Esau. He had previously married two Canaanite wives, Adah and Oholibamah. When Esau "realized how displeasing the Canaanite women were to his father Isaac...he went to Ishmael and married Mahalath, the sister of Nebaioth and daughter of Ishmael son of Abraham, in addition to the wives he already had" (Gen. 28:8–9). So the circle of pain and rejection was completed in the mingling of the blood lines of Esau and Ishmael—two orphan spirits, two disinherited and rejected firstborn sons, who for all generations would be linked together in their anger and hatred and bitterness.

MOAB AND AMMON, THE SONS OF ABRAHAM'S NEPHEW, LOT

The final branches of Abraham's dysfunctional family tree mentioned in Genesis are Moab and Ammon, the sons of Abraham's nephew, Lot. After the destruction of Sodom and Gomorrah, seeking the preservation of their family line, the two daughters of Lot plotted:

> "Let's get our father to drink wine and then lie with him"....So both of Lot's daughters became pregnant by their father. The older daughter had a son, and she named him Moab ["from father"]; he is the father of the Moabites of today. The younger daughter also had a son, and she named him Ben-Ammi ["Son of my people"]; he is the father of the Ammonites of today.
> —GENESIS 19:32, 36–38

In our day Moab and Ammon, on the eastern side of the Jordan Valley, make up the Hashemite Kingdom of Jordan, Israel's closest eastern neighbor. And at the time of this writing, we find ourselves watching with concern as the Muslim Brotherhood, the mother of all terrorist organizations, is seeking to destabilize Jordan as they did Egypt, turning Jordan into an enemy of Israel, as they are seeking to do in Egypt.

Eight hundred years after the saga of Abraham and his many sons, Asaph, King David's psalmist (1 Chron. 6:31, 39), wrote of the ongoing eight-hundred-year-long hostility of the surrounding Arab world against Israel. Asaph's words are so accurate in describing our current situation that many have taken this psalm as a prophetic end-time psalm written for today:

> O God, do not keep silent; be not quiet, O God, be not still. See how your enemies are astir, how your foes rear their heads. With cunning they conspire against your people; they plot against those you cherish. "Come," they say, "let us destroy them as a nation, that the name of Israel be remembered no more." With one mind they plot together; they form an alliance against you—the tents of Edom [who live to the south of Jordan] and the Ishmaelites [who live on the Arabian peninsula], of Moab [who live in Central Jordan] and the Hagrites [Egypt], Gebal [Lebanon], Ammon [who live in northern Jordan] and Amalek [who dwell in Sinai], Philistia [which is modern-day, troublesome Gaza], with the people of Tyre [Lebanon]. Even Assyria [which includes modern-day Syria, Iraq and Iran] has joined them to lend strength to the descendants of Lot [to Moab and Ammon]....who said, "Let us take possession of the pasturelands of God"....Cover their faces with shame so that men will seek your name, O Lord....Let them know that you, whose name is the Lord—that you alone are the Most High over all the earth.
>
> —Psalm 83

Millennia have now passed and though some of the names have changed, the orphan spirit of rejection and murder has remained and increased to terrifying proportions. Yet throughout the Arab world a promised destiny for the Arab peoples remains unfulfilled, and as we shall shortly see, the prophets of God declare an awesome redemption not only for Israel but for the Arab world in these last days!

Chapter 3

SONGS OF THE KINGDOM

THE PSALMS, TEHILLIM in Hebrew, are the praise songs of Israel. Psalm 90, the earliest psalm, is attributed to Moses, and nearly a dozen other psalms come from the same time period, ascribed to the sons of Korah (possibly descendants of the notorious rebel Korah, who perished in the wilderness in Numbers 16). But by far King David and his prophetic influence permeate the Psalter. Seventy-three psalms, nearly half of the book of songs, are attributed to David. Psalms 72 and 127 carry the name of David's son Solomon, and twelve other psalms are ascribed to Asaph, one of David's choir directors. Two excellent psalms (88 and 89) are attributed to the Ezrahites, Ethan and Heman, musicians in David's court (1 Chron. 15:19).

Consequently, a number of the psalms are *prophetic kingdom songs,* for David was a *prophetic kingdom man* who composed these *kingdom lyrics* in the Spirit. We will look at twelve of these kingdom songs as part of our ongoing inquiry, *Are these the last days?*

PSALM 2

Reflecting on this psalm, a commentary on the Mishnah declares, that we are "...to firmly believe in the advent of Messiah, although he tarries, to wait for him, nonetheless. One must believe that the excellence and prestige of Messiah will surpass that of all kings who ever lived."[1]

Along this line, Psalm 2 has four prophetic movements—the antichrist rage of the nations and their rulers against Jehovah and His Messiah (vv. 1–3), the messianic declaration from the Enthroned One in heaven (vv. 4–6), the proclamation of the Messiah Himself

(vv. 7–9), and the final call to the rulers of the nations to repent before the Messiah (vv. 10–12).

In the first movement (vv. 1–3), we look with anguish as "the nations rage" (NKJV) and "the rulers gather together against the LORD and against his Anointed One [literally, against his Christ, his Messiah]" (NIRV).

Then in verses 4–6, the Enthroned One, the eternal Father, "rebukes them in his anger," sovereignly declaring, "I have installed my king on Zion, my holy mountain."

In verses 7–9, the Messiah makes this proclamation, "He said to me, 'You are my son; today I have become your father.'" This statement is quoted in Hebrews 1:5 and undoubtedly refers to the day of Messiah's physical incarnation—the day "when God [brought] his firstborn into the world" (Heb. 1:6). The Messiah has been promised to receive the nations for His inheritance, and He "will rule them with an iron scepter."

Finally, in verses 10–12, the rulers of the earth are warned: "Serve the LORD with fear...Kiss the Son, lest he be angry.... [for] Blessed are all who take refuge in him"! Psalm 2 is an excellent kingdom song!

PSALM 22

David's Psalm 22 is likewise messianic. Its words are found in the mouth of our Lord Jesus as He hung impaled in agony on the cross: "My God, my God, why have you forsaken me?" (Ps. 22:1; Matt. 27:46). The further words of Psalm 22:8, "He trusts in the LORD; let the LORD rescue him. Let him deliver him since he delights in him," are also found in the mouths of his enemies as they mocked Him as He hung on the cross (Matt. 27:41, 43). The description of Messiah's agonies is also vividly described in Psalm 22:14–18: "I am poured out like water, and all my bones are out of joint. My heart has turned to wax; it has melted away within me [for He died of a broken heart]...my tongue sticks to the roof of my mouth ['I am thirsty,' John 19:28]...they have pierced my hands and my feet...people stare and gloat over me. They divide my garments among them and cast lots for my clothing [John 19:24]."

The psalm then fast forwards from the sufferings of the Messiah to His kingdom glory, acknowledged both by Israel and by all the nations of the earth.

> All you descendants of Jacob, honor him! Revere him, all you descendants of Israel....All the ends of the earth will remember and turn to the LORD, and all the families of the nations will bow down before him, for dominion belongs to the LORD and he rules over the nations.
>
> —PSALM 22:23, 27–28

What an excellent psalm this is, portraying both Messiah's first and second coming. An excellent kingdom psalm!

PSALM 45

Psalm 45 is quoted at length in Hebrews chapter 1 as fulfilled in Yeshua, Jesus, the Messiah. Psalm 45 is a wedding song, and, as such, pictures the Wedding of the Lamb, as recorded in Revelation 19.

> You are the most excellent of men and your lips have been anointed with grace, since God has blessed you forever....In your majesty ride forth victoriously...Let your sharp arrows pierce the hearts of the king's enemies; let the nations fall beneath your feet. Your throne, O God, will last for ever and ever; a scepter of justice will be the scepter of your kingdom. You love righteousness and hate wickedness; therefore God, your God, has set you above your companions by anointing you with the oil of joy....at your right hand is the royal bride in gold of Ophir....[the bride is then addressed:] the king is enthralled by your beauty; honor him, for he is your Lord....[Messiah is then also addressed:] I will perpetuate your memory through all generations; therefore the nations will praise you for ever and ever.
>
> —PSALM 45:2, 4–7, 9, 11, 17

Amen!

Psalms 46, 47, 48

These three psalms by the Sons of Korah are most surely kingdom psalms!

> Nations are in uproar, kingdoms fall....I will be exalted among the nations, I will be exalted in the earth.
>
> —Psalm 46:6, 10

> How awesome is the Lord Most High, the great King over all the earth! He subdued nations under us, peoples under our feet....God is the King of all the earth; sing to him a psalm of praise. God reigns over the nations; God is seated on his holy throne. The nobles of the nations assemble as the people of the God of Abraham, for the kings of the earth belong to God; he is greatly exalted.
>
> —Psalm 47:2-3,7-9

> Great is the Lord, and most worthy of praise, in the city of our God, his holy mountain...Mount Zion [is] the city of the Great King....your praise reaches to the ends of the earth.
>
> —Psalm 48:1-2, 10

Psalm 72

Psalm 72 is a kingdom psalm ascribed to Solomon, the son of David. Solomon's words are most clearly messianic, speaking of the coming Messiah, the Son of David.

> Endow the king with your justice, O God, the royal son with your righteousness....He will endure as long as the sun, as long as the moon, through all generations....He will rule from sea to sea and from the [Euphrates] River to the ends of the earth. The desert tribes [the Arab nations] will bow before him and his enemies will lick the dust. The kings of Tarshish [Spain] and of distant shores will bring tribute to him; the kings of Sheba [Yemen] and Seba [Ethiopia] will present him gifts. All kings will bow down to him and all nations will serve him....May his name endure forever; may it continue as long as the sun. All nations will be blessed through him, and they will call him blessed....Praise be to his glorious name

forever; may the whole earth be filled with his glory. Amen and Amen.

—Psalm 72:1, 5, 8–11, 17, 19

Psalm 89

We have already commented in this book on Psalm 83, and we will touch on Psalm 87 in our final study in Zechariah 14. These are two great kingdom psalms. Ethan's Psalm 89 is also a powerful kingdom psalm, which ultimately focuses on David's greater Son, the Messiah:

> I will set his hand over the sea, his right hand over the rivers. He will call out to me, "You are my Father, my God, the Rock my Savior [Deliverer]." I will also appoint him my firstborn, the most exalted of the kings of the earth. I will maintain my love to him forever, and my covenant with him will never fail. I will establish his line forever, his throne as long as the heavens endure [this is most clearly speaking of Messiah].
>
> —Psalm 89:25–29

Psalm 98

> The Lord has made his salvation known and revealed his righteousness to the nations. He has remembered his love and his faithfulness to the house of Israel; all the ends of the earth have seen the salvation of our God....let them sing before the Lord, for he comes to judge the earth. He will judge the world in righteousness and the peoples with equity.
>
> —Psalm 98:2–3, 9

Psalm 105

Psalm 105 is a celebration of God's covenant promise to the patriarchs.

> He is the Lord our God; his judgments are in all the earth. He remembers *his covenant forever*, the word he commanded, for a thousand generations, *the covenant he made* with Abraham, *the oath he swore* to Isaac. He confirmed it to Jacob

as a decree, to Israel as *an everlasting covenant*: "To you I will give the land of Canaan as *the portion you will inherit*."
—Psalm 105:7-11, EMPHASIS ADDED

And God is not a man that He should ever lie, nor is He a son of man that He should ever change His mind (Num. 23:19)!

PSALM 110

Psalm 110 is one of the most frequently quoted psalms in the New Testament, pointing to Jesus, the messianic King-Priest.

> The LORD says to my Lord, "Sit at my right hand until I make your enemies a footstool for your feet. The LORD will extend your mighty scepter from Zion; you will rule in the midst of your enemies."…The LORD has sworn and will not change his mind: "You are a priest forever, in the order of Melchizedek"…he will crush kings on the day of his wrath. He will judge the nations…crushing the rulers of the whole earth.
—Psalm 110:1-2, 4-6

PSALM 145

Psalm 145 is the final recorded song ascribed to David in the Psalter, a kingdom song of majestic excellence.

> I will exalt you, my God the King; I will praise your name for ever and ever.…All you have made will praise you, O LORD; your saints will extol you. They will tell of the glory of your kingdom and speak of your might, so that *all men* may know of your mighty acts and the glorious splendor of your kingdom. Your kingdom is an everlasting kingdom, and your dominion endures through all generations. The LORD is faithful to all his promises and loving toward all he has made.…*Let every creature praise his holy name for ever and ever.*
—Psalm 145:1, 10-13, 21, EMPHASIS ADDED

This psalm is most surely fulfilled in the words of John in Revelation 5:13: "I heard every creature in heaven and on earth and under the earth and on the sea, and all that is in them, singing: 'To him who sits on the throne and to the Lamb be praise and honor and glory and power, for ever and ever!" Amen and amen!

Chapter 4

THE ROAR OF ISRAEL'S YOUNG PROPHETIC LIONS

The LORD will roar from on high; he will thunder from
his holy dwelling and roar mightily against his land.
—JEREMIAH 25:30

THE FIRST SEVENTEEN books in our Old Testament, from Genesis through Esther, are the books of Israel's history. These are followed by the five books of Israel's poetry: Job, the Psalms, Proverbs, Ecclesiastes, and the Song of Songs. The rest of our Old Testament is made up of seventeen prophetic books. The first of these prophetic writings, Isaiah, Jeremiah, Ezekiel, and Daniel, are major in size and major in content. These are Israel's young prophetic lions, for all of these prophets started their prophetic careers as young men. Though they each prophetically spoke to the impending crisis of their day—the invasion of Judah, the destruction of both Jerusalem and the temple by Babylon, and then the restoration after seventy years—they each also had a clear vision of the Day of the Lord, the end times, that final prophetic hour of human history. Because of the prophetic nature of our inquiry, *Are these the last days?* we will focus on various major end-time themes articulated by Isaiah, Jeremiah, Ezekiel, and Daniel.

THE PROPHECIES OF ISAIAH

The prophecies of Isaiah concerning the Messiah are profound, making the Book of Isaiah one impressive unfolding of redemption through our Lord Jesus Christ! Among the early prophecies of Isaiah we have the promise of the virgin-born Son, "Immanuel," in Isaiah 7:14, the "Wonderful Counselor, Mighty God, Everlasting Father, Prince of Peace" prophecy of Isaiah 9:6, and the profound "shoot…from the stump of Jesse" prophecy of Isaiah 11:1. Also in all these earlier chapters of Isaiah we find an eschatological, or end-time, theme. In the first thirty-nine chapters (which make up part one of the whole Book of Isaiah), the eschatological expression "in that day" appears no fewer than thirty-nine times—all pointing to the Day of the Lord. Among Isaiah's last days prophecies we find words such as these: "In the last days the mountain of the Lord's temple will be established as chief among the mountains; it will be raised above the hills, and all nations will stream to it" (Isa. 2:2). Some may spiritualize this passage away, making it refer to something other than what is apparent, but that is not a wise pathway to follow, as we shall see. In this passage a clear reference is made to "the last days," which actually began with the first coming of our Lord Jesus (Heb. 1:2; 1 Pet. 1:20). The last days, however, were to continue on until the second coming of our Lord Jesus—and that is the theme of these last days prophecies.

Another "in that day" prophecy is found in Isaiah 4:2–6:

> *In that day* the Branch of the Lord will be beautiful and glorious, and the *fruit of the land* will be the pride and glory of the *survivors* in Israel. Those who are *left* in Zion, who *remain* in Jerusalem, will be called holy, all who are recorded among the living in Jerusalem. The Lord will wash away the filth of the women of Zion; he will cleanse the bloodstains from Jerusalem by a spirit of judgment and a spirit of fire. Then the Lord will create over all of Mount Zion and over those who assemble there a cloud of smoke by day and a glow of flaming fire by night; over all the glory will be a canopy. It will be a shelter and shade from the heat of the day, and a refuge and hiding place from the storm and rain. (emphasis added)

Three things stand out in this prophecy, underscoring its end-time nature. Mention is made of the survivors in Israel and "those who are left in Zion" and those "who remain in Jerusalem." This is a note frequently sounded by the prophets, as they see the conflict of the ages involving Israel in the last days; but out of that conflict *a glorious remnant will remain.*

Isaiah also called attention to the cleansing of that remnant—"The LORD will wash away the filth of the women of Zion; he will cleanse the bloodstains from Jerusalem." This redemptive theme is also an ongoing theme that runs throughout the utterances of the prophets. Finally, Isaiah spoke of the glory—another recurring theme of a glorious restoration that also runs throughout the prophets—when he wrote, "Over all the [Shekinah] glory will be a [wedding] canopy." These are clearly prophetic words for the last days.

Yet another "in that day" prophecy appears in Isaiah 11. Note the end-time nuance of these words:

> They will neither harm nor destroy on all my holy mountain, for the earth will be *full* of the knowledge of the LORD as the waters cover the sea. *In that day* the Root of Jesse [speaking of Messiah] will stand as a banner for the peoples; *the nations will rally to him, and his place of rest will be glorious. In that day* the LORD will reach out his hand a second time to reclaim *the remnant* that is left of his people.
>
> —ISAIAH 11:9–11, EMPHASIS ADDED

What inspiring end-time words!

Another fascinating last days prophecy is found in Isaiah 19:23–24: "In that day there will be a highway from Egypt to Assyria [present day Syria/Iraq/Iran]…In that day Israel will be the third, along with Egypt and Assyria [Syria/Iraq/Iran], a blessing on the earth." What eager expectation there is for this to be fulfilled, especially as we see the present, almost uncontrollable hostility of Syria, Egypt, Iraq, and Iran against Israel!

As we turn our eyes toward the second main section of Isaiah (chapters 40–66), we are again impressed with the high degree of messianic content in these chapters, especially in the five beautiful Servant Songs found in Isaiah 42:1–7; 49:1–9; 50:4–11; 52:13–53:12; and 61:1–3. Nothing in all of prophetic Scripture describes Calvary more clearly than the fourth Servant Song from Isaiah 52 and 53!

> He was pierced for our transgressions, he was crushed for our iniquities; the punishment that brought us peace was upon him, and by his wounds we are healed.
>
> —Isaiah 53:5

As in the first main section of Isaiah, references to the last days also abound in the second section of Isaiah:

> The glory of the LORD will be revealed, and all mankind together will see it. For the mouth of the LORD has spoken.
>
> —Isaiah 40:5

> Turn to me and be saved, *all you ends of the earth;* for I am God, and there is no other. By myself I have sworn, my mouth has uttered in all integrity a word that will not be revoked: Before me *every knee will bow;* by me *every tongue will swear.* They will say of me, 'In the LORD alone are righteousness and strength'…in the LORD *all the descendants of Israel will be found righteous and will exult.*
>
> —Isaiah 45:22–25, EMPHASIS ADDED

END-TIME PROMISES FOR THE ARAB WORLD

Isaiah 60 is a powerful end-time prophecy concerning the end-time restoration of many in the Arab world. First, Israel was promised: "Arise, shine, for your light has come, and the glory of the LORD rises upon you….Nations will come to your light, and kings to the brightness of your dawn" (Isa. 60:1, 3). That declaration is followed by this word in verse 6 regarding the Arab world: "Herds of camels will cover your land, young camels of Midian and Ephah." We recall from Genesis 25:1–4 that Midian was one of the sons of Abraham by Keturah and Ephah was Abraham and Keturah's grandson. Midian settled on the western coast of Saudi Arabia with his son Ephah. What an amazing prophecy concerning them!

Isaiah continues in chapter 60, verses 6 and 7: "And all from Sheba [modern-day Yemen] will come, bearing gold and incense [famous in Yemen] and *proclaiming the praise of the Lord.* All *Kedar's* flocks will be gathered to you [Kedar was Ishmael's second born son, who settled in Saudi Arabia; the clan from which, we are told, Mohammad, Islam's prophet was born], the rams of Nebaioth

[Ishmael's firstborn son] will serve you; they will be accepted as offerings on my altar, and I will adorn my glorious temple." And so this becomes a snapshot of the destiny of the Arab world in the last days. The promises to Israel and Jerusalem continue:

> The glory of Lebanon will come to you [there will be no more terrorist strikes from Hezbollah]...The sons of your oppressors will come bowing before you; all who despise you will bow down at your feet and will call you the City of the LORD, Zion of the Holy One of Israel....Then will all your people be righteous and they will possess the land forever...I am the LORD; in its time I will do this swiftly.
> —ISAIAH 60:13–14, 21–22

What wonderful prophetic words of destiny are given to those in the Arab world as well as to Israel!

These prophecies concerning the miraculous restoration of Israel's last-days remnant to the land are perhaps what prompts Isaiah's final questions: "Who has ever heard of such a thing? Who has ever seen such things? Can a country be born in a day or a nation be brought forth in a moment? Yet no sooner is Zion in labor than she gives birth to her children" (Isa. 66:8). The miraculous rebirth of Israel in the earth is a marvel! And Israel's restoration is a divine stroke of holy genius!

In Isaiah 66:18–20 a most unusual prophecy appears:

> I...am about to come and gather all nations and tongues, and they will come and see my glory...I will *send* [as on an apostolic mission] *some of those who survive* to the nations— to Tarshish [west to Spain], to the Libyans [south to north Africa] and Lydians [north to Turkey]...to Tubal [to the Black Sea area] and Greece [to the west], and to the distant islands that have not heard of my fame or seen my glory. They will proclaim my glory among the nations. And they will bring all your brothers, from all the nations, to my holy mountain in Jerusalem as an offering to the LORD.

Isaiah concluded his words with prophetic finality concerning Israel and concerning all mankind: "'As the new heavens and the new earth that I make will endure before me,' declares the LORD, 'so will your name and descendants endure [a promise for Israel]. From one New Moon to another and from one Sabbath to another, all mankind will come and bow down before me,' says the LORD" (Isa. 66:22–24).

So we see that God has given promises to the people of Israel and to the Arab world and to all mankind that He most surely will personally keep, for "God is not a man, that he should lie, nor a son of man, that he should change his mind. Does he speak and then not act? Does he promise and not fulfill?...He has blessed, and [men] cannot change it" (Num. 23:19–20).

THE PROPHET JEREMIAH

Jeremiah's prophecies concerning Israel's physical and spiritual restoration in the last days are clear, as he spoke of the Messiah: "'The days are coming,' declares the LORD, 'when I will raise up to David a righteous Branch, a King who will reign wisely and do what is just and right in the land. In his days Judah will be saved and Israel will live in safety. This is the name by which he will be called: The LORD Our Righteousness [Jehovah Tsidkenu]'" (Jer. 23:5–6).

However, this restoration of Israel in the last days cannot happen apart from great conflict and tribulation, for, "How awful that day will be! None will be like it. It will be a time of trouble for Jacob ['Jacob's trouble,' NKJV], but he will be saved out of it" (Jer. 30:7)!

Chapter 31 of Jeremiah continues to declare several wonderful truths. First of all, God has promised to "make a new covenant with the house of Israel and with the house of Judah" (Heb. 8:8). That New Covenant is now shared by all the redeemed people of God, both Jews and Gentiles, according to Hebrews 8:8–12. Then on the heels of the promise of the New Covenant, these words of prophetic revelation come through Jeremiah concerning the restoration of Israel:

> This is what the LORD says, he who appoints the sun to shine by day, who decrees the moon and stars to shine by night, who stirs up the sea so that its waves roar—the LORD Almighty is his name: "Only if these decrees vanish from my

sight," declares the LORD, "will the descendants of Israel *ever cease to be a nation before me.*" This is what the LORD says: "Only if the heavens above can be measured and the foundations of the earth below be searched out will *I reject all the descendants of Israel* because of all they have done," declares the LORD.

—JEREMIAH 31:35–37, EMPHASIS ADDED

Then at the conclusion of this wonderful promise to Israel we read: "'The days are coming,' declares the LORD, 'when this city [Jerusalem] will be rebuilt for me....The city will never again be uprooted or demolished'" (Jer. 31:38, 40). Some believe that this promise was fulfilled in the return of the people of Judah from the seventy-year Babylonian captivity to rebuild Jerusalem. This cannot be, for God promised that the city would never again be demolished, and in A.D. 70 the city was again destroyed by the Roman General Titus. No, this prophecy is reserved for the last days when Jerusalem will be rebuilt for God, *never again* to be uprooted or demolished! *Never again!*

This end-time prophetic section of Jeremiah contains these powerful words over Israel:

I will make an everlasting covenant with them: I will never stop doing good to them, and I will inspire them to fear me, so that they will never turn away from me. I will rejoice in doing them good and will assuredly plant them in this land with all my heart and soul.... The days are coming," declares the LORD, 'when I will fulfill the gracious promise I made to the house of Israel and to the house of Judah."

—JEREMIAH 32:40–41; 33:14

And all of these promises will be literally fulfilled, for our "God is not a man, that he should lie, nor a son of man, that he should change his mind" (Num. 23:19)!

Chapter 5

THE FIRST OF DANIEL'S FIVE
END-TIME VISIONS
Daniel 2

O F THE FOUR Major Prophets, Isaiah was the *earliest,* prophesying one hundred and fifty years *before* the Babylonian
invasion under the hand of its emperor, Nebuchadnezzar.
In time sequence Jeremiah came on the scene next, prophesying
during the Babylonian invasion, "when the people of Jerusalem
went into exile" (Jer. 1:3). The Lamentations that follow after his
prophecies were Jeremiah's laments over the horrible destruction
of Jerusalem. Daniel came next in time, actually prophesying *from
Babylon* as a part of the exile. His impressive writings are dated
from "the third year of the reign of Jehoiakim king of Judah" (Dan.
1:1), 607 B.C. Finally, Ezekiel the priest began his prophetic ministry
in "the fifth year of the exile of King Jehoiachin" (Ezek. 1:2), the son
of Jehoiakim, in the year 595 B.C. Like Daniel, Ezekiel was one of
the exiles deported from Judah to Babylon. Our focus in these next
chapters will be on Daniel and his profound end-time visions.

THE STERLING CHARACTER OF DANIEL

Daniel, probably in his late teens during the events of chapter 1 of
the book that bears his name, was a youth of sterling character. In
Daniel 1:8 we read that "Daniel resolved not to defile himself" in
the midst of the corrupt and corrupting courts of Nebuchadnezzar,
emperor of Babylon. His sterling character and God-given wisdom
earned him a place in the administration of the government of
Babylon over the seventy years of Babylon's existence. Daniel
served as a government worker and continued on into the administration of the empire that followed—the empire of the Medes and

25

Persians. By doing the math we conclude that Daniel was well into his nineties when he went to his rest, awaiting the resurrection at the second coming of Messiah (Dan. 12:13).

Daniel's was a long and productive life, but his *greatest* achievement was the recording of his five amazing end-time prophetic visions, leaving for us some of the sharpest, clearest insights into the last days that we have. Daniel's five prophetic visions are the large statue in Nebuchadnezzar's night dreams given in 604 B.C. and recorded in chapter 2. This was followed by Daniel's night vision of the four beasts in 555 B.C., found in chapter 7. Then followed Daniel's vision in 551 B.C. of the ram and the goat, in chapter 8, followed by Daniel's revelation of the "seventy sevens," given to him by the angel Gabriel in 539 B.C., recorded in chapter 9. And finally, we have Daniel's fifth vision, a vision of the great war, a powerful revelation revealed to him by an awesome heavenly messenger in chapters 10, 11, and 12. This final vision was given to Daniel in 536 B.C.

Three very important principles emerge from Daniel's five visions. First of all, these five visions do not run in consecutive order. In other words, one vision does not follow the other in sequence of time. The five visions run *parallel* to each other. The vision of chapter 7 runs parallel to the vision of chapter 2; and the vision of chapter 8 runs parallel to the visions of chapters 2, 7, 9, and 10 through 12. Second, all five visions conclude on the same note—the final overthrow of all evil and the final triumph of the glorious kingdom of our God in the Person of the Messiah. Third, each successive vision brings with it *further insights* that are then added to what has already been spoken, so that the prophetic picture *increases* in content and revelation from vision to vision. These three principles will help us to interpret the similar visions of John's *Revelation* when we will conclude our prophetic study with an overview of John's five visions.

THE VISION OF THE GREAT STATUE IN CHAPTER 2

It was the year 604 B.C. Nebuchadnezzar had been on the throne as emperor of Babylon for just two years, and Daniel had been in training for his government post in Nebuchadnezzar's court for just over a year. One night Nebuchadnezzar had a most troubling dream. Though no one else in the court could tell Nebuchadnezzar about his dream, "During the night the mystery was revealed to Daniel in a vision" (Dan. 2:19). Daniel's humble explanation for his insights was this: "There is a God in heaven who reveals mysteries. He has shown King Nebuchadnezzar what will happen in days to come ['in the latter days,' NKJV]" (v. 28). Nebuchadnezzar's dream was prophetic; it was a latter-days revelation, a word for the end times!

Daniel 2:31–33 tells us Nebuchadnezzar saw:

> A large statue—an enormous dazzling statue, awesome in appearance. The head of the statue was made of pure gold [a snapshot of Babylon, for Daniel said to Nebuchadnezzar, "*You* are that head of gold," (v. 38)], its chest and arms of silver [Daniel prophesied to Nebuchadnezzar, "*After you, another kingdom* will rise, inferior to yours" (v.39), the dual kingdom of the Medes and Persians], its belly and thighs of bronze [and Daniel explained, "A *third kingdom*, one of bronze, will rule over the whole earth" (v. 39), Alexander the Great's kingdom of Greece], [and finally] its legs of iron."

On this Daniel declared, "Finally, there will be a fourth kingdom, strong as iron—for iron breaks and smashes everything—and as iron breaks things to pieces, so it will crush and break all the others" (v. 40), an apt description of the Roman Empire with the later overlay of the Islamic Caliphate (A.D. 632–A.D. 1923), which covered much of the *same* basic land area of the Roman Empire, to the east and in North Africa.

The Roman Empire
East and West, First Century

For years, as one trained in evangelical circles I saw only the western European theater of the Roman Empire. Even though I knew from church history that the Roman Empire was a *dual empire* with two legs—picturing both the west (Europe), with its capital at Rome and the east (the Middle East) with its capital at Constantinople—I never connected that church history information to the statue of Daniel 2. Just recently, however, the Lord spoke a clear word to my heart: "You have only been looking at one leg." I realized in an instant that for years I had been doing exactly that, focusing on the western, or Latin, part of the Roman Empire, the European theater, with its capital at Rome. That nudge from the Lord started me on a prophetic search, and I quickly uncovered "the other leg," the eastern part of the Roman Empire, the Middle Eastern arena. And then I realized that it was exactly *this* geography that was making headlines in the news each day for the past several years!

Then the final part of the vision of the statue made more sense than ever before, regarding "its feet partly of iron and partly of baked clay" (Dan. 2:33). Daniel gave a lengthy explanation of that part of the vision:

> Just as you saw that the feet and toes were partly of baked clay and partly of iron, so this will be a divided kingdom; yet it will have some of the strength of iron in it, even as you saw iron mixed with clay. As the toes were partly iron and partly clay, so this kingdom will be partly strong and partly

brittle. And just as you saw the iron mixed with baked clay, so the people will be a mixture and will not remain united, any more than iron mixes with clay.

—DANIEL 2:41–43

The lengthy detail of this part of the vision, and what follows, makes it clear that *this* was the main focus of the whole vision—a focus, as we shall see, that centers on *the last days.*

The two feet and the ten toes of the statue have in them the strength of the iron, which, like the iron of the legs, the ancient Roman Empire itself, speaks of *authoritarian rule.* The clay in the feet and the toes, however, depicts the opposite—the will of the people, easily broken by the iron of authoritarian rule. To try to mix both the iron and the clay simply would not work. These two entities, the iron and the clay, "will not remain united, any more than iron mixes with clay" (v. 43).

In the Arab Spring of 2011 we watched with dismay as we saw the clay of restless humanity clash with the iron of radical Islam's authoritarianism. We saw the Egyptian democracy movement, for example, subverted by the authoritarian Muslim Brotherhood, as the "Arab Spring" transitioned to become the "Arab Winter." And we continue to watch as the populace continues to rise up to oppose authoritarian rule in Egypt. In other Mideastern nations we also see the same struggle with radical Islam, as it seeks to subvert the various democracy movements of the Middle East.

When we then look to the West, to the European front, we see the same dilemma; we see those Mediterranean nations whose economies are literally collapsing because of their lack of financial discipline and spending restraint, threatening to bring down the European Economic Community with them. It is important for us to keep our eyes wide open, for we see in Europe, as we see in the Middle East, the same "iron mixed with clay"—the clash of two ideologies. On November 6, 2012, while I was in Qatar, I was impressed in reading this statement regarding the European Union in the *Gulf Times:*

The core principle of democracy is the ability of citizens to guide the direction of public policy. But today, across Europe, citizens feel impotent. With the economic crisis, the phenomenon is particularly pronounced in Europe's south, where voters sense uneasily that they have little influence in Berlin, where the real decisions are being made.[iii]

The lengthy conclusion to the vision of the statue, which is the final point of the vision, deeply thrills us:

> While you were watching, a rock was cut out, but not by human hands. It struck the statue on its feet of iron and clay and smashed them. Then the iron, the clay, the bronze, the silver and the gold were broken to pieces at the same time and became like chaff on a threshing floor in the summer. The wind swept them away without leaving a trace. But *the rock that struck the statue became a huge mountain and filled the whole earth.*
> —DANIEL 2:34–35, EMPHASIS ADDED

The interpretation of this part of the vision is more awesome than the vision itself:

> In the time of those [final] kings, the God of heaven will set up a kingdom that will never be destroyed, nor will it be left to another people. It will crush all those kingdoms and bring them to an end, but it will itself endure forever. This is the meaning of the vision of the rock cut out of a mountain, but not by human hands.
> —DANIEL 2:44–45

As to the timeline, Daniel told Nebuchadnezzar, "The great God has shown the king what will take place in the future. The dream is true and the interpretation is trustworthy" (Dan. 2:45).

There are those evangelical, biblical scholars who believe that God's establishment of a kingdom that will never be destroyed actually happened when Jesus cried out on the Cross, "It is finished!" They say this kingdom was then literally birthed on the earth when Jesus rose in triumph from the grave. When from His

---

iii Ana Palacio, "Europe's Regional Revolts." *Gulf Times*, November 6, 2012.

ascended glory He then poured out His Holy Spirit, it was upon His people, who would expand this heavenly kingdom everywhere throughout this earth! *And we could not agree more!* That is *exactly* what happened when Jesus went from the cross through the empty grave into His ascended glory, filling everything from the highest heavens to the lowest earth with Himself, the sovereign Lord of all! But we can also believe that we are now at the *finale* of the last days, which began at Jesus' first coming. We now "eagerly await a Savior from [heaven], the Lord Jesus Christ, who by... [His] power... [will] bring everything under his control" (Phil. 3:20–21). The victory *was procured* by Jesus at Calvary, *was provided for* by Jesus at Pentecost, and *will be consummated* by Jesus at His coming!

In the impressive language of 1 Corinthians 15:24–25, 28, our Lord Jesus must continue His sovereign "reign until he has put all his enemies under his feet," and He "hands over the kingdom to God the Father after he has destroyed all dominion, authority and power....so that God may be all in all." According to Daniel 2:44, the Day of the Lord will see this final and complete destruction of every dominion, authority, and power—a victory that was *procured* at Calvary and will be *consummated* at Jesus' appearing. His kingdom will be openly and universally manifest and established as "a kingdom that will never be destroyed, nor will it be left to another people... [for] it will itself endure forever"! Praise God! This is the first prophetic vision recorded by Daniel, and what a vision it is!

Chapter 6

DANIEL'S PROPHETIC EXPERIENCES
IN CHAPTERS 3-6

THE PROPHETIC VISIONS of Daniel are found in chapter 2, and then, leaping over four chapters, in chapters 7 through 12. Interestingly, the language itself changes in chapter 8 from Aramaic (Chaldee) to Hebrew, as if to say that chapters 1 through 7 are for the Babylonians to read and understand in their own language, but the deeper revelation, which begins with chapter 8 and runs through chapter 12, has been written in the Hebrew language for the people of God alone to understand.

However, the chapters between the first and second vision, between chapters 2 and 7, are not simply superfluous material, children's bedtime stories, as we previously thought. These four chapters (3, 4, 5, and 6), contain valuable prophetic truths, illustrated in the real-life experiences of Daniel and his three Hebrew friends. So let us briefly consider them.

GOD'S PROMISE TO KEEP HIS OWN
IN THE HOUR OF TRIAL:
THE PROPHETIC EXPERIENCE OF DANIEL 3

The Lord had previously given an encouraging promise to His people through Isaiah the prophet: "I will be with you...When you walk through the fire, you will not be burned; the flames will not set you ablaze. For I am the LORD, your God, the Holy One of Israel, your Savior" (Isa. 43:2-3). That promise of divine protection was literally fulfilled in the lives of the three Hebrew friends of Daniel in Daniel 3.

Nebuchadnezzar apparently had been quite impressed with his

own vision in Daniel 2, especially that he was that head of gold. So, Nebuchadnezzar erected an image of gold for himself on the plains of Dura that was sixty cubits high and six cubits wide, ninety feet high and nine feet wide in our measurements. It was an image sixty by six, before which everyone was to bow in worship. Sounds similar to the six–six–six image of Revelation 13, before which the world will be required to bow in the last days! But three young men—Shadrach, Meshach, and Abednego—*refused to bow!* They declared, "If we are thrown into the blazing furnace, the God we serve is able to save us from it, and he will rescue us from your hand, O king. But even if he does not, we want you to know, O king, that we will not serve your gods or worship the image of gold you have set up" (Dan. 3:17–18)!

I continually hear from Christians, especially in our effete western world, that they are terrified at the thought of living in the last days. However, there is only one response we should have. If, by the power of the Holy Spirit within us we will take *an unyielding stand* in the midst of whatever Satan may throw at us, we can be assured that our God will come and dance with us in the fire and deliver us out of the trial to His heavenly kingdom! In this we *will* be the living fulfillment of the last-days promise given by Peter, apostle of Jesus: You, "who through faith are shielded ['kept,' NKJV] by God's power until the coming of the salvation that is ready to be revealed in the last time" (1 Pet. 1:5). This is the awesome point of Daniel 3. Our God keeps and shields His own in the fire!

AT THE NAME OF JESUS EVERY KNEE SHALL BOW: THE PROPHETIC EXPERIENCE OF DANIEL 4

The end-time truth found in Daniel 4 in the humiliation of the proud and arrogant Babylonian emperor Nebuchadnezzar, is articulated in his own words: "Now I, Nebuchadnezzar, praise and exalt and glorify the King of heaven, because everything he does is right and all his ways are just. And those who walk in pride he is able to humble" (Dan. 4:37). As we trace the ongoing work of the Holy Spirit in Nebuchadnezzar's life—from his acknowledgement in Daniel 2:47, to his admonition in Daniel 3:28–29, to his personal testimony in Daniel 4:1–3 and 4:34–37, we are impressed that

Nebuchadnezzar, as a result of the patient witness of Daniel and his three Hebrew friends, experienced a genuine conversion. We can believe he is in the kingdom of God today!

The apostolic writers also assure us that in the last days we will see the determination of a sovereign God to *subject all things beneath the feet of Jesus!* What a thrill it is to hear the testimonies of terrorists and suicide bombers, and of mullahs and imams, who have been apprehended by visions of our Lord Jesus Christ and transformed by His saving grace, and who are now living for His honor and glory! Though the judgments of God are severe on the earth in the last days against all those who refuse the final tug of His Holy Spirit, we must *never* lose sight of the fact that there comes out of the tribulation of the last days "a great multitude that no one could count, from every nation, tribe, people and language.... [who] have washed their robes and made them white in the blood of the Lamb" (Rev. 7:9, 14). Islam, for example, represents over one fourth of all the peoples of the earth, and so it is out of Islamic nations and tribes and peoples as well that a good segment of the redeemed multitude will come—so vast a number that no one could count them! In these last days the salvation of our God will be great. And this is the message of Daniel 4. Before our Lord Jesus Christ, every knee will bow and every tongue will confess that He is Lord to the glory of God the Father (Phil. 2:9–11).

THE LORD WATCHES OVER HIS PROPHETIC WORD TO FULFILL IT: THE PROPHETIC EXPERIENCE OF DANIEL 5

The Lord watches over His prophetic word to fulfill it (Jer. 1:12). That is what we learn from Daniel 5. At this same time in history, Ezra testified that "in order to fulfill the word of the LORD spoken by Jeremiah, the LORD moved the heart of Cyrus king of Persia" (Ezra 1:1). Jeremiah himself testified in Lamentations 2:17 that "The LORD has done what he planned; he has fulfilled his word, which he decreed."

Concerning Daniel 5, simply stated, the Lord *predicted* the overthrow of the Babylonian Empire seventy years before it fell. And in September 539 B.C. God fulfilled His word! Verses 30–31 explain, "That very [September] night [in 539 B.C.] Belshazzar, king of the Babylonians, was slain, and Darius the Mede took over the kingdom, at the age of sixty-two." So we today can be assured that *every* aspect of God's end-time plan *will* come to pass. Every end-time prophecy *will* be fulfilled; every word regarding the last days *will* happen as He said. God had prophetically shown Daniel that following Babylon would come the empire of the Medes and the Persians. God identified the Medes and the Persians by name in a prophecy given in 551 B.C., *twelve years before they came to power* (Daniel 8:1, 20), and He named their emperor, Cyrus, by name in Isaiah 44:28 and 45:1, one hundred and seventy-five years before his birth, as the one who would order the rebuilding of the temple of God in Jerusalem! Thus we can be *assured* that because God watches over His Word to fulfill it, *all* that He has spoken concerning these last days *will* come to pass, as He said it would! That is the lesson for us in Daniel 5!

STRUCK DOWN BUT NOT DESTROYED: THE PROPHETIC EXPERIENCE OF DANIEL 6

Paul gives an amazing Daniel-like testimony in 2 Corinthians 4:8–9, 11:

> We are hard pressed on every side, but not crushed; perplexed, but not in despair; persecuted, but not abandoned; struck down, but not destroyed....For we who are alive are always being given over to death for Jesus' sake, so that his life may be revealed in our mortal body.

These verses in *The Message* so powerfully read:

> We've been surrounded and battered by troubles, but we're not demoralized...we've been spiritually terrorized, but God hasn't left our side; we've been thrown down, but we haven't broken....Our lives are at constant risk for Jesus' sake, which makes Jesus' life all the more evident in us.

This is what Daniel 6 is all about. Betrayed by ambitious men, innocent yet condemned to death, Daniel came out of the lion's den more than a conqueror through Him who loved him!

We note that the prophetic Scriptures strangely speak of two seemingly opposite end-time happenings at the same time. Jesus stated concerning these last days: "You will be betrayed even by parents, brothers, relatives and friends, and they will put some of you to death" (Luke 21:16). It is true that if we are not willing to lay down our very lives for Him who laid down His very life for us, we are not worthy to be called His disciples (Matt. 16:24–25). Yet in the same breath Jesus tells us, "Be always on the watch, and pray that you may be able to escape ['to pass safely through'] all that is about to happen, and that you may be able to stand before the Son of Man" (Luke 21:36). So both apparently will be true—some will be put to death; others will "escape all that is about to happen." And our only stand in all of this, as His loyal disciples, is to confess that "Christ will be exalted in my body, whether by life or by death" (Phil. 1:20).

It is interesting to me that I found myself writing these very words while I was concluding a mission to Niger in northwest Africa in the late fall of 2012. We had just learned that two hours away a band of relief workers had been kidnapped by Al-Qaeda terrorists who came across the Mali border. To be truthful, as an American, which is to be high profile in Niger, I was concerned; but I settled the matter in prayer in the presence of the Master, declaring "whether by life or by death," let Christ be exalted in my body. The same is true day by day of the many who continue to serve Jesus in dangerous places such as these, and the same will be true of many in these last days. This is Daniel's testimony in Daniel 6; this is his commitment in the lion's den: "By life or by death, let Messiah be exalted." Chapter 6 brings to us this powerful end-time truth!

We have examined the treasures buried in Daniel chapters 3 through 6. These are not just nice children's stories. These are rich treasures, truths that will strengthen us in the last days!

Chapter 7

DANIEL'S VISION OF THE FOUR BEASTS

Daniel 7

THE BACKGROUND

It was 553 B.C., the first year of the reign of Belshazzar, the final king of Babylon, and fourteen years before the fall of Babylon to the Medes and the Persians. The great city of Babylon, sitting astride the river Euphrates, would fall to the Medes and Persians in September of 539 B.C. The armies of Cyrus would divert the Euphrates River just as the Lord had predicted one hundred and seventy-five years before through the prophet Isaiah in a word given for the yet-unborn Cyrus the Persian, recorded in Isaiah chapters 44:27 through 45:6. As the Euphrates was diverted, its riverbed ran dry, the brass gates in the riverbed that guarded the city from intruders were opened by insiders, the Persian army took the city, and that very night the Babylonian empire fell! Then Cyrus appointed Darius the Mede, the son of Ahasuerus, to the throne (Dan. 5:30).

THE VISION

In 553 B.C., "Daniel had a dream, and visions passed through his mind as he was lying on his bed" (Dan. 7:1). In his vision Daniel saw four great beasts rising up from the Mediterranean. In Daniel 7:4 he writes, "The first was like a lion, and it had the wings of an eagle." Daniel "watched until its wings were torn off and it was lifted from the ground so that it stood on two feet like a man, and the heart of a man was given to it" (v. 4). This wording is similar to the wording used to describe Nebuchadnezzar's insanity and his restoration in Daniel 4. During Nebuchadnezzar's insanity, "his hair grew like the feathers of an eagle and his nails like the claws of a bird" (Dan. 4:33). Nebuchadnezzar described his restoration in

these words: "At the end of that time, I, Nebuchadnezzar, raised my eyes toward heaven, and my sanity was restored. Then I praised the Most High; I honored and glorified him who lives forever" (Dan. 4:34). God had changed Nebuchadnezzar's heart: "The heart of a man was given to [him]" (Dan. 7:4). So we may reasonably conclude that this first beast is clearly a picture of Babylon, and the eagle's wings being torn off and it being given the heart of a man is a picture of the conversion of its first emperor, Nebuchadnezzar.

It is of interest to note that in the similar vision in chapter 2, the four empires were pictured for Nebuchadnezzar as an "enormous, dazzling statue, awesome in appearance" (Dan. 2:31). This is how an unregenerated man would understand the kingdoms of this world. In chapter 7, however, Daniel saw the same world empires as God sees them, as ravaging beasts! The second beast in Daniel's vision was "like a bear" (Dan. 4:5). We believe this to be the empire of the Medes and the Persians. Daniel explained that "it was raised up on one of its sides [depicting the ascendancy of the Persians over the Medes], and it had three ribs in its mouth between its teeth [depicting the Medo-Persian conquest of Lydia, Babylon and Egypt]" (v. 5). This second beast corresponded to the chest and the arms of silver of the statue—the dual empire of the Medes and the Persians.

The third beast that Daniel saw in his night vision was "like a [swift] leopard. And on its back it had four wings like those of a bird [picturing the swiftness of this empire's conquests in all four directions of the world]. This beast also had four heads [indicating the four-fold break up of this kingdom to the east, to the west, to the north, and to the south]" (Dan. 7:6). This beast corresponds to the belly and thighs of bronze of the awesome statue. This third beast was in every detail the Grecian Empire of Alexander the Great, swiftly expanding in all four directions until Alexander was cut down in an untimely death in 323 B.C. at the age of thirty-three. Alexander's empire was then parceled out to his four generals—to the west, to the east, to the north, and to the south.

The fourth and final beast, the beast with iron teeth, depicts the fourth and final empire of the dazzling statue, the iron empire, with its two legs of iron. Daniel's description of this fourth beast empire was "terrifying and frightening" (Dan. 4:7). This fourth beast was "very powerful," and we believe it to be the Roman Empire—including both the European western leg and the Middle Eastern leg. In Daniel's chapter 7 vision, this beast "had large *iron* teeth; it crushed and devoured its victims and trampled underfoot whatever was left. It was different from all the former beasts, and it had ten horns" (Dan. 7:7), corresponding to *the ten toes* of the enormous statue of chapter 2.

So far the two visions run parallel; the four-part statue runs parallel to the four beasts. But now, in the vision of chapter 7, a new component is added to the overall vision. Daniel recorded, "While I was thinking about the [ten] horns [corresponding to the statue's ten toes], there before me was another horn, a little one, which came up among them; and three of the first horns were uprooted before it. This horn had eyes like the eyes of a man and a mouth

that spoke boastfully" (Dan. 7:8). We then see that this "little horn"
actually becomes the main focus of this vision. Daniel said:

> I…wanted to know about the ten horns on [the fourth beast's]
> head and about the other horn that came up, before which
> three of them fell—the horn that looked more imposing than
> the others and that had eyes and a mouth that spoke boastfully.
> As I watched, this horn was waging war against the saints and
> defeating them [a defeat similar to what happened to the three
> young men in the fiery furnace and then to Daniel in the lion's
> den. This would continue] until the Ancient of Days came and
> pronounced judgment in favor of the saints of the Most High,
> and the time came when they possessed the kingdom.
>
> —DANIEL 7:20–22

Then a more comprehensive description of the blasphemous
"little horn" was given to Daniel in these words: "He will speak
against the Most High and oppress his saints and try to change
the set times and the laws [for he is the *lawless one*]. The saints
will be handed over to him for a time [one year], times [two years]
and half a time [half a year]. But the court will sit, and his power
will be taken away and completely destroyed forever" (Dan. 7:25–
26). We see that the focus of Daniel's night vision was clearly this
monstrous "little horn," who came out of the iron beast. And we
have come to know this blasphemous one by various names—the
Antichrist, the lawless one, the man of sin, the beast, the son of
perdition.

The judgment of the Antichrist is then clearly pictured in the
heart of this chapter in verses 9 through 14, and what an awesome
scene this is! In verses 9 and 10 we are transported to a courtroom,
and the Judge is seated:

> As I looked, thrones were set in place, and the Ancient of Days
> took his seat. His clothing was as white as snow; the hair of
> his head was white like wool. His throne was flaming with fire,
> and its wheels were all ablaze [wheels because this is a "mobile"
> throne similar to the one pictured in Ezekiel 1, a "mobile"
> throne enabling God to be in every place and in every age
> at once]. A river of fire was flowing, coming out from before

him [creating the lake of fire spoken of in Revelation 19:20]. Thousands upon thousands attended him; ten thousand times ten thousand [100 million] stood before him. The court was seated, and the books were opened.

Daniel "continued to watch because of the boastful words the horn was speaking" (v. 11). Then Daniel wrote: "I kept looking until the beast [the head of this antichrist empire] was slain and its body destroyed and thrown into the blazing fire" (v. 11). Paul's description of the demise of this man of sin reads: "And then the lawless one [the one of Daniel 7:25 who would 'try to change the set times and the laws'] will be revealed, whom the Lord Jesus will overthrow with the breath of his mouth and destroy by the splendor of his coming" (2 Thess. 2:8). John in Revelation 19:20 also described the beast's final fate: he, along with the false prophet, will be "thrown alive into the fiery lake of burning sulfur."

Daniel, in chapter 7, verse 12, then continues with an interesting sidebar from the courtroom scene—"The other beasts had been stripped of their authority, but were allowed to live for a period of time." We may deduct from that statement that though the original ancient world empires of Babylon, Medo-Persia, Greece, and Rome are historically gone, the spirit that motivated them continues to live on in this present day. The lion we can recognize as England (for the lion is its present-day symbol). The eagle wings torn off the lion would be the colonies of America (for the eagle is the present-day symbol of America). It is important to note that only to this first two-part beast, the lion and the eagle, was "the heart of a man" given. The revival history of England in the 1700s–1800s was the history of a nation whose tender heart was set on God. In the 1900s, this revival torch was passed on to America, who then became God's channel of spiritual blessing worldwide. The bear could well be Russia, for the bear is its symbol, and the leopard, China, the present, fast-moving, economic and military dynamo of Asia. Ultimately only God fully knows what the statement in Daniel 7:12 refers to, but it is possible to see in these four beasts the major power brokers of our time.

Daniel continued with his vision, describing another most powerful turn of events:

In my vision at night I looked, and there before me was one like a son of man ["the Son of Man," KJV], coming with the clouds of heaven…[This is the Messiah Himself!] He approached the Ancient of Days and was led into his presence. He was given authority, glory and sovereign power; all peoples, nations and men of every language worshiped him. His dominion is an everlasting dominion that will not pass away, and his kingdom is one that will never be destroyed.

—Daniel 7:13–14

In the angel's interpretation of the vision, Daniel is also told that not only the Son of Man, but "the saints of the Most High will receive the kingdom and will possess it forever—yes, for ever and ever" (Dan. 7:18), causing us to wonder, who exactly is this Son of Man who receives this everlasting kingdom? We can confidently say that this Son of Man is *the corporate Christ,* made up of Jesus the Head and His many-membered Body, the Church!

This astounding vision concludes with these breathtaking words: "The court will sit, and [the final beast's] power will be taken away and completely destroyed forever. Then the sovereignty, power and greatness of the kingdoms under the whole heaven will be handed over to the saints, the people of the Most High. [Messiah's] kingdom will be an everlasting kingdom, and all rulers will worship and obey him" (Dan. 7:26–27)! "This is the end of the matter," Daniel declared (v. 28). Indeed it is, for "the kingdom of the world has become the kingdom of our Lord and of his Christ, and he will reign forever and ever" (Rev. 11:15), and His saints will reign with Him forever and ever (Rev. 22:5)!

Chapter 8

DANIEL'S VISION OF THE TWO-HORNED RAM AND THE SHAGGY GOAT

Daniel 8

ACCORDING TO DANIEL 8:1, it was "the third year of King Belshazzar's reign," the year 551 B.C., two years after the vision of the four beasts and twelve years before the fall of Babylon to the Medes and the Persians. At this time, Daniel, who was now seventy-two, had another vision, his third one. Though he was in Babylon, in the vision Daniel saw himself transported to Susa, the capital of Persia, in the province of Elam, and in this vision he saw himself standing beside the Ulai Canal (Dan. 8:2).

Daniel 8:3 begins, "I looked up, and there before me was a ram with two horns." From the interpretation that the angel Gabriel gave to Daniel recorded in verse 20, we learn that the two-horned ram represents the kings of Media and Persia. Daniel notes that "one of the horns [Persia] was longer than the other but grew up later. I watched the ram [Medo-Persia] as he charged toward the west and the north and the south...He did as he pleased and became great" (Dan. 8:3–4). But Daniel continues, "As I was thinking about this, suddenly a goat with a prominent horn between his eyes came from the west [from Greece], crossing the whole earth [in rapid conquest] without touching the ground" (v. 5). Gabriel, in 8:21, interpreted for Daniel the meaning of the swift goat with the large horn: "The shaggy goat is the king of Greece, and the large horn between his eyes is the first king [Alexander the Great]." The rapidity of Alexander's conquest of the whole Middle East in just three years is reflected in the statement about the goat rapidly "crossing the whole earth without touching the ground" (Dan. 8:5).

43

Daniel continued:

[The goat with the large horn, Greece's Alexander the Great] came toward the two-horned ram [Medo-Persia] . . . and charged at him in great rage. I saw him [Alexander the Great] attack the ram [Medo-Persia] furiously, striking the ram [Medo-Persia] and shattering his two horns. The ram was powerless to stand against him; the goat [Greece's Alexander the Great] knocked him to the ground and trampled on him, and none could rescue the ram from [Alexander the Great's] power.

—DANIEL 8:6–7

Secular history records that in two decisive battles Alexander the Great literally destroyed the military might of Persia—first at Granicus in the spring of 334 B.C., and then at Issus in the fall of 333 B.C., where Alexander decimated the six-hundred-thousand-man Persian army of Darius III.

And the vision continues: "The goat [the Grecian empire] became very great, but at the height of his power his large horn [Alexander the Great] was broken off" (Dan. 8:8). Alexander the Great, after his great military campaign that took him all the way to India, died an untimely death of a fever at age thirty-three in 323 B.C.

Having no viable heir to his throne, Alexander's four military generals each received part of Alexander's empire. The "large horn [Alexander the Great] was broken off, and in its place four prominent horns grew up toward the four winds of heaven" (Dan. 8:8). That is why we read in verse 22 that "four kingdoms . . . will emerge from his nation but will not have the same power." Antipater and his son Cassander took the western part of Alexander's empire, Greece and Macedonia. Lysimachas took Thrace and Asia Minor to the east. Ptolemy I took Palestine and Egypt to the south, and Seleucus

I took the Syrian kingdom to the north. Of the four, the Egyptian kingdom of the south and the Syrian kingdom of the north would rise to greater prominence, and would play a prophetic role in the end-time scheme of things.

THE SYRIAN KINGDOM OF SELEUCUS

The Syrian kingdom of Seleucus was destined to play a major role in end-time events. With the fourfold breakup of Alexander the Great's empire as a backdrop, Daniel 8:9–11 declares of the four kingdoms:

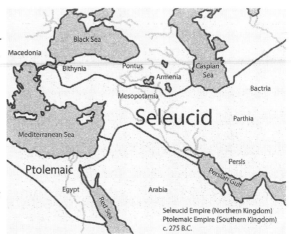

> Out of one of them [Syria] came *another horn,* which started small but grew in [hostile] power to the south [against Egypt] and to the east and toward the Beautiful Land [Israel]. It grew until it reached the host of the heavens, and it threw some of the starry host down to the earth and trampled on them [this "horn" would obviously move in the same satanic powers described for us in Revelation 12:4]. [The horn] set itself up to be as great as the Prince of the host [the Messiah]; it took away the daily sacrifice from him, and the place of his sanctuary was brought low.

Historically, these events that were being described for Daniel took place in 168 B.C. in the defiling of the temple in Jerusalem by one of the Seleucid kings, Antiochus IV Epiphanes Theos (an arrogant title meaning "god manifest").

In the face of the blasphemous activities of this ancient Syrian Antichrist, an anxious cry goes up among the angels, "How long?" (Dan. 8:13). Antiochus IV Epiphanes Theos had defiled the holy place, setting up an abomination of desolation, an altar to the god Zeus Olympus. The inquiry was quickly answered: "It will take

2,300 evenings and mornings [or 1,150 days; about three and a half years]; then the sanctuary will be reconsecrated [which happened on December 25, 165 B.C., when the freedom-fighting Maccabees recaptured the Temple Mount, cleansed the holy place, and drove the Syrian army to the very borders of Israel]" (Dan. 8:13–14). In Israel that victory would be celebrated from then on as Hanukkah, the Festival of the Dedication!

However, in a surprise statement Daniel was told by Gabriel that "the vision [really] concerns the time of the end" (Dan. 8:17) and that Daniel was actually being told "what will happen later in the time of wrath, because the vision concerns the appointed time of the end" (v. 19)! Apparently, all the blasphemous actions of Antiochus IV Epiphanes Theos in 168–165 B.C. were but a picture of something even more abominable that would yet happen in the last days, of which the career of Antiochus Epiphanes was but a preview. Jesus Himself, in His Matthew 24 end-time teaching on the Mount of Olives, indicated that this would be the case. Two hundred years *after* the infamous career of Antiochus Epiphanes ("god manifest") ended, Jesus refers to it *as still future, as part of the last-days scenario:* "So when you see standing in the holy place 'the abomination that causes desolation,' spoken of through the prophet Daniel—let the reader understand—then let those who are in Judea flee to the mountains.... For then there will be great distress ['tribulation,' KJV], unequaled from the beginning of the world until now—and never to be equaled again" (Matt. 24:15–16, 21). In a similar word spoken to Daniel, these things would happen "later in the time of wrath," at "the appointed time of the end" (Dan. 8:19).

Daniel 8:23–25 brought Daniel's third vision to its close by focusing on the last days:

> In the latter part of their reign, when rebels have become completely wicked, a stern-faced king, a master of intrigue, will arise. He will become very strong, but not by his own power [he will be inspired and empowered by Satan himself]. He will cause astounding devastation and will succeed in whatever he does. He will destroy the mighty men and the holy people. He will cause deceit to prosper, and he will consider himself superior. When they feel secure, he will destroy many

and take his stand against the Prince of princes [the Messiah]. Yet he will be destroyed, but not by human power.

Writing to the Thessalonians, Paul speaks of "the lawless one...whom the Lord Jesus will overthrow with the breath of his mouth and destroy by the splendor of his coming" (2 Thess. 2:8). This grand vision closes with this injunction: "seal up the vision, for it concerns the distant future" (Dan. 8:26).

We have now considered the first three of Daniel's five visions. From the first vision we learned that in the last days we will see a revival of the original Roman Empire. Ten kings will come into prominence; however, in the days of those kings the God of heaven will act. A stone will come hurling out of heaven, which will destroy all these other kingdoms and then will grow to become a mountain, a kingdom without end that will fill the whole earth!

From the second vision we learn something new—out of these ten kingdoms, pictured as ten horns, an abominable "little horn" will appear who will blaspheme God and wage war against the saints, even to the point of defeating them. But God will miraculously intervene on behalf of the saints, delivering them and putting into their hands His everlasting Kingdom! In this second vision we are then introduced for the first time, in graphic form, to the end-time Antichrist, the man of sin, the lawless one. And so we see that Daniel's end-time vision continued to grow.

In Daniel's third vision yet more of this end-time scenario is made know by God. We are now given *the geography* from which the Antichrist will come. Out of the vast area of the Roman Empire, our sights are directed to the Middle East, the formerly forgotten other leg of the statue. And in the Middle East, our sights are directed toward the area of the ancient Seleucid, or Syrian, kingdom of Antiochus IV Epiphanes Theos, which, not coincidentally, is also the geography of the vast Islamic Caliphate (c. 632–1923), known to us in recent days as the Ottoman Empire. Somewhere in this part of the Mideastern world that stretches from the Black Sea to the Persian Gulf, a man will be satanically prepared to become the supreme figure in the politics, economics, and religion of the Middle East. Winsome and appealing yet deceptive and cunning, this one will work all ends together until he has established himself as the unrivaled and supreme leader of mankind! And who might this one be?

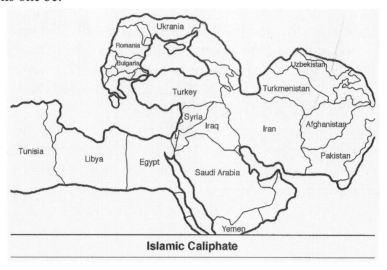

Islamic Caliphate

Looking for the Possible Identity of the End-Time Antichrist

When Iran's former President Mahmoud Ahmadinejad addressed the United Nations General Assembly in New York City on September 26, 2012, most of what he had to say went right over the heads of most of those assembled and surely over the heads of American news reporters. President Ahmadinejad declared that the world would soon see new global management by the Twelfth Imam, also know as the "Mahdi," and his deputy, Jesus Christ. These are excerpts from President Ahmadinejad's speech:

> Creating peace and lasting security with decent life for all, can be accomplished. The Almighty God has not left us alone in this mission and has said that it will surely happen. If it doesn't, then it will be contradictory to his wisdom.
>
> God Almighty has promised us a man of kindness, a man who loves people and loves absolute justice, a man who is a perfect human being and is named Imam Al-Mahdi, a man who will come in the company of Jesus Christ (PBUH) and the righteous. He will lead humanity into achieving its glorious and eternal ideals.
>
> The arrival of the Ultimate Savior will mark a new

beginning, a rebirth and a resurrection. It will be the beginning of peace, lasting security and genuine life.

His arrival will be the end of oppression, immorality, poverty, discrimination and the beginning of justice, love and empathy.

He will come and he will cut through ignorance, superstition and prejudice by opening the gates of science and knowledge. He will establish a world brimful of prudence and he will prepare the ground for the collective, active and constructive participation of all in the global management.

He will come to grant kindness, hope, freedom and dignity to all humanity.

He will come so that hands will be joined, hearts will be filled with love and thoughts will be purified to be at the service of security, welfare and happiness for all.

He will come to return all children of Adam irrespective of their skin colors to their innate origin after a long history of separation and division, linking them to eternal happiness.

The arrival of the Ultimate Savior, and Jesus Christ, and the Righteous will bring about an eternally bright future for mankind, not by force or by waging wars, but through thought awakening and developing kindness in everyone. Their arrival will breathe a new life in the cold and frozen body of the world. He will bless humanity with a spring that puts an end to our winter of ignorance, poverty and war with the tidings of a season of blooming.

Now we can sense the sweet scent and the soulful breeze of the spring, a spring that will soon reach all the territories in Asia, Europe, Africa and the US.

Let us join hands and clear the way for his eventual arrival with empathy and cooperation, in harmony and unity. Let us march on this path to salvation for the thirsty souls of humanity to taste immoral joy and grace.[iv]

It becomes virtually impossible to match the above "Peace, peace" rhetoric of President Ahmadinejad with his own prior words—and

iv. The full transcript of President Ahmadinejad's speech may be found at "Ahmadinejad UN General Assembly Speech Full Transcript 2012 (Video)." *Latinos Post*. September 25, 2012. Accessed at http://www.latinospost.com/articles/4606/20120926/ahmadinejad-un-general-assembly-speech-full-transcript-video-united-nations.htm (November 21, 2013).

those of Iran's clerical leaders—calling for the complete destruction of Israel. For example, in early February of 2012 Iran's supreme
leader Ayatollah Ali Khamenei declared:

> Israel is a cancerous tumor in the Middle East…. Israel is a
> satanic media outlet. Every Muslim is required to arm them-
> selves against Israel…. The usurper state of Israel poses
> a grave threat to Islam and Muslim countries. Islam and
> Muslim states must not lose this opportunity to remove the
> corruption from our midst. All of our problems are because
> of Israel.
>
> The first step should be the absolute destruction of Israel. To
> this end, Iran could make use of long-range missiles. The dis-
> tance between us is only 2,600 km. It can be done in minutes.
>
> Defensive Jihad justifies annihilating Israel and targeting
> its civilian population, because Israel has spilled Muslim
> blood and oppresses its Muslim neighbors.
>
> With regard to the fake state of Israel in Palestine, we must
> defend the sacred blood of Muslims in Islamic Palestine using
> any means necessary.[v]

Author Joel Rosenberg comments on this seeming disparity
between the contradicting "Peace, peace" rhetoric about the Mahdi
and the "absolute destruction of Israel" rhetoric coming from Iran's
leaders:

> Islamic theologians say Muslim political leaders today are
> supposed to set into motion the annihilation of the Judeo-
> Christian civilization as we know it and *create the condi-
> tions* of chaos and carnage to hasten the arrival of the Twelfth
> Imam. Then the Mahdi is supposed to turn all these wars and
> killings to his advantage and establish justice and peace…It
> is this Shia End Times theology that is driving Iranian foreign
> policy today. This is why the mullahs in Tehran are working
> so hard to pursue nuclear weapons and the means to deliver
> them, to prepare the way for the rise of this Islamic kingdom
> or caliphate.[2]

---

v. Gabe Kahn, "Iran: Genocide a Moral Obligation," IsraelNationalNews.com, February 6, 2012, http://www.israelnationalnews.com/News/News.aspx/152478#.Uta-
83JuA3lU (accessed January 15, 2014).

A powerful and enlightening observation!

To underscore the seriousness of this situation, a new Pew Research poll recently affirmed that "two-thirds of a billion Muslims expect the Mahdi—the last Islamic Imam they believe will come and rule the world—to arrive in their lifetimes."[3]

ISLAMIC ESCHATOLOGY

In the Hadith [the Sayings], Muhammad, the prophet of Islam declared:

> The world will not come to pass until a man from among my family, whose name will be my name, rules over the Arabs...The Mahdi will be from my family and will be exactly forty years of age. His face will shine like a star...A peace agreement will be mediated...and will be upheld for seven years...The Mahdi will fill the earth with equity and justice as it was filled with oppression and tyranny, and he will rule for seven years.

Ayatullah Baqir Al-Sadr and Ayatullah Murtada Mutahhari, Shi'a scholars, write about the Mahdi: "He has been the vision of the visionaries in history. He has been the dream of all the dreamers of the world. For the ultimate salvation of mankind he is the Pole Star of hope on which the gaze of humanity is fixed...the Mahdi himself is universal...He belongs to everybody."[4]

President Ahmadinejad, in his U.N. speech, alluded to Jesus as the Mahdi's deputy: "Imam Al-Mahdi...will come in the company of Jesus Christ (PBUH) and the righteous." Muhammad, founder and prophet of Islam, describes this coming of Isa Al-Maseeh, Jesus the Messiah, in these words: "Isa ibn Maryam [Jesus son of Mary] shall descend as equitable judge and fair ruler. He shall...come to my grave to greet me, and I shall certainly answer him...Jesus will descend...He will break the cross...Allah will [cause to] perish all religions except Islam." Islamic scholars Al-Sadr and Mutahhari have interpreted Muhammad's words in this fashion: "Jesus will descend from heaven and espouse the cause of the Mahdi...The Christians will abandon their faith in his godhead[5]...Isa [Jesus] will declare 'that he is alive…he is not God nor the Son of God but [Allah's] slave and messenger.'"[6]

Joel Richardson in his two excellent *New York Times* bestsellers, *The Islamic Antichrist* and *Mideast Beast*, has made the case most clearly that presently Islam's Imam Al-Mahdi is the most viable candidate for the biblical Antichrist and that presently Islam's Isa Al- Maseeh, Jesus the Messiah, is the most viable candidate for the biblical false prophet. So we are encouraged with our Master's words: "When you see all these things, you know that [He] is near, right at the door…this generation will certainly not pass away until all these things have happened" (Matt. 24:33–34)!

Chapter 9

DANIEL'S VISION OF THE DAY
MESSIAH THE PRINCE DIED
Daniel 9

ANIEL 9 IS a marvelous study in the power of prevailing
prayer. Its message becomes an encouragement to all who
are given to prayer, all who will not let God go, who will
"give him no rest" (Isa. 62:6–7), until He answers from heaven.

It was 539 B.C., "the first year of Darius son of Xerxes ['Ahasuerus']
(a Mede by descent), who was made ruler [by the emperor Cyrus]
over the Babylonian kingdom" (Dan. 9:1). Daniel tells us, "In the first
year of [Darius'] reign, I, Daniel, understood from the Scriptures,
according to the word of the LORD given to Jeremiah the prophet,
that the desolation of Jerusalem would last seventy years" (v. 2).
(As a sidebar to this, it is interesting to note that Jeremiah's recent
prophecies were already being looked upon by God's people as "the
Scriptures.")

The specific "seventy years" prophecy to which Daniel referred
is recorded in both Jeremiah 29:10 and 2 Chronicles 36:21: "This is
what the LORD says: 'When seventy years are completed for Babylon,
I will come to you and fulfill my gracious promise to bring you
back to this place'" (Jer. 29:10). And so, "The land enjoyed its sabbath rests; all the time of its desolation it rested, until the seventy
years were completed in fulfillment of the word of the LORD spoken
by Jeremiah" (2 Chron. 36:21).

Nebuchadnezzar, Emperor of Babylon, lay siege to the city of
Jerusalem three times, in 606 B.C., in 598 B.C., and then in 589–
587 B.C. Jerusalem finally fell and was completely destroyed in 587
B.C. Daniel knew, according to his words in Daniel 9:2, that "the

desolation of Jerusalem would last seventy years," and so in the first year of Darius the Mede, in 539 B.C., Daniel began to pray for God's mercy upon the temple and upon the city of Jerusalem. However, when we do the math, subtracting 539 B.C. (the first year of Darius' reign) from 587 B.C. (the year Jerusalem was destroyed), we come up with only forty-six years—twenty-four years short of the prophesied seventy years! But, surprisingly, God nonetheless answered Daniel's fervent prayers, for "in the first year of Cyrus king of Persia [539 B.C.], in order to fulfill the word of the LORD spoken by Jeremiah, the LORD moved the heart of Cyrus king of Persia to make a proclamation" to rebuild the temple in Jerusalem (2 Chron. 36:22). The final order to rebuild the city of Jerusalem itself would come later, in April of 445 B.C., "In the month of Nisan in the twentieth year of King Artaxerxes" (Neh. 2:1). What was *begun* in 539 B.C. in answer to Daniel's fervent prayers would be completed in 445 B.C. in answer to Nehemiah's fervent prayers!

The urgency of Daniel's prayer is reflected in his *commands* addressed to the sovereign Lord of heaven. Perhaps Daniel took seriously the Lord's invitation through Isaiah: "Concerning the work of My hands, you command Me" (Isa. 45:11, NKJV). Consequently, these are Daniel's commands:

> Now, our God, *hear* the prayers and petitions of your servant. For your sake, O LORD, *look with favor* on your desolate sanctuary. *Give ear*, O God, and *hear*; *open your eyes and see* the desolation of the city that bears your Name...O LORD, *listen!* O LORD, *forgive!* O LORD, *hear and act!* For your sake, O my God, *do not delay*, because your city and your people bear your Name.
>
> —DANIEL 9:17–19, EMPHASIS ADDED

Perhaps never before had a mere man been so impassioned in his intercessions before God so as to command the Lord of heaven! But God heard him and answered him! Twenty-four years before the appointed seventy-year deadline, God *heard* Daniel's pleas, and He began to answer them! I have pondered the possible reason for Daniel's sense of urgency in his prayers. In the inspired record, Daniel's *final* vision came three years later, in 536 B.C. At the conclusion of that final vision, it was clear that the nearly ninety-year-old Daniel, whose life covered two empires, was going to die. Twice he was told: "Go your way, Daniel...go your way till the end. You will rest, and then at the end of the days you will rise to receive your allotted inheritance" (Dan. 12:9, 13). But apparently Daniel, like Simeon five hundred years later, was determined to see the Lord's salvation *before* he died (Luke 2:29–30)!

Now let us carry this matter one step further. We are told by Jesus that the day of His return is a day only known and kept in the secret counsels of the Father: "No one knows about that day or hour...only the Father" (Matt. 24:36). Yet we are told by Peter of a people in the last days who will "look forward to the day of God and speed its coming" (2 Pet. 3:12). The New King James Version fine-tunes the King James Version of 1611 by its words: "looking for and hastening the coming of the day of God." Conservative Greek scholar Kenneth Wuest makes this arresting observation on the phrase, "Looking for and hastening the coming of the day of God," when he quotes Greek scholar M.R. Vincent:

> I am inclined to adopt, with Alford...and Trench, the transitive meaning, *hastening on*; i.e., "causing the day of the Lord to come more quickly by helping to fulfil those conditions without which it cannot come; that day being no day inexorably fixed, but one the arrival of which it is free to the church to hasten on by faith and by prayer" (Trench). See Matthew 24:14: "the gospel of the kingdom shall be preached in all the world; for a witness unto all nations; and then shall the end come."[7]

One of these conditions is most clearly spelled out for us by Jesus in Matthew 24:14. In answer to the question, "What will be the sign of your coming and of the end of the age?" Jesus responded, "This gospel of the kingdom will be preached in the whole world as a testimony to all nations [*ethnos*, "ethnic groups"], and then the end will come." In this statement we can see the very heart of our LORD, who is "not wanting anyone to perish, but everyone to come to repentance" (2 Pet. 3:8).

Prayer *can* move forward the clock of heaven! Obedience *does* hurry along the plans and purposes of a sovereign God! What a challenge for us, then, to always pray and not give up, not faint, not lose heart, never quit; and what a challenge for us to obey His final command.

Heaven's answer to Daniel's strong pleas came quickly, and in a more surprising answer than Daniel could ever have imagined. Gabriel told Daniel: "As soon as you began to pray, an answer was given, which I have come to tell you, for you are highly esteemed" (Dan. 9:23). This Hebrew word for "highly esteemed", *chamudoth*, is also translated in the KJV as "precious" in Daniel 11:43. The NIV translates it as "treasure" in this passage. Daniel was precious to his God, a treasure, greatly beloved (KJV), a man whom God loved "very much" (TLB)!

Daniel was then told that he stood at the juncture of two seventy-year periods of time. The first seventy years were the seventy accumulated Sabbath years that had been neglected by a greedy people over the prior four hundred and ninety years (Lev. 26:33–35; 2 Chron. 36:21). And now a new four-hundred-and-ninety-year span was about to begin—the "seventy 'sevens'" spoken of in Daniel 9:24. I have compiled the following explanatory commentary on Daniel 9:24–27 to help us navigate our way through this somewhat complicated but amazing prophecy, one which *actually pinpoints when Messiah the Prince would die!* The prior two visions of Daniel, in chapters 7 and 8, had introduced us to this grand messianic figure— the Son of Man. Daniel 7:14 tells us that to Him would be "given authority, glory and sovereign power; [as] all peoples, nations and men of every language worshiped him. His dominion [will be] an everlasting dominion that will not pass away, and his kingdom is one that will never be destroyed." This grand messianic figure is then seen again in Daniel 8 as "the Prince of the host" of heaven (v. 11), the very "Prince of princes" Himself (v. 25)! In this current vision of chapter 9, this Prince stands front and center as the one through whom God's eternal purposes will be fulfilled!

COMMENTARY ON DANIEL 9:24–27, THE "SEVENTY 'SEVENS'"

(24) Seventy "sevens" [490 years][vi] are decreed for your people [Israel] and your holy city [Jerusalem] to [1] finish transgression, to [2] put an end to sin, to [3] atone for wickedness, to [4] bring in everlasting righteousness, to [5] seal up vision and [6, seal up] prophecy and to [7] anoint the most holy [place, or Most Holy One].

(25) Know and understand this: From the issuing of the decree to restore and rebuild Jerusalem [which happened in Nisan (April) 445 B.C., Neh. 2:1, 4–5, 9] until the Anointed One, the ruler ["Messiah the Prince," KJV], comes, there will be seven "sevens,"[vii] and sixty-two "sevens" [a total of sixty-nine "sevens," or four hundred and eighty-three years—from 445 B.C. to A.D. 33, leaving five years for a necessary calendar adjustment].[viii]

(26) After the sixty-two "sevens" [in Nisan (April) A.D. 33], the Anointed One ["the Messiah," KJV; literally, "the Christ"]

---

vi. "Weeks" (KJV) in the original Hebrew is literally "sevens." There are seventy "sevens," or four hundred and ninety years in this prophecy. As we already noted, Daniel stands in the middle of two four-hundred-and-ninety-year spans of times—the first four hundred and ninety years are all the years the land did not keep its seventh year of Sabbath. Every seventh year the land was to lay fallow, but in its greed, Israel neglected this Sabbath seventy times over a period of four hundred and ninety years. During Israel's Babylonian captivity the LORD gave the land seventy years of "catch-up" rest (2 Chron. 36:20–21). Now that the catch-up was almost fulfilled, God would return them, and even early, to their land in answer to Daniel's prayer. But something unexpected was also going to happen in the *next* four hundred and ninety years! That is the theme of this prophecy.

vii. The initial "seven sevens" block of time, forty-nine years, actually may refer to the time it took for the initial complete restoration of Jerusalem. To these forty-nine years are added "sixty-two 'sevens,'" making a total of sixty-nine sevens, or four hundred and eighty-three years.

viii. The era *Anno Domini* was first fixed by a monk in A.D. 532. Years later it was discovered to be five years off! The Newberry Bible, therefore, places the birth events of Jesus in Matthew 1 as taking place in "the fifth year *before* the Common Era called *Anno Domini.*"[8] Consequently, when one starts from April 445 B.C. and subtracts four hundred and eighty-three years (sixty-nine "sevens") and then subtracts five years for the necessary calendar adjustment, one comes exactly to Nisan (April) A.D. 33, the precise time when Messiah was violently cut off, but not for Himself!

will be cut off [in a violent death] and will have nothing ["but not for Himself," KJV]. The people of the [evil] ruler who will come will destroy the city and the sanctuary. [This actually was foreshadowed in A.D. 70 under General Titus of Rome.]ⁱˣ [Then, projecting into the last days] The end will come like a flood: War will continue until the end, and desolations have been decreed.

(27) He [the Antichrist] will confirm a covenant with many for one "seven" [for seven years].ˣ In the middle of the "seven" [three and a half years] he [the Antichrist, like Antiochus Epiphanes before him] will put an end to sacrifice and offering. On a wing [of the temple] he will set up an abomination that causes desolation [predicted by Jesus in Matthew 24:15], until the end that is decreed is poured out on him [spoken of by Paul in 2 Thessalonians 2:8].

A marvelous prophecy! This stands as one of the most amazing prophecies about the Messiah, predicting not only His comprehensive work of redemption, but when He would actually accomplish that work (in mid-April of A.D. 33) and also the events of the last days!

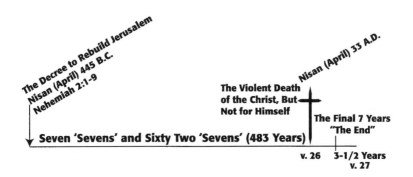

Daniel 9:24-27, the "Seventy 'Sevens'" of Years

---

ix. Author Joel Richardson, in his second book, *Mideast Beast,* makes an observation on "the people of the ruler [Titus] who will come" (Dan. 9:27) that in the army of Titus in A.D. 70, "The overwhelming majority of the [recruited] soldiers that destroyed the Temple were primarily Syrians, Arabs, and Eastern peoples" rather than Romans, a foreshadow of what is yet to come in the last days!"9

x. It is important to remember Muhammad's prophetic words about the Mahdi: "A peace agreement will be mediated…and will be upheld *for seven years*…and he will rule for *seven years*" (emphasis added).

Chapter 10

DANIEL'S FIFTH AND FINAL
VISION OF THE GREAT WAR
Daniel 10–12

WE NOW COME to Daniel's fifth and final vision—the vision of the "great war." Daniel was an old man by this time. The first vision of the great statue was given in 604 B.C. Daniel, as a young man, was probably in his late teens or early twenties at that time. Later in his life he would see three more visions—two when he was possibly in his early seventies and one when he was probably in his mid-eighties. Now it was 536 B.C., "the third year of Cyrus king of Persia," (Dan. 10:1), and Daniel was close to ninety years old. As we already noted, at the end of *this* vision, Daniel would be summoned home by the Lord: "Go your way till the end" (Dan. 12:13). So this would be Daniel's final vision. We have seen how each successive vision brought a further clarity to Daniel's whole end-time understanding, and to ours as well. Now in this final vision we will see *most clearly* the climax of the ages—the great tribulation, the second coming of Messiah, the overthrow of the Antichrist, and the final judgment of good and evil. This final message "was true and it concerned a great war" (Dan. 10:1).

Daniel had been in fasting and prayer for three weeks, unaware that a great battle was going on in the heavenlies, as he was interceding on the earth. In this tenth chapter of Daniel the foundations of the understandings of spiritual warfare are laid down for us. I believe Paul had this tenth chapter of Daniel in mind when he wrote to the Ephesians: "Our struggle is not against flesh and blood, but against the rulers, against the authorities, against the powers of this dark world and against the spiritual forces of evil in the heavenly realms" (Eph. 6:12). The earthly scene was clear—it was "the third year of Cyrus king of Persia." The Persian Empire was the ruling Gentile empire in the earth in those days, but in the heavenlies was the demonic "prince of the Persian kingdom," who was engaged in battle against Gabriel, preventing him for twenty-one days from reaching Daniel with the answer to his intercessions. The deadlock was finally broken when God dispatched the arch-angel "Michael, one of the chief princes" (Dan. 10:13), to join with Gabriel in the battle against the demonic prince of Persia. Just note these powerful statements from Gabriel:

> Do not be afraid, Daniel. Since the first day...your words were heard, and I have come in response to them. But the prince of the Persian kingdom resisted me twenty-one days. Then Michael, one of the chief princes, came to help me, because I was detained there with the [demonic] king of Persia. Now I have come to explain to you what will happen to your people *in the future,* for the vision concerns *a time yet to come.*
> —DANIEL 10:12–14, EMPHASIS ADDED

The New King James Version, more accurate to the Hebrew text, translates the final statement of verse 14: "I have come to make you understand what will happen to your people [Israel] *in the latter days,* for the vision refers to many days yet to come." The vision that would then be unfolded for Daniel in chapters 11 and 12 Spotlights the last days, and as such is the grand climax of this book of five visions.

The glorious being described by Daniel in chapter 10, verses 5–9 is considered by some to be the pre-incarnate Christ. However, the *dependency* of that glorious being on Michael the archangel for vic-tory requires this to be another than our Lord. Gabriel may well be that glorious one (Dan. 9:21). If, however, the glorious one of Daniel 10:5–9 *is* our Lord, then most surely the speaker shifts in 10:10 to Gabriel, for the aforestated reason.

We note from Daniel 10:20–21 and 11:1 The principle of spiritual warfare. Earthly kingdoms rise and advance because of the corre-sponding demonic powers in the heavenlies that sustain and uphold them, but when a demonic power is overthrown in the heavenlies through spiritual warfare, the corresponding kingdom falls on the earth. Soon the Grecian Empire would replace the Persian Empire on the earth—but only after a shift first took place in the heavenlies. Hear the words of Gabriel in this passage:

> Soon I will return to fight against the [heavenly] prince of Persia, and when I go ["and when I get him out of the way," THE MESSAGE], the [heavenly] prince of Greece will come [and at that time the Grecian Empire will emerge on the earth] ... (No one supports me against them except Michael, your prince. And in the first year of Darius the Mede, I [Gabriel] took my stand to support and protect him) [or else the Persian Empire on earth would have failed to come forth, and Cyrus would not have been able to release the Jewish exiles to return to the land to rebuild the Temple and the city of Jerusalem in answer to Daniel's intercessions (Ezra 1:1–3)].

These all form amazing insights into the importance of spiritual warfare in the furtherance of God's kingdom on the earth.

In Appendix Two at the end of this book I have provided a running commentary of Daniel 11:2–35, which traces the history of the world empires from Persia to Greece to the breakup of Alexander's empire; to the reign of the demonic Selucid king, Antiochus IV Epiphanes Theos, and his devastation of the temple in 168 B.C. This follows the same history recorded in Daniel's third vision in Daniel 8:9–14. We already noted that in Daniel's third vision, the demonic career of Antiochus Epiphanes became a springboard into the last days and the final Antichrist ruler; so now in this fifth vision we will see the same springboard projecting us into the last days, except with more detail and greater clarity than in any of the previous four visions.

Daniel 11:36–45 spotlight the last days, the Antichrist, and the end of all things. The details of this section actually do not fit what is historically known of Antiochus IV Epiphanes, underscoring the shift to the Antichrist of the last days.

> [36] The king [Antichrist] will do as he pleases. He will exalt and magnify himself above every god and will say unheard-of things against the God of gods. He will be successful until the

time of wrath is completed [an end-time happening], for what has been determined must take place.

[37] He will show no regard for the gods of his fathers or for the one desired by women [this may be a reference to the Messiah, the one desired by every woman in Israel], nor will he regard any god, but will exalt himself above them all.

[38] Instead of them, he will honor a god of fortresses [a powerful demonic god of supernatural strength]; a god unknown to his fathers he will honor with gold and silver, with precious stones and costly gifts.

[39] He will attack the mightiest fortresses with the help of a foreign god and will greatly honor those who acknowledge him. He will make them rulers over many people and will distribute the land at a price.

[40] At the time of the end [an end-time reference] the king of the South [Egypt] will engage him in battle, and the king of the North [Syria] will storm out against him with chariots and cavalry and a great fleet of ships. [The Antichrist] will invade many countries and sweep through them like a flood. [We note with interest that Syria, to Israel's north and Egypt, to Israel's south are main players in today's unfolding drama in the earth, and that Egypt and Syria are presently in opposition to one another.]

[41] He will also invade the Beautiful Land [Israel]. Many countries will fall, but Edom, Moab and the leaders of Ammon [the present-day kingdom of Jordan] will be delivered from his hand.

[42] He will extend his power over many countries; Egypt will not escape.

[43] He will gain control of the treasures of gold and silver and all the riches of Egypt, with the Libyans and Nubians [the northern Sudanese] in submission.

[44] But reports from the east and the north will alarm him, and he will set out in a great rage to destroy and annihilate many.

[45] He will pitch his royal tents [similar to the way Muammar Gaddafi often did, even when he came to New York City] between the seas [the Mediterranean and the Dead Seas] at the beautiful holy mountain [Mount Moriah in Jerusalem]. Yet he will come to his end, and no one will help him. [Note: Antiochus Epiphanes died in Persia; the Antichrist will be overthrown in Israel—destroyed on Mount Moriah, in the temple where he will stand declaring that he is god, destroyed by the brightness of Jesus' coming, according to Paul in 2 Thessalonians 2:8.]

Chapter 12 Then continues on with the grand conclusion of this vision, describing in greater detail than the preceding visions, the great tribulation, the deliverance of the saints, the resurrection from the dead, and the final reward of the faithful.

CHAPTER 12: THE PROPHETIC FINALE TO THE BOOK

Chapter 12 begins with this important signpost: "*At that time* Michael, the great prince who protects your people [Israel], will arise" (Dan. 12:1, emphasis added). This ties the end-time events of chapter 12 to the final verses of the preceding chapter, concerning the destruction of the Antichrist.

"At that time" Michael arises to protect the battered Jewish nation. These are the days of the great tribulation, for "there will be a time of distress such as has not happened from the beginning of nations until then" (Dan. 12:1). *The Message* translates this statement as "a time of trouble, the worst trouble the world has ever seen." The Great Tribulation is clearly in view here.

Yet, encouraging news follows: "At that time your people—everyone whose name is found written in the book—will be delivered" (v. 1). The use of the word "everyone" may broaden the vision to include the grafted-in Gentiles, for the whole church seems to be in view in the next statement concerning the resurrection:

"Multitudes who sleep in the dust of the earth will awake: some to everlasting life, others to shame and everlasting contempt" (v. 2). This verse appears to telescope together both the resurrection of the just and the unjust, just as in Jesus' statement in John 5:28–29, though there is a time period between the first and last resurrection, according to Revelation 20.

Then follows some very special promises to God's end-time people: "Those who are wise [those who are teachers, 'those who impart wisdom,'] will shine like the brightness of the heavens, and those who lead many to righteousness, like the stars for ever and ever" (v. 3). Special mention is made of anointed end-time teachers and evangelists. They receive God's special "Oscars" on that day of grand reward! These rewards are the crowns promised to those who have been faithful as they "have longed for his appearing" (2 Tim. 4:8)! With this, the final vision ends.

In Daniel 12:4, Daniel is told to "close up and seal the words of the scroll until the time of the end." And in Daniel 12:9 the seer is again told, "Go your way, Daniel, because the words are closed up and sealed until the time of the end." Perhaps the reason why the "sealed" message of Daniel is now becoming clearer to us is that the words of this scroll are now being unsealed and opened for us as never before, for these are the last days! Then the final three and a half years (or 1,290 days) are highlighted for us one last time, since *that is the most critical piece of prophetic time during which the final drama of humanity will be worked out* (Dan. 12:7, 11). In conclusion, Daniel himself was given a very special personal promise from God: "As for you, go your way till the end. You will rest, and then at the end of the days you will rise to receive your allotted inheritance" (Dan. 12:13)! And so closes one of the most profound prophetic books in the Old Testament.

Chapter 11

THE PROPHET EZEKIEL

THE FINAL MAJOR prophet to prophesy was Ezekiel. Like Daniel, Ezekiel wrote in exile, but he wrote later than Daniel. He was the last of the four young prophetic lions. Also, like Isaiah and Jeremiah and Daniel before him, Ezekiel began his prophetic ministry as a young man: "In ['my,' NIV margin] thirtieth year, in the fourth month on the fifth day, while I was among the exiles by the Kebar River [a canal of the Euphrates], the heavens were opened and I saw visions of God" (Ezekiel 1:1). *The Message* reads: "When I was thirty years of age, I was living with the exiles on the Kebar River...and I saw visions of God." Verses two and three add these facts: "On...the fifth year of the exile of King Jehoiachin [597 B.C.]—the word of the LORD came to Ezekiel the priest, the son of Buzi, by the Kebar River in the land of the Babylonians." As a priest this thirtieth year would be Ezekiel's year of holy ordination. What a way to begin one's ministry—with visions of God! Ezekiel's vision of God's mobile throne in chapter 1 is similar to Daniel's vision of that throne in Daniel 7, a throne with wheels, a *mobile* throne able to sovereignly move from age to age and from nation to nation in an instant of time. This is our awesome God, the same yesterday, today, and forever!

The Book, or scroll, of Ezekiel has two main parts: Ezekiel's vision of the *departing* glory (found in chapters 1 through 35) and his vision of the *returning* glory (found in chapters 36 through 48). This second section, the returning glory, is primarily eschatological, or end-time, in nature, as we shall see.

In part one, concerning the departing glory, we trace the "glory of the God of Israel [as it went up] from above the cherubim, where it had been, and moved to the threshold of the temple" (Ezek. 9:3).

From there "the glory of the LORD departed from over the threshold of the temple" (Ezek. 10:18), and in Ezekiel 11:23, "The glory of the LORD went up from within the city and stopped above the mountain east of [the Mount of Olives]." The departing glory moved ever so slowly from the holy of holies to the threshold of the temple, and from there into the city, finally departing to the Mount of Olives. Perhaps the Lord was hoping, as He slowly moved from place to place, that someone would notice that He was departing and would run after Him, but no one did. As a forsaken lover, the Lord was soon forgotten (Ezek. 16).

THE RETURNING GLORY

Ezekiel 36 begins with a stunning prophecy to "the mountains of Israel," which is known today in Israel as the West Bank. The enemies of Israel had said about the mountains of Israel, the West Bank: "Aha! The ancient heights have become our possession" (Ezek. 36:2). But the Lord overruled the greed of their land-grab and declared of *the West Bank:* "But you, O mountains of Israel, will produce branches and fruit *for my people Israel, for they will soon come home*" (v. 8, emphasis added).

God then told Israel that their restoration to the land would be "not for your sake, O house of Israel...but for *the sake of my holy name...*I will show the holiness of *my great name...*Then the nations will know that I am the LORD...For I will take you out of the nations; I will gather you from all the countries and bring you back into your own land" (Ezek. 36:22–24).

Then came a most wonderful promise to Israel: "I will give you a new heart and put a new spirit in you; I will remove from you your heart of stone and give you a heart of flesh. And I will put my Spirit in you and move you to follow my decrees…You will live in the land I gave your forefathers; you will be my people, and I will be your God" (Ezek. 36:26–28).

God's promise of a new heart and a new spirit is what the symbolism of Ezekiel 37 is all about—the valley of dry bones will experience the outpouring of the Holy Spirit and the dry bones will live! That is what is meant by Ezekiel 37:14: "I will put my Spirit in you and you will live, and I will settle you in your own land." The eschatological nature of this end-time revival is borne out in these powerful "forever" promises to Israel:

> They will live in the land I gave to my servant Jacob, the land where your fathers lived. They and their children and their children's children will live there *forever*, and David my servant will be their prince *forever*. I will make a covenant of peace with them; it will be an *everlasting* covenant. I will establish them and increase their numbers, and I will put my sanctuary among them *forever*. My dwelling place will be with them; I will be their God, and they will be my people. Then the nations will know that I the LORD make Israel holy, when my sanctuary is among them *forever*.
>
> —EZEKIEL 37:25–28, EMPHASIS ADDED

These are forever promises involving Israel, and the land, and the temple, and the resurrected David!

Chapters 38 and 39 of Ezekiel then record a riveting prophecy "against Gog, of the land of Magog, the chief prince of Meshech and Tubal" (Ezek. 38:1). Genesis 10:2 Tells us that Magog, Tubal, and Meshech were "sons of Japheth," who was Noah's eldest son. A study of geography reveals that these grandsons of Noah settled in what is modern-day Turkey—in the eastern part of the ancient Roman Empire (that formerly forgotten right leg of the great statue of Daniel, the center of the Islamic Caliphate of the Middle Ages). Gog, the ruler of Magog, Meshech, and Tubal is none other than the violent one of Daniel's visions. The Antichrist, Gog, in military union with "Persia [Iran], Cush [the Sudanese] and Put [Libya]" (Ezek. 38:5), along with Gomer (the firstborn son of Japheth) with all its troops and Beth Togarmar (modern-day Armenia), will invade Israel "in future years" (v. 8). Ezekiel 38:14–16 reads, "In that day, when my people Israel are living in safety...You will come from your place in the far north, you and many nations with you...You will advance against my people Israel like a cloud that covers the land."

The Gog/Magog prophecy is believed by a number of Bible scholars to refer to Russia, though geography places this scene in Turkey. It is undeniable, however, that Russia will play a major role in the Middle East in the last days. We have witnessed repeatedly Russia, along with Iran and China, backing the rogue Assad government of Syria. Russia also blocked UN Security Council resolutions proposing sanctions against Assad, and recently brokered the supposed dismantling of Syria's weapons chemical weapons to avert a military strike by the US.

However, "'When Gog attacks the land of Israel, my hot anger will be aroused,' declares the Sovereign LORD...'I will execute judgment upon him with plague and bloodshed; I will pour down torrents of rain, hailstones and burning sulfur on him and on his troops and on the many nations with him. And so I will show my greatness and my holiness, and I will make myself known in the sight of many nations. Then they will know that I am the LORD'" (Ezekiel 38:18, 22–23). Ezekiel 39 then describes the gruesome extent of the devastation of this antichrist army: "On the mountains of Israel [they] will fall...For seven months the house of Israel will be burying them in order to cleanse the land...and the day I am glorified will be a memorable day for them,' declares the Sovereign LORD" (v. 4, 12–13).

THE GLORIOUS TEMPLE OF EZEKIEL 40–48

"In the twenty-fifth year of our exile," Ezekiel wrote, "In visions of God he took me to the land of Israel" (Ezek. 40:1–2). There Ezekiel saw the restored holy city and the rebuilt temple of God within that city. The reinstitution of the blood sacrifices in this temple (Ezek. 40:39) poses no small problem in view of the clear New Testament teaching on the finished work of Christ, especially in Hebrews. It has been suggested that these sacrifices could be for Israel what the Lord's Table is for the wider body of Christ—a memorial celebration of the finished work of Christ on the cross. But we will have to patiently wait to see what God will say to us in that day on this matter.

Then Ezekiel saw the return of the glory of God to His temple: "I saw the glory of the God of Israel coming from the east...The glory of the LORD entered the temple through the gate facing east...and the glory of the LORD filled the temple" (Ezek. 43:2, 4–5). Then the Lord said to Ezekiel, "Son of man, this is the place of my throne and the place for the soles of my feet. This is where I will live among the Israelites forever" (v. 7).

"The Gate Facing East"

A fascinating prophecy is given in Ezekiel 44:1–3. Speaking of what is known as the eastern gate of the Temple Mount, "the gate facing east" (Ezek. 43:4), Ezekiel wrote:

> The man brought me back to the outer gate of the sanctuary, *the one facing east,* and *it was shut.* The LORD said to me, "This gate is to *remain shut.* It *must not be opened; no one may enter through it.* It is to *remain shut* because the LORD, the God of Israel, has entered through it [Jesus actually did this on Palm Sunday, A.D. 33]. The prince himself [in the last days] is *the only one* who may...enter by way of the portico of the gateway and go out the same way."
>
> —Ezekiel 44:1–3, emphasis added

Learning about this prophecy of the Prince coming through this gate, the Turks of the Ottoman Empire ordered masons to seal up the eastern gate, and it remains sealed to this day. Little did they know that they were actually fulfilling this ancient prophecy! The eastern gate is destined to remain shut until Messiah the Prince Himself comes and enters again through it, as He first did in A.D. 33 on Palm Sunday!

And as Joel 3:18 and Zechariah 14:8 both stated, Ezekiel himself also prophesied about the river that will flow from the temple of God, bringing healing everywhere. He wrote, "Fruit trees of all kinds will grow on both banks of the river. Their leaves will not wither, nor will their fruit fail...Their fruit will serve for food and their leaves for healing" (Ezek. 47:12)!

The prophecy of Ezekiel closes with a description of the new boundaries of the restored land of Israel, with a very special promise to the Palestinians and a snapshot of the new city of Jerusalem, renamed Jehovah Shammah: "And the name of the city from that time on will be: THE LORD IS THERE" (Ezek. 48:35).

Describing the boundaries of the restored land, "the Sovereign LORD says: 'These are the boundaries by which you are to divide the land for an inheritance among the twelve tribes of Israel, with two portions for Joseph. You are to divide it equally among them. Because I swore with uplifted hand to give it to your forefathers, this land will become your inheritance'" (Ezek. 47:13–14). Yes, our "God is not a man, that he should lie, nor a son of man, that he should change his mind...Does he promise and not fulfill?" (Num. 23:19) He is a God who keeps His promises. His word will never fail!

But He is also a God of great compassion. And He has provided an answer to the nagging Palestinian question that haunts us today, and that answer is not missiles or suicide bombers; nor is the answer with the PLO or Hamas or Hezbollah or the Muslim Brotherhood. The answer to the Palestinian question is found in Jehovah's compassionate promise:

> "You are to distribute this land among yourselves according to the tribes of Israel. You are to allot it as an inheritance for yourselves and for the aliens [the strangers, the sojourners, such as the Palestinians] who have settled among you and

who have children. You are to consider them as native-born Israelites; along with you they are to be allotted an inheritance among the tribes of Israel. In whatever tribe the alien [the stranger, the sojourner] settles, there you are to give him his inheritance," declares the Sovereign LORD.

—EZEKIEL 47:21–23

And this wonderful God is our God and shall be the God of both Jews and Palestinians forever! Amen!

to offer Refuge + hope

protection + peace for refugees, immigrants coming to her (Israel)

Chapter 12

THE MINOR PROPHETS: HOSEA
THROUGH MICAH

HOSEA THROUGH MALACHI are the twelve Minor Prophets, minor only because their words are generally shorter. Of the twelve, all but one has clear eschatological revelation. That exception is Jonah, but he shares a powerful end-time truth with us, as we shall see. In this chapter, we will consider Hosea through Micah, the first six of the twelve Minor Prophets.

HOSEA, SON OF BEERI

Hosea, along with Zechariah, are the longest books of the Minor Prophets. Hosea, in particular, has powerful end-time revelation concerning Israel in the last days. He was a prophet to the northern ten tribes of Israel and a contemporary in time with Isaiah. Hosea prophesied on the backdrop of a deep personal tragedy in his own life in which his wife, Gomer, had forsaken him for other men. He felt the pain of Jehovah's heart, who also had been abandoned by His wife, Israel, who had gone whoring after other gods. So we have two broken hearts—Jehovah's and Hosea's. Thus the grieving Hosea became the sympathetic spokesman for the brokenhearted God of Israel, who mourns over his fallen people.

Even as Hosea began to see the prospect of restoring his own fallen wife (Hosea 4:1–3), the promises of restoration began to come from Jehovah for Israel in the last days.

> *In that day* [a prophetic signpost signifying the last days]...I will betroth you to me *forever*...I will betroth you in faithfulness, and you will acknowledge the LORD. *In that day*...I will plant her for myself in the land; I will show my love to the

one I called 'Not my loved one.' I will say to those called "Not my people," "You are my people"; and they will say, "You are my God."

—HOSEA 2:18–21, 23, EMPHASIS ADDED

Both Paul in Romans 9:24–25 and Peter in 1 Peter 2:10 expanded these promises to include both Israel and the Gentiles, consistent with Paul's understanding that now the "Gentiles are heirs together with Israel…sharers together in the promise in Christ Jesus" (Eph. 3:6).

The further end-time promise in Hosea 3:5 is also very powerful: "Afterward the Israelites will return and seek the LORD their God and David their king. They will come trembling to the LORD and to his blessings in the last days." A number of the prophets, like Hosea, spoke of the place of King David in God's end-time plan for Israel. Though David had been dead for five hundred years, Hosea declared Israel will "seek the LORD their God and David their king." In understanding this we have one of two options—that this promise is a veiled prophecy concerning the Messiah, David's greater Son, or that this is spoken of David himself, resurrected at the coming of our Lord Jesus Christ.

A powerful end-time prophetic word about the "third day" is next given in Hosea 5:14–6:3. The rejected, brokenhearted Messiah spoke in Hosea 5:15 "I will go back to my place until they admit their guilt. And they will seek my face; in their misery they will earnestly seek me." And Israel will say, "Come, let us return to the LORD. He has torn us to pieces but he will heal us; he has injured us but he will bind up our wounds. After two days he will revive us; on the third day he will restore us, that we may live in his presence…As surely as the sun rises, he will appear; he will come to us…like the spring rains that water the earth" (Hosea 6:1–3). The rejected Messiah, the great Lion of Judah, returns to His place. Then, after two days He comes and *revives* His broken and repentant people, and on the third day He *restores* them to live in His presence.

Moses had already established the prophetic insight that with the LORD "a thousand years in your sight are like a day" (Ps. 90:4). Peter in 2 Peter 3:4, 8 built on Moses' prophetic insight in answering the scoffers' ridicule, "Where is this 'coming' he promised?" Peter

declared "With the LORD a day is like a thousand years, and a thousand years are like a day." In other words, for us today, for example,
the Lord has actually only been gone two days (two thousand
years)! Hosea made a similar observation—the rejected Messiah left,
but He will return to revive a broken, repentant Israel "after two
days," after two thousand years of being gone. "On the third day,"
in the thousand-year reign of the coming kingdom, He will *restore*
Israel to live in His presence. This is a most marvelous prophecy,
especially for us who live at the end of that second day, at the end
of those two thousand years since the first century. We sense we are
indeed living in the last days!

JOEL, SON OF PETHUEL

Joel lived at the time of a fierce natural disaster. The land was being
devastated by a plague of locusts. On that backdrop Joel prophesied concerning the coming disaster of "the day of the LORD" (Joel
2:1). In the face of the impending catastrophe, the people of Israel
were called to repentance, to return to Jehovah with all their hearts
(Joel 2:12). As repentance comes, the promise of restoration comes
also: "Then the LORD will be jealous for his land and take pity on
his people... *never again* will I make you an object of scorn to the
nations.... *never again* will my people be shamed... *never again*"
(Joel 2:18–19, 26–27). Some Bible expositors feel that these promises of restoration were fulfilled in the return of Israel from the
Babylonian Exile in 538 B.C. However, these promises state that this
kind of devastation will "never again" happen to the nation. When
we realize that such destruction did happen again in A.D. 70 under
the Roman general Titus, we believe we must seek a future end-
time fulfillment for these promises.

In Joel 2:28–32 we find the original verses of the Acts
2:17–21 promise of a last days outpouring, but it is important for us
to notice the wording found in this Joel passage. Here God pledged:
"And afterward, I will pour out my Spirit on all people. Your sons
and daughters will prophesy... Even on my servants, both men and
women, I will pour out my Spirit in those days... before the coming
of the great and dreadful day of the LORD. And everyone who calls
on the name of the LORD will be saved." Joel spoke of "the great and

dreadful day of the LORD," but Peter changed the word to "the great and glorious day of the Lord." Joel, seeing the judgments of that day, saw that day as *dreadful;* Peter saw it as *glorious* for "everyone who calls on the name of the LORD will be saved"! The prophecy in Joel continued on: "For on Mount Zion and in Jerusalem there will be deliverance ["a great rescue," THE MESSAGE], as the LORD has said, among the survivors ["the remnant," NKJV] whom the LORD calls" (Joel 2:32). These words clearly spell out for us that though the last days will be for Israel "the time of Jacob's trouble...he shall be saved out of it" (Jer. 30:7, KJV).

Joel continued, "In those days and at that time, when I restore the fortunes of Judah and Jerusalem, I will gather all nations and bring them down to the Valley of Jehoshaphat [the Valley of "Judgment," literally]. There I will enter into judgment against them concerning my inheritance, my people Israel, for they scattered my people among the nations and divided up my land" (Joel 3:1–2). Verse 4 is commanding. The Lord asks, "Now what have you against me, O Tyre and Sidon [modern-day Syria and Lebanon to the north of Israel, powerbase for Hezbollah with its hatred against Israel] and all you regions of Philistia [modern-day Gaza to the south of Israel, powerbase for Hamas with its hatred against Israel]. Are you repaying me for something I have done? If you are paying me back, I will swiftly and speedily return on your own heads what you have done." These are powerful warnings for the people to the north and to the south of present-day Israel!

The conclusion of Joel's end-time prophecy is awesome:

> "Then you will know that I, the LORD your God, dwell in Zion, *my* holy hill. Jerusalem will be holy; *never again* will foreigners invade her. *In that day* [an end-time signpost] the mountains will drip new wine, and the hills will flow with milk...A fountain will flow out of the LORD's house...But Egypt will be *desolate,* Edom [northwestern Saudi Arabia] a *desert waste, because of violence done to the people of Judah,* in whose land they shed innocent blood. Judah will be *inhab-ited forever* and Jerusalem *through all generations.* Their

bloodguilt, which I have not pardoned, *I will pardon*." THE LORD DWELLS IN ZION!

—JOEL 3:17–21, EMPHASIS ADDED

Yes, our God is not a man, that He should lie, nor a son of man, that He should change His mind! He has promised these things, and He will fulfill His promises!

AMOS, ONE OF THE SHEPHERDS OF TEKOA

Amos was a prophet primarily to Israel, a contemporary in time with Isaiah (Amos 1:1). Amos spoke much about the Day of the Lord. The Lord promised that "in that day I will restore David's fallen tent," a pledge claimed by James in Acts 15:16 for the Gentiles who have become inheritors together with Israel of the vast promises of God!

Concerning Israel itself, Amos declared that the Lord promised: "'I will bring back my exiled people Israel; they will rebuild the ruined cities and live in them…I will plant Israel in their own land, *never again* to be uprooted from the land I have given them,' says the LORD your God" (Amos 9:14–15). And we confess it again: our God is not a man that He should lie or change His mind. He has given promises, and He will fulfill His promises!

THE VISION OF OBADIAH

Obadiah declared, "The day of the LORD is near for all nations" (Obad. 1:15). Addressing Edom [northwest Saudi Arabia] the LORD said: "As you have done [to Israel], it will be done to you; your deeds will return upon your own head.…But on Mount Zion will be deliverance; it will be holy, and the house of Jacob will possess its inheritance.…Deliverers will go up on Mount Zion to govern the mountains of Esau [in Saudi Arabia]. And the kingdom will be the LORD's" (Obad. 1:15, 17, 21). Hallelujah!

JONAH, SON OF AMITTAI

Jonah is the only minor prophet with no end-time word, but Jonah himself learned a valuable lesson that is essential for us in the last days. Initially, Jonah refused to go to Nineveh, the capital of Assyria, to preach repentance. But the Lord made Jonah willing to go! And "when God saw...how [the people of Nineveh] turned from their evil ways, he had compassion and did not bring upon them the destruction he had threatened" (Jon. 3:10). At first Jonah could not understand God's merciful compassions to these vicious enemies of Israel. He "was greatly displeased and became angry" (Jon. 4:1), but God held Jonah's feet to the fire until, I believe, Jonah's anger gave way to understanding God's merciful heart.

Therefore, what is the lesson in this for us today? Simply this: It is important for us not to be upset as God pours out His Spirit on the very enemies of Israel. We are beginning to see showers of revival blessing falling on the Arab world—on the Palestinians in Israel, on those in Egypt, on the Iranians, on the Pakistanis, and on the Afghans. Saudis are coming to know Him, and Syrians as well. Our God is "a gracious and compassionate God, slow to anger and abounding in love, a God who relents from sending calamity" (Jon. 4:2). So we are to expect powerful moves of the Spirit upon those who once were ruthless enemies, and believing for those powerful moves is to be part of our daily intercessions before God!

MICAH OF MORESHETH

Micah was a contemporary of Isaiah. His prophecy of the last days in Micah 4:1–5 was mirrored in Isaiah's same word in Isaiah 2:2–5: "In the last days the mountain of the LORD's temple will be established as chief among the mountains...and peoples will stream to it. Many nations will come...to the mountain of the LORD...[for] The law will go out from Zion, the word of the LORD from Jerusalem." And all of this will be possible because of what happened one silent night in Bethlehem in Judah. The Lord said:

> But you, Bethlehem Ephrathah, though you are small among the clans of Judah, out of you will come for me one who will be ruler over Israel, whose origins ["whose goings forth," NKJV] are from of old, from ancient times [literally, "from days of eternity"]....He will stand and shepherd his flock in the strength of the LORD, in the majesty of the name of the

Lord his God…His greatness will reach to the ends of the
earth. And he will be their peace.

—Micah 5:2, 4–5

We note from Micah 5:4 that Jehovah is called the Messiah's *God*.
That God should be Jesus' God is not a foreign thought to New
Testament Christology. In John 20:17 Jesus called the Father "my
God," and in John 20:28 Thomas called Jesus "my God." How can
Jesus be God and yet the Father be His God? The mystery is solved
once we see Him as the great God-Man. As perfect God, Jesus is
worthy of Thomas' worship, and because Jesus is also a perfect man,
Jesus would indeed acknowledge His Father as His God!

Micah closed his prophecy with this amazing declaration about
the Lord: "You will be true to Jacob, and show mercy to Abraham,
as you pledged on oath to our fathers in days long ago" (Mic. 7:20).
Jehovah has "pledged on oath" to redeem and to restore His people
Israel, and in the words of the author of Hebrews, "Because God
wanted to make the unchanging nature of his purpose very clear
to the heirs of what was promised, he confirmed it with an oath.
God did this so that, by two unchangeable things in which it is
impossible for God to lie, [those two unchangeable things are His
promise and His oath, so that] we who have fled to take hold of the
hope offered to us may be greatly encouraged" (Heb. 6:17–18). And
so we are very encouraged; praise God!

Chapter 13

THE MINOR PROPHETS: NAHUM THROUGH MALACHI

Nahum the Elkoshite

NAHUM PROPHESIED JUDGMENT on the Assyrians. Years had passed since the revival in the Assyrian capital of Nineveh under the reluctant Jonah. In the years that followed the revival, the Assyrians had gone back to their vicious and oppressive ways. For this reason Nahum prophesied against them, declaring that God "will make an end of [Nineveh]; he will pursue his foes into darkness" (Nah. 1:8). Assyria, with its capital, Nineveh, covered the eastern part of the Roman Empire, the geography of the later Islamic Caliphate; it is today's Syria, Iran, and Iraq. But, even as there was judgment on Nineveh and Assyria, there will be judgment on its modern-day counterparts. But there will also be blessing on Israel, whom these adversaries oppressed: "Look, there on the mountains, the feet of one who brings good news, who proclaims peace...No more will the wicked invade you; they will be completely destroyed" (Nah. 1:15). Nahum 2:2 Tells us, "The LORD will restore the splendor of Jacob...though destroyers have laid them waste and have ruined their vines."

HABAKKUK THE PROPHET

Habakkuk was the prophet who argued with God over His management of the world. He called God into account. The Prime Minister of Israel, Benjamin Netanyahu, in an article in *Time* commented that "the Jews are not so much God's chosen people as His argumentative ones. They don't take things on faith...They argue with God...Islam is about submission; Judaism is about arguing."[10] Habakkuk is a good example of this. That is why he was told, "The just will live by faith" (Hab. 2:4).

And that is why the Lord gave Habakkuk fuel for his faith—a promise that "the earth will be filled with the knowledge of the glory of the LORD, as the waters cover the sea" (Hab. 2:14). This is the vision spoken of in chapter 2, verse 3, a vision that "speaks of the end and will not prove false...it will certainly come and will not delay." And that is how Habakkuk became a changed man, able to declare in faith, "Though the fig tree does not bud and there are no grapes on the vines...yet I will rejoice in the LORD, I will be joyful in God my Savior" (Hab. 3:17–18). This is a valuable lesson for us. At times we can perceive things so negatively that we begin calling God into account for His management of the world. However, He *does* have a sovereign plan that will "certainly come and will not delay." So for this reason we can rejoice in the Lord and be joyful in God our Savior, even in trying times!

ZEPHANIAH, SON OF CUSHI

Zephaniah prophesied during the reign of King Josiah (640–609 B.C.). King Josiah had become God's instrument in bringing a godly reformation to Judah, and Zephaniah stood by him, assisting in the renewal. But Zephaniah's vision is primarily for *the Day of the Lord*. In the Spirit, Zephaniah saw that "the great day of the LORD is near—near and coming quickly...That day will be a day of wrath, a day of distress and anguish, a day of trouble and ruin, a day of darkness and gloom, a day of clouds and blackness" (Zeph. 1:14–15). Yet in the midst of the outpouring of God's anger on a deeply fallen humanity, God extends a promise to His faithful: "Seek the LORD, all you humble of the land...Seek righteousness, seek humility; perhaps you will be sheltered on the day of the LORD's anger" (Zeph. 2:3).

Then these precious promises are given to the nation of Israel in their hour of great trial:

> Sing, O Daughter of Zion; shout aloud, O Israel! Be glad and rejoice with all your heart, O Daughter of Jerusalem! The

LORD has taken away your punishment, he has turned back your enemy. The LORD, the King of Israel, is with you; *never again* will you fear any harm. *On that day* they will say to Jerusalem, "Do not fear, O Zion...The LORD your God is with you, he is mighty to save. He will take great delight in you, he will quiet you with his love, he will rejoice over you with singing."

—ZEPHANIAH 3:14–17, EMPHASIS ADDED

Zephaniah's inspiring words end with this grand promise to Israel: "At that time I will gather you; at that time I will bring you home. I will give you honor and praise among all the peoples of the earth when I restore your fortunes before your very eyes,' says the LORD" (Zeph. 3:20). It doesn't take much for us to realize that this has not yet happened. Though the modern state of Israel is impressive, it is not yet glorious. Modern-day Israel is a reproach among the nations, but God has promised Israel "honor and praise among all peoples of the earth." And it shall be, for the sovereign Lord has given His word!

THE PROPHET HAGGAI

The next two prophetic voices, that of Haggai and Zechariah, were heard as Judah returned to the land from the Babylonian exile. These two prophets were spoken of by name in Ezra 5:1 and 6:14 as the encouraging voices that spurred the people on to complete the rebuilding of the temple in Jerusalem. However, when we read the prophecies of both Haggai and Zechariah, we sense their deepest burden was for the Day of the Lord. For example:

> Thus saith the LORD of hosts; yet once, it is a little while, and I will shake the heavens, and the earth, and the sea, and the dry land [This "once more" promise of Haggai 2:6 is repeated in Hebrews 12:26–29 as yet future for us.]; and I will shake all nations, and the desire of all nations [He whom the nations were looking for and longing for all along but didn't realize that it was He! He] shall come: and I will fill this house with glory, saith the LORD of hosts...The glory of this latter house

shall be greater than of the former, saith the LORD of hosts:
and in this place will I give peace, saith the LORD of hosts.
—HAGGAI 2:6–7, 9, KJV

ZECHARIAH, SON OF BEREKIAH

In October of 520 B.C., two months after Haggai began his prophetic ministry, Zechariah began his. Zechariah's themes also went
beyond the immediate issue of completing the rebuilding of the
temple at Jerusalem. Zechariah, as Haggai, saw the coming great
and glorious Day of the Lord.

> "Shout and be glad, O Daughter of Zion. For *I am coming*, and
> I will live among you," declares the LORD. "Many nations
> will be joined with the LORD *in that day* and will become my
> people…The LORD will inherit Judah as his portion in the
> holy land and will again choose Jerusalem."
> —ZECHARIAH 2:10–12, EMPHASIS ADDED

It was reported that in November of 2007 a government delegation from West Papua New Guinea arrived in Jerusalem with a
substantial gift of gold for the building of the third temple. They
had been reading Zechariah together and felt the Lord had spoken
to them from Zechariah 6:15: "Those who are far away will come
and help to build the temple of the LORD, and you will know that
the LORD Almighty has sent me to you." Indeed, "many peoples
and powerful nations will come to Jerusalem to seek the LORD
Almighty and to entreat him" (Zech. 8:22)!

The beautiful Palm Sunday messianic prophecy of Zechariah
9:9–10 blends together both the first and the second coming of our
Lord Jesus Christ:

> Rejoice greatly, O Daughter of Zion! Shout, Daughter of
> Jerusalem! See, your king comes to you, righteous and having
> salvation, gentle and riding on a donkey, on a colt, the foal of
> a donkey. He will proclaim peace to the nations. His rule
> will extend from sea to sea and from the River [Euphrates] to
> the ends of the earth.

The concluding three chapters of Zechariah, chapters 12 Through 14, are so prophetically powerful that we will fully devote the next chapter of this book to just these three chapters of Zechariah.

MALACHI, JEHOVAH'S MESSENGER

The final minor prophet, Malachi, likewise had his eyes fixed on the last days. He envisioned that blessed day when, in the words of the Lord, "'My name will be great among the nations, from the rising to the setting of the sun. In every place incense and pure offerings will be brought to my name, because my name will be great among the nations,' says the LORD Almighty" (Mal. 1:11).

Concerning His coming, Malachi also heard the Lord say:

> "See, I will send my messenger, who will prepare the way before me. Then suddenly *the Lord you are seeking will come* to his temple; the messenger of the covenant, whom you desire, *will come*," says the LORD Almighty. But who can endure *the day of his coming*? Who can stand when *he appears*? For he will be like a refiner's fire or a launderer's soap. He will sit as a refiner and purifier of silver; he will purify the Levites and refine them like gold and silver. Then the LORD will have men who will bring offerings in righteousness, and the offerings of Judah and Jerusalem will be acceptable to the LORD, as in days gone by, as in former years.
>
> —MALACHI 3:1–4, EMPHASIS ADDED

Malachi's prophecies end with a grand vision of the Day of the Lord, showing both the severity and the goodness of the Lord:

> "Surely *the day is coming*; it will burn like a furnace. All the arrogant and every evildoer will be stubble, *and that day that is coming* will set them on fire...But for you who revere my name, the sun of righteousness will rise with healing in [His] wings. And you will go out and leap like calves released from the stall. Then you will trample down the wicked; they will be ashes under the soles of your feet *on the day* when I do these things," says the LORD Almighty.
>
> —MALACHI 4:1–3, EMPHASIS ADDED

Finally, "I will send you the prophet Elijah before that great and dreadful day of the LORD comes" (Mal. 4:5). In His first coming, Jesus came as *a single man*, preceded by *a single forerunner*, John the Baptist, who came in the spirit and power of Elijah (Luke 1:17). In His second coming, Jesus comes "to be glorified in his holy people" (2 Thess. 1:10); and in that sense Jesus will be revealed as the head of *a corporate man*. We can, therefore, reasonably expect that the forerunner for Jesus in His second coming will be *a corporate Elijah, a company of saints* preparing the way of the Lord!

Father, come and empower us as an Elijah task force as we ourselves look forward to the day of God and speed its coming. In Jesus' name. Amen.

Chapter 14

ZECHARIAH 12-14

T HE FINAL THREE chapters of Zechariah are so powerful in themselves that we will now consider them in a separate and focused way in this study on the last days. These chapters begin with the announcement: "This is the word of the LORD concerning Israel" (Zech. 12:1). And we will surely want to know what *He* has to say about His people. In these three chapters we notice seven climactic happenings in the earth concerning Israel in the last days. The first of these is the attack against Jerusalem and Judah and the divine intervention from heaven.

THE ATTACK AGAINST JERUSALEM AND JUDAH AND THE DIVINE INTERVENTION FROM HEAVEN

In Zechariah 12:2–3 the Lord declares:

> I am going to make Jerusalem a cup that sends all the surrounding peoples reeling. Judah will be besieged as well as Jerusalem. *On that day* [a prophetic signpost signaling the last days], when all the nations of the earth are gathered against her, I will make Jerusalem an immovable rock for all the nations. All who try to move it will injure ["rupture," THE MESSAGE] themselves.

To see these Scriptures presently happening before our eyes is a wonder to us. For nearly twenty-five hundred years, the fulfillment of these Scriptures was not even possible, but since the rebirth of the State of Israel in 1948, the ongoing hostilities of the surrounding Arab world against Israel's rebirth, and the united voice of virtually all the nations of the world against Israel, we see these prophecies actually beginning to take shape! Zechariah spoke of the hostilities of "all the surrounding peoples." Let's consider them.

North of Israel we see Turkey, a nation torn between the iron of authoritarian rule and the clay of democratic reform. In mid-August of 2013, the Turkish Prime Minister, Erdogan, who has a history of making anti-Israeli and anti-Semitic remarks, blamed Israel for the events that brought about Egypt's President Mohamed Morsi's ouster from power. Closer to Israel lies Syria, fortified by Russia, with its own evil intent against Israel. Syria, with its stockpile of chemical weapons, possibly the largest in the world, continues to be a threat to northern Israel. From Lebanon, directly north of Israel, Hezbollah, the front for Syria, continues to strike out at Israel, particularly threatening Haifa, Israel's third largest city.

To the east of Israel lies Jordan, considered to be one "friend" Israel has in the Middle East. However, Jordan is in turmoil, spurred on by the Muslim Brotherhood, who wants nothing more than to radicalize Jordan and complete the circle of hate that surrounds Israel.

Directly to the south of Israel is Palestinian Gaza, where the hatred of Hamas, fortified by Iran, results in the nearly daily shelling of southern Israel. And just beyond Gaza lies Egypt, ramping up its hate and threats against Israel as the Arab Spring revolution fell into the hands of the Muslim Brotherhood, only to see a surprising swing back toward democracy in the summer of 2013!

Southeast of Israel lies Saudi Arabia, the holy land of Islam and the seedbed of Al-Qaeda in its relentless hatred of Israel and the West for its support of Israel. Yet further to the east is Iran, which boldly declares its intent to wipe Israel off the map and is relentlessly building its nuclear potential for that very purpose.

Yet our Sovereign God has given His promise, "I am going to make Jerusalem a cup that sends all the surrounding peoples reeling…I will make Jerusalem an immovable rock for all the nations. All who try to move it will injure themselves" (Zech. 12:2–3). Five times in this initial passage in Zechariah reference is made to "on that day" (vv. 3–4, 6, 8–9). That day is the Day of the Lord, the great and terrible Day of the Lord, when He arises to act on behalf of the people of Israel.

We are impressed with verse 8 of Zechariah 12: "On that day

the LORD will shield [by a divine 'iron dome'] those who live in Jerusalem," and then in verse 9: "On that day I will set out to destroy all the nations that attack Jerusalem." This is God's irrevocable commitment. "This is the word of the LORD concerning Israel" (v. 1). Then the second climactic happening in the earth concerning Israel is addressed—the outpouring of the Holy Spirit on the house of David and on Jerusalem.

THE OUTPOURING OF THE HOLY SPIRIT ON THE HOUSE OF DAVID AND ON JERUSALEM

Our Lord personally promised, "And I will pour out on the house of David and the inhabitants of Jerusalem a spirit of grace and supplication. They will look on [or, to] me, the one they have pierced, and they will mourn for him as one mourns for an only child, and grieve bitterly for him as one grieves for a firstborn son" (Zech. 12:10). *The Message* translates these words: "They'll then be able to recognize me as the One they so grievously wounded—that piercing spear-thrust!" Then we see the overwhelming grief that this revelation will cause: "On that day the weeping in Jerusalem will be great, like the weeping of Hadad Rimmon in the plain of Megiddo" (Zech. 12:11), where the people mourned the untimely death of the godly King Josiah in 2 Chronicles 35:22–25.

Zechariah continues to describe the redemptive effects of the deep grief of the people of Israel: "On that day a fountain will be opened to the house of David and the inhabitants of Jerusalem, to cleanse them from sin and impurity" (Zech. 13:1). Eighteenth-century hymn writer William Cowper from Olney, England, described that fountain: "There is a fountain filled with blood drawn from Immanuel's veins, and sinners plunged beneath its flood lose all their guilty stains."

Zechariah 13:6 is also an arresting verse. If we link it to verse 7, which follows, then verse 6 clearly becomes messianic: "If someone asks him [the pierced one of 12:10], 'What are these wounds on your body? ['in your hands,' KJV] he will answer, 'The wounds I was given at the house of my friends.'" Verse 7 then describes how this wounding happened: "Awake, O sword, against my shepherd, against the man who is close to me! ['my companion,' NKJV; 'my fellow,' KJV; 'my close associate,' THE MESSAGE]...Strike the shepherd, and the

sheep will be scattered." This Scripture was quoted by our Lord
Jesus in Matthew 26:31 Concerning His final sufferings. Oh, what
powerful pictures of the suffering Messiah, so similar to the graphic
prophecies of Isaiah 53! Then the third climactic prophetic happening emerges for us in Zechariah 13:8–9.

THE REMNANT OF ISRAEL—A COMPLETELY SAVED NATION

Paul, in Romans 11:26, made a profound statement concerning
Israel in the last days: "And so *all Israel* will be saved, as it is
written: 'The *deliverer* will come from Zion; he will turn godless-
ness away from Jacob'" (emphasis added). The best explanation of
Paul's statement, as grievous as it is in its wider implications, is
found in Zechariah 13:8–9:

> "In the whole land," declares the LORD, "two-thirds will be
> struck down and perish; yet one-third will be left in it. This
> third I will bring into the fire; I will refine them like silver
> and test them like gold. They will call on my name and I will
> answer them; I will say, 'They are my people,' and they will
> say, 'The LORD is our God.'"

The anguish of the implications of this passage is crushing: "two-
thirds will be struck down and perish." We can hardly grasp the
enormity of this loss. When we consider Zechariah's statement, we
recall the vengeful words of Iran's Ayatollah Ali Khamenei in his
February 2012 address in which he declared it legally and morally
justified to wipe Israel off the map. In his address he also stated that
Tel Aviv, Jerusalem, and Haifa could be hit by Shahab-3 ballistic
missiles, which could kill much of the population. Out of Israel's
total population of around 8 million, two-thirds of the population
live in Tel Aviv, Jerusalem, and Haifa! In the air strikes between
Gaza and Israel in November 2012, missiles, believed to be supplied
by Iran, reached as far as Tel Aviv and Jerusalem!

The only ray of hope in this otherwise abysmal darkness is the
Lord's unfailing promise: "One-third will be left in [the land]. This
third I will bring into the fire; I will refine them like silver and test
them like gold. They will call on my name and I will answer them;'

I will say, 'They are my people,' and they will say, 'The LORD is our God.'" The remnant nation will *all* be saved! This is what Paul saw regarding God's people when he wrote the words: "And so all Israel will be saved" (Rom. 11:26). The fourth climactic happening in the earth is then presented—our Lord's personal return from heaven.

OUR LORD'S PERSONAL RETURN FROM HEAVEN

Zechariah prophesied: "A day of the LORD is coming" (Zech. 14:1). And the Lord Himself declared:

> I will gather all the nations to Jerusalem to fight against it; the city will be captured, the houses ransacked, and the women ["ravished," KJV]. Half of the city will go into exile, but the rest of the people will not be taken from the city. *Then* the LORD will go out and fight against those nations, as he fights in the day of battle. *On that day* his feet will stand on the Mount of Olives, east of Jerusalem.
> —ZECHARIAH 14:2–4, EMPHASIS ADDED

What an amazement to think that the sovereign Lord from heaven has *feet!* He has feet that were pierced by nails on an old, rugged cross, and those "feet will stand on the Mount of Olives, east of Jerusalem."

When our Lord Jesus ascended into heaven to His Father, it was from the Mount of Olives (Acts 1:9–12). His disciples were then told by the two men dressed in white: "This same Jesus, who has been taken from you into heaven, will come back in the same way you have seen him go into heaven" (v. 11). We believe Zechariah 14:4 is the fulfillment of that promise. Zechariah further told us that as His feet touch the mount, "The Mount of Olives will be split in two from east to west, forming a great valley."

While on a recent journey to Israel, as we were going up to Jerusalem via a tunnel that had been blasted through the Mount of Olives, we were told by our Israeli guide that the blasting of the tunnel actually caused a cleavage in the mount—a cleavage awaiting the feet of the Messiah, when "the Mount of Olives will be split in two from east to west, forming a great valley…Then the LORD my God will come, and all the holy ones with him [His gathered saints along with the angels of heaven]" (Zech. 14:4–5). This is the promised second coming of our Lord Jesus Christ!

The *Los Angeles Times* carried a report on October 1, 2012, that, "America's two biggest Christian broadcasters [Daystar Television Network and Trinity Broadcasting Network] have positioned themselves to catch any messianic action on the Mount of Olives, such as is described in the Bible of Jesus' return."[11] Amazing! And so Jesus' return will trigger the fifth climactic happening in the earth.

THE GREAT AND GLORIOUS DAY OF THE LORD

In the last three chapters of Zechariah the phrase "on that day," referring to the great and glorious Day of the Lord, appears no fewer than seventeen times, half of which appear in chapter 14 alone. Verses 6 and 7 say, "On that day there will be no light, no cold or frost. It will be a unique day, without daytime or nighttime—a day known to the LORD. When evening comes, there will be light." We are further told, "On that day living water will flow out from Jerusalem, half to the eastern [the Dead] sea and half to the western [the Mediterranean] sea" (v. 8). The vision of this river flowing out of Jerusalem was also prophesied by both Ezekiel (Ezek. 47:1–12) and Joel (Joel 3:18). But, the centerpiece of the Day of the Lord is found in Zechariah 14:9: "The LORD will be king over the whole earth. On that day there will be one LORD, and his name the only name." This is our great and glorious God, Jehovah (Yahweh)!

In the next several verses (Zech. 14:10–11), a very special promise is spoken over Jerusalem—the city that has come under such violent attack at the hand of her enemies: "Jerusalem will be raised up and remain in its place…It will be inhabited; never again will it be destroyed. Jerusalem will be secure." *"Never again"*—a promise from God that appears over and over again in the prophetic writings regarding the last days. "Never again"! Then comes the sixth climactic happening in the earth in the last days.

GOD'S JUDGMENT ON THOSE NATIONS WHO FOUGHT AGAINST JERUSALEM

Almost like a scene from the end of the *Raiders of the Lost Ark*, we are told: "This is the plague with which the LORD will strike all the nations that fought against Jerusalem: Their flesh will rot while they are still standing on their feet, their eyes will rot in their sockets, and their tongues will rot in their mouths. *On that day* men will be stricken by the LORD with great panic," so much so that they will turn on one another and attack each other (Zech. 14:12–13). And spoils and tribute, "the wealth of all the surrounding nations will be collected—great quantities of gold and silver and clothing" (v. 14).

How fearful and awesome are the judgments of our God! "How unsearchable his judgments, and his paths beyond tracing out," Paul declares in Romans 11:33! "To him be the glory forever! Amen" (Rom. 11:36), which brings us to the seventh and final climactic happening in the last days.

THE CELEBRATION OF THE FEAST OF TABERNACLES BY THE ATTACKING NATIONS

In this concluding section of Zechariah, Zechariah 14:16–19, we witness the redemptive heart of God even toward those who were His enemies—"Then the survivors from all the nations that have attacked Jerusalem will go up year after year to worship the King, the LORD Almighty, and to *celebrate* the Feast of Tabernacles" (v. 16). Tabernacles, or Succoth, was originally intended to be the festival of the nations, and this will actually happen. The surviving nations will go annually to Jerusalem to worship the Lord. The Saudis will be there and the Syrians and the Iranians and the Turks. They will come to Jerusalem from Yemen and Egypt and Sudan "to worship the King, the LORD Almighty" (v. 17) and to celebrate together before Him! Marvelous grace that can turn enemies into worshipers and foes into friends!

The Sons of Korah sang of this day in their powerful prophetic song, Psalm 87:

> On the holy mountain stands the city founded by the LORD.
> He loves the city of Jerusalem more than any other city in
> Israel. O city of God, what glorious things are said of you!
> I will record Egypt and Babylon [modern-day Iraq] among
> those who know me—also Philistia [modern-day Gaza] and

Tyre [modern-day Lebanon], and even distant Ethiopia. They have all become citizens of Jerusalem! And it will be said of Jerusalem, "Everyone has become a citizen here." And the Most High will personally bless this city. When the LORD registers the nations, he will say, "This one has become a citizen of Jerusalem." At all the festivals the people will sing, "The source of my life is in Jerusalem [for the LORD Himself will be there]!" (NLT)

Yet some will drag their heels in going up to Jerusalem, for whatever reason. Consequently, "If any of the peoples of the earth do not go up to Jerusalem to worship the King, the LORD Almighty, they will have no rain" (Zech. 14:17). And, by special mention, in view of the recent hate coming from the Muslim Brotherhood of Egypt against Israel: "If *the Egyptian* people do not go up and take part, they will have no rain…This will be the punishment of Egypt and the punishment of all the nations that do not go up to celebrate the Feast of Tabernacles" (v. 18–19).

The concluding two verses of this powerful end-time prophecy have to be the strangest statements to conclude such an extraordinary prophetic vision—strange, that it is, until we look a little closer. These two final verses speak about bells on the collars of the horses, cooking pots of Jerusalem, and Canaanites no longer being found in the house of God—strange references, but wonderful ones! "On that day" everything—down to the least, most insignificant item will declare the awesome holiness of the Lord! Everything profane and defiling and secular will be gone, and He alone will be seen to be holy! In the words of Paul, as he concludes that great section on God's end-time purposes for Israel in Romans 9, 10, and 11: "From him and through him and to him are all things. To him be the glory forever! Amen" (Rom. 11:36). This sentiment is in the concluding two verses of Zechariah, and to this we say, "Amen, so be it!" Amen and amen!

PART TWO: A PROPHETIC HANDBOOK OF END-TIME PROPHECIES FROM THE NEW TESTAMENT IN LIGHT OF TODAY'S EVENTS

Chapter 15

JESUS' END-TIME TEACHINGS

INTRODUCTION

S O FAR WE have walked through the Old Testament on an end-time pilgrimage, beginning with God's promises to Abraham, Isaac, and Jacob in Genesis and concluding with those grand prophecies of Zechariah 12, 13, and 14 concerning the last days. In our journey we noted again and again God's unfailing commitment to His promises to Israel, but we have also witnessed again and again the hostility of the surrounding nations against Israel and against those promises.

A clear example of both of these realities is found in Numbers 23. One of the eastern nations hostile to Israel was Moab, one of the descendants of Lot (Gen. 19:36–37), living on the site of what is modern-day Jordan. The then king of Moab, Balak, hired a jaded "prophet" by the name of Balaam to declare the demise of Israel: "Curse them for me" (Num. 23:13). In the process, however, "The LORD met with Balaam and put a message in his mouth" (v. 16). And what a message it was! These words became a high-water mark in the Old Testament concerning the veracity of God's promises: "Then [Balaam] uttered his oracle: 'Arise, Balak [king of Moab], and listen…God is not a man, that he should lie, nor a son of man, that he should change his mind. Does he speak and then not act? Does he promise and not fulfill? I have received a command to bless; [and the reason is because] he has blessed, and I cannot change it'" (Numbers 23:18–20).

A similar statement on the unchangeableness of God's promise to Abraham is given to us, as we already noticed, in Hebrews 6:13: "When God made his promise to Abraham, since there was no one greater for him to swear by, he swore by himself, saying, 'I will surely bless you and give you many descendants.'" The reference is undoubtedly to Genesis 22:16–18, where the Lord promises, "I swear by myself, declares the LORD, that...I will surely bless you and make your descendants as numerous as the stars in the sky and as the sand on the seashore. Your descendants will take possession of the cities of their enemies [the land of promise], and through your offspring [your Seed] all nations on earth will be blessed." These are wonderful promises concerning the nation of Israel, concerning the land of promise, and concerning the Messiah, through whom "all nations on earth will be blessed." And God is a God who always keeps His word. The author of Hebrews continues in Hebrews 6:16–18:

> Men swear by someone greater than themselves, and *the oath* confirms what is said and puts an end to all argument. Because God wanted to make *the unchanging nature of his purpose very clear to the heirs of what was promised, he confirmed it with an oath. God did this so that, by two unchangeable things in which it is impossible for God to lie, we who have fled to take hold of the hope offered to us may be greatly encouraged.* (emphasis added)

In other words, *we know beyond a shadow of a doubt* that God will *never* break His promises and His commitments *to us* as new covenant believers, because of His track record in faithfully keeping His promises and His commitments to His covenant people Israel!

JESUS' TEACHING ON HIS SECOND COMING: MATTHEW 23:36–24:31

We now begin our end-time walk through the New Testament, and we begin with Jesus' teachings on the last days given during His final week before His crucifixion and resurrection.

Jesus had been grieving over Jerusalem: "Upon you will come all the righteous blood that has been shed on earth, from the blood of righteous Abel to the blood of Zechariah son of Berekiah, whom you murdered between the temple and the altar" (Matt. 23:35). (This Zechariah is the one whose end-time prophecies we just finished studying; we would not have known how he died except for these words of Jesus.)

Jesus continued, "O Jerusalem, Jerusalem, you who kill the prophets and stone those sent to you, how often I have longed to gather your children together, as a hen gathers her chicks under her wings, but you were not willing. Look, your house is left to you desolate" (Matt. 23:37–38). Jesus reiterated this awful judgment in His next statement concerning the temple: "Not one stone here will be left on another; every one will be thrown down" (Matt. 24:2). This prophecy was literally fulfilled in A.D. 70 in the destruction of Jerusalem—both the city and the temple—by the armies of the Roman general Titus, son of Vespasian, the Emperor of Rome.

The concluding words of Jesus over Jerusalem, found in Matthew 23:39, become for us the first of a series of signs that point to the end-times and assure us that we are in the last days! Jesus said, "I tell you, you will not see me again until you say, 'Blessed is he who comes in the name of the Lord.'"

When, after nearly two thousand years of non-existence, Israel became a state in 1948 and the Jewish people began to return to their homeland, they virtually all returned in unbelief—at least toward Yeshua[xi]—just as spoken in Jeremiah 3:14, "Return, faithless people."

When my wife, Dotty, and I first visited Israel in 1977 there were very few messianic believers in Yeshua (and these were mainly westerners), and there were only a handful of small messianic congregations in *the whole land*. Today, we were recently told that it is believed that across Israel there are upwards to twenty thousand messianic believers in Yeshua, meeting in nearly two hundred messianic congregations! God has begun to pour out His Spirit as He promised in Zechariah 12:10, and throughout the land the cry is going up from the faithful concerning Yeshua: "Blessed is he who comes in the name of the Lord"! And, according to Jesus, that cry will trigger His return, for "you will not see me again *until you say*, 'Blessed is he who comes in the name of the Lord'"! This is the first great sign pointing to Jesus' near return!

The narrative continues in Matthew 24:3: "As Jesus was sitting

---

xi. *Yeshua* is Jesus' name in Aramaic, the native tongue of first-century Israel.

on the Mount of Olives, the disciples came to him privately. 'Tell us,' they said, 'when will this happen,'" referring to the immediate destruction of Jerusalem and the temple, which did happen in A.D. 70. Jesus, actually, did not respond to this part of their question, for they would actually see that destruction within their very own life-times. He responded rather to the more pertinent end-time part of their question, "What will be the sign of your coming and of the end of the age?" (v. 3).

Beginning Signs

In Matthew 24:4–8 Jesus cited three major preliminary signs of the end of the age. We call these beginning signs because of Jesus' own words: "Such things must happen, but the end is still to come" (v. 6) and "these are the beginning of birth pains" (v. 8), the *beginning* birth pangs of God's new age! These are the three beginning signs:

- Spiritual deception: "Watch out that no one deceives you...many will come in my name, claiming: 'I am the Christ,' and will deceive many" (Matt. 24:4–5). Deception will be a snare in the lasts days.[xii]

- Ethnic wars: "You will hear of wars and rumors of wars...Nation [ethnic group, literally] will rise against nation [ethnic group], and kingdom against kingdom" (Matt. 24:6–7). The outbreak of ethnic wars will proliferate in the last days, even as we are seeing such conflicts unfold before us in the news today.

- Natural disasters: "Famines [such as the devastating famines we are seeing in Africa] and earthquakes in various places" (Matt. 24:7). It has been reported that in the past nineteen hundred years, since Jesus gave this prediction, there have been thirty major earth-quakes in the world; however, in the past half-century there have been *sixty major earthquakes worldwide*, killing millions. One of the reasons for the increased death toll is that in 1800, for example, there was only

---

xii. See Appendix Five for a brief discussion on "Other Christs."

one city, Beijing, with more than a million people; today there are well over one hundred eighty urban areas with at least one million people, and some of these exist on serious fault lines.

MORE INTENSE SIGNS

Jesus continued, "Then you will be handed over to be persecuted and put to death, and you will be hated by all nations because of me" (Matt. 24:9). Over the past nearly two thousand years it has been estimated that 50 million martyrs have been slain for Jesus' sake. But half of these have been killed in *the past century alone,* and many of these in Islamic lands! And because of persecution, "Many will turn away from the faith and will betray and hate each other, and many false prophets will appear and deceive many people.....[And] the love of most will grow cold." (Matt. 24:10, 12). The exponential increase in these signs causes them to become *signs of the times,* indicating *the last days.* In the intensity of these last days, only the one "who stands firm to the end will be saved" (Matt. 24:13)!

THE SIGN OF THE END

One of the questions the disciples had asked Jesus was, "What will be the sign of your coming and of the end of the age?" (Matt. 24:3). Jesus told us: "And this gospel of the kingdom will be preached in the whole world as a testimony to all nations [Greek, *ethne*, meaning 'ethnic groups'] and then the end will come" (v. 14).

For nearly two thousand years Jesus' final command to His followers has gone unfulfilled: "Go and make disciples of all nations" (Matt. 28:19). The generation of believers that is alive today, however, with its passionate commitment to bring the message of Jesus to every yet-unreached ethnic group in the world, is actually within reach of completing this task—for the first time in history! Missionary leaders feel that this mission is possible to complete before the end of the next decade!

Peter, who personally heard the Olivet teachings from the lips of Jesus on these end-time events, asks us this salient question in 2 Peter 3:11: "What kind of people ought you to be?" The answer is clear: "You ought to live holy and godly lives as you look forward to the day of God and speed its coming" (2 Pet. 3:11–12). We have already noted that the New King James Version translates this amazing statement, "Looking for and hastening the coming of the day of God." The salvation of mankind is foremost in our Lord's thinking, for He is "not wanting anyone to perish, but everyone to come to repentance" (2 Pet. 3:9), and obedience to our Lord's final command in worldwide evangelism is the key to "hastening the coming of the day of God" as the saints "speed its coming." Jesus has already shown us through his servant John that at the end of the days before the throne of God there will be "a great multitude that no one could count, from every nation, tribe, people and language" (Rev. 7:9). Amen!

THE RISE OF THE ANTICHRIST KINGDOM

Jesus continued: "So when *you see* standing in the holy place 'the abomination that causes desolation,' spoken of through the prophet Daniel—let the reader understand" (Matt. 24:15). First of all, the mention of the holy place plainly tells us that the temple *will* be rebuilt, the temple that Titus' army tore down so that "not one stone [was] left on another" (v. 2). (We will discuss this third temple in more detail later.) Second, the mention of "'the abomination that causes desolation,' spoken of through the prophet Daniel," makes it clear that the prophecies of Daniel about the "abomination that causes desolation" (Dan. 8:13; 9:27; 11:31; 12:11) were not fulfilled (except as a type) in the career of Antiochus IV Epiphanies Theos in 168 B.C. but await a final end-time fulfillment in these last days.

The rise of the Antichrist kingdom from the surrounding nations will mean great persecution against the people of Israel, as we have already noted from the Old Testament prophecies. Consequently, Jesus declared: "Let those who are in Judea flee to the mountains," and, "Pray that your flight will not take place in winter or on the Sabbath. For then there will be great distress ['great tribulation,' NKJV], unequaled from the beginning of the world until now—and never to be equaled again...but for the sake of the elect those days will be shortened" (Matt. 24:16, 20–22). From references in this passage ("let those who are in Judea"), it becomes clear that the vortex of the Great Tribulation will be the Middle East, though from there the effects of the Great Tribulation will reach to all nations on earth.

The next section of Jesus' teaching in Matthew 24:23–28 becomes intriguingly clearer, especially when we understand it in the light of Islamic eschatology. Jesus taught:

> At that time if anyone says to you, "Look, here is the Christ [the Messiah]!" or, "There he is!" *do not believe it.* For false Christs [especially, *the* Antichrist] and false prophets [especially, *the* false prophet] will appear and perform great signs and miracles to deceive even the elect—if that were possible. See, I have told you ahead of time. So if anyone tells you, "There he is, *out in the desert," do not go out;* or, "Here he is, *in the inner rooms," do not believe it.* For as lightning that comes from the east is visible even in the west [instantaneously streaking across the sky], so will be the coming of the Son of Man. Wherever there is a carcass [a Slain One], there the vultures will gather ["the eagles will be gathered together," NKJV]." (emphasis added)

The reason why we are not to go out to the desert when we hear the report that the Messiah has come is simply because at His coming, which will be instantaneous as a lightning flash in the sky, we will be gathered to Him. All the eagles will be gathered together to the Slain One when He appears! Plainly stated, His saints will be raptured to meet Him in the air when He appears, as eagles gathering around a freshly slain carcass.

As previously explained, the reference to the coming of the Messiah *to the desert* is a significant reference in Islamic eschatology. As we already noticed, Muhammad, the prophet and founder of Islam, spoke clearly of the last days, as recorded in his sayings, the Hadith:

> The world will not come to pass until a man from among my family, whose name will be my name, rules over the Arabs. The Mahdi [Islam's awaited lord and savior, Mahdi al-Muntadhar]…will be from my family and will be exactly forty years of age. His face will shine like a star…[He] will govern the people by the Sunnah [Islamic teachings] and establish Islam on earth. He will remain *seven years…*The Mahdi will fill the earth

with equity and justice as it was filled with oppression and tyranny, and he will *rule for seven years.* (emphasis added)

We take note from Daniel 9:26–27 that "the [Antichrist] ruler
who will come…will confirm a covenant with many for one 'seven'
[for seven years]."

As for the *desert* appearance of the Messiah, note these predic-
tions from Islam's sacred traditions about Isa Al-Maseeh (Jesus, the
Islamic Messiah): "At this very time Allah would send Christ, son of
Mary, and he will descend at the white minaret in the eastern side
of Damascus wearing two garments lightly dyed with saffron."[12]

Muhammad himself prophesied, "Jesus son of Mary would
descend and their commander [the Mahdi] would invite him to
come and lead them in prayer, but he would say, No," for, "Jesus
will come and will perform the obligatory prayers behind the
Mahdi and follow him."[13] This reference to the prayer activity in
the mosque at Damascus may be what Jesus alluded to when He
said, "So if anyone tells you… 'Here he is in the inner rooms,' do
not believe it" (Matt. 24:36). The phrase "the inner rooms" has been
translated "the hidden, secret chamber" and may refer to the place
for prayer in the mosque, off limits to everyone but Muslims.

Muhammad further states of Jesus, "Isa ibn Maryam [Jesus son
of Mary] shall descend as equitable judge and fair ruler. He shall
come to my grave [in the deserts of Saudi Arabia] to greet me, and
I shall certainly answer him."[14] So much for the "desert" appear-
ances of the Christ! We are speaking here of a false Christ, the one
described for us in Revelation 13:11–17 as the false prophet!

Concerning this false Messiah other Islamic commentators note
that: "Jesus will descend from heaven and espouse the cause of
the Mahdi. The Christians and the Jews will see him and recognize his true status. The Christians will abandon their faith in his
godhead…Isa [Jesus] will declare that he is alive and has not died,
and he is not God nor the Son of God, but Allah's slave and messenger…Allah will [cause to] perish all religions except Islam."[15]
These end-time Islamic prophecies fit the last-days scriptures as a
glove fits a hand and give us reasonable ground to believe that the
radical Islamic world may very well be the antichrist kingdom of
the last days!

THE SECOND COMING OF OUR LORD, JESUS CHRIST

The true believers in Jesus, God's elect, will not be deceived into going out to the desert to see a false Messiah. They will be caught up together to meet Him in the air, for as Jesus taught us:

> Immediately after the distress ["tribulation," KJV] of those days 'the sun will be darkened, and the moon will not give its light; the stars will fall from the sky, and the heavenly bodies will be shaken.' At that time the sign of the Son of Man will appear in the sky, and all the nations of the earth will mourn. They will see the Son of Man coming on the clouds of the sky, with power and great glory. And he will send his angels with a loud trumpet call, and they will gather his elect from the four winds, from one end of the heavens to the other.
>
> —MATTHEW 24:29–31

This is our blessed hope! In the words of James H. McConkey:

> Suddenly in mid-heaven, without a second's warning, is staged by God the most stupendous sight upon which human eyes have ever gazed—the outflashing, the dazzling, awful splendor of the personal coming of the Lord Jesus Christ in His glory.
>
> *The earth beholds* and thrills with the first ecstatic moment of her deliverance from the bondage of corruption into the glorious liberty of the sons of God.
>
> *The angels behold* and cry, "The kingdoms of this world are become the kingdom of our Lord and His Christ."
>
> *The kings and princes of the world behold* and cry to the rocks and hills to fall upon them and hide them from His presence.
>
> *The anti-christ beholds* and falls palsied and helpless before the breath of His mouth and the glory of His coming.
>
> *The nations of the earth behold* and cry out because of Him.
>
> Not since the skies were stretched by the omnipotent hand of God in the ages that are past, has their blue canopy been the setting for such a scene as now floods them with its glory![16]

Chapter 16

JESUS' TEACHING ON PREPARING
FOR HIS RETURN

Matthew 24:32–25:46

I N THE LAST chapter we considered the teachings of our Lord
Jesus on the last-days signs of the times. According to Him the
final and greatest sign of the last days will be "the sign of the
Son of Man [that] will appear in the sky" when all on earth "will
see the Son of Man coming on the clouds of the sky, with power
and great glory" (Matt. 24:30). This is an open and glorious coming
seen by all the world. Revelation 1:7 describes it this way: "Look,
he is coming with the clouds, and *every eye* will see him, even
those who pierced him; and *all the peoples of the earth* will mourn
because of him. So shall it be! Amen." Also at that time, "He will
send his angels with a loud trumpet call, and they will gather his
elect from the four winds, from one end of the heavens to the other"
(Matt. 24:31). And this is the Rapture of the church! Jesus has now
fully answered the question the disciples originally asked, "What
will be the sign of *your coming*?" (Matt. 24:3).

We note from His answer that this is His *only* coming. There is
no earlier coming; there is *no* secret coming; there is *no* other rapture. Only this one found in Matthew 24:29–31. And Jesus expected
His disciples to take *these teachings of His* to all the nations (Matt.
28:19–20).

On the heels of this teaching, our Lord Jesus made some startling statements. First of all, He taught, "Learn this lesson from the
fig tree: As soon as its twigs get tender and its leaves come out, you
know that summer is near. Even so, when you see all these things,
you know that it ['He,' margin] is near, right at the door" (Matt.

24:32–33). We are impressed with His words "you know," used twice over. Our Lord Jesus was fully expecting His followers to be careful observers of end-time events and for them to *know* from the unfolding of those events that His second coming was near at hand. Jesus was quick to tell His followers that no one knows the *exact day or hour* of His return (Matt. 24:36, 42, 44), but, on the other hand, believers are not to be ignorant of "the times and the seasons" leading up to His return (1 Thess. 5:1, NKJV).

The second startling statement Jesus made was: "I tell you the truth, this generation [the generation that begins to see all these things] will certainly not pass away until all these things have happened" (Matt. 24:34). The generation that begins to see the fulfillment of these end-time signs will not pass away until they are all fulfilled. That generation will indeed witness the second coming of our Lord! All that He taught us will be fulfilled, for He promised, "Heaven and earth will pass away, but my words will never pass away" (Matt. 24:35). Everything will happen *exactly as He said!* The elect *will know* what is happening; others—as in the days of Noah—will *know nothing* of what is about to happen until it is too late, and they are suddenly swept away (vv. 37–41). Indeed, "one will be taken and the other left" behind (v. 40). In the next section, Matthew 24:42–44, we believers are, therefore, commanded twice to "keep watch" and "to be ready," for we know neither the day nor the hour when our Lord will come!

Matthew 24:45–51 is a sober warning to those in leadership in the last days, those "whom the master has put in charge of the servants in his household." The faithful and wise servant leader who serves well in the household will be richly rewarded! But the servant leader who is authoritarian and heavy handed, beating his fellow servants, along with the servant leader who is compromising and backslidden, who "eats and drinks with drunkards," will both be assigned "a place with the hypocrites, where there will be weeping and gnashing of teeth." *The Message* translates this: "the Master…[will] make hash of him. He'll end up in the dump with the hypocrites, out in the cold shivering, teeth chattering." A sober warning to all servant leaders!

MATTHEW 25: THREE STORIES ON
BEING READY FOR JESUS' RETURN

The Story of the Ten Virgins

The three stories told by Jesus in Matthew 25 tell us how we can be ready and "keep watch, because [we] do not know on what day [our] Lord will come" (Matt. 24:42). In the first story we are introduced to ten virgins, who by that very designation are a picture of believers. These "took their lamps and went out to meet the bridegroom" (Matt. 25:1). Five of the ten were foolish and the other five were wise. The foolish took their lamps but "did not take any oil with them"; the "wise, however, took oil in jars along with their lamps" (Matt. 25:2–4). "Oil" in the Scriptures is a picture of the Holy Spirit, and "oil in jars" speaks of the abundance that the five wise virgins had. Paul speaks of being wise in Ephesians 5:15–18: "Be very careful, then, how you live—not as unwise but as wise...do not be foolish...be [ever] filled with the Spirit." The Greek verb used here shows abundance, as believers are commanded to be filled with the Spirit—day by day, hour by hour. This is the way we can be found ready when Jesus comes!

Almost prophetically, Jesus predicted in Matthew 25:5, "The bridegroom was a long time in coming"; and nearly two thousand years *is* a long time! Consequently, "They all became drowsy and fell asleep." This is an accurate description of the state of the professing church—asleep! But "at midnight the cry rang out: 'Here's the bridegroom! Come out to meet him!'" (v. 6) May our voices be part of that midnight cry that will awaken a slumbering church to the reality of the nearness of Jesus' return! Paul may have had this very story in mind when he admonished the Romans to understand the present *kairos* time: "The hour has come for you to wake up from your slumber, because our salvation is nearer now than when we first believed" (Rom. 13:11). Then according to Matthew 25:7, "All the virgins woke up and trimmed their lamps," and an oil crisis arose! The foolish virgins' lamps were "going out," and as they were scurrying around trying to find more oil, "the bridegroom arrived. The virgins who were ready went in with him to the wedding banquet. The door was shut," and outside were the unprepared. What sober words: "'I don't know you.' 'Therefore keep watch, because you do not know the day or the hour' (Matt. 25:8, 10–13)!

The Story of the Talents

The point of the first story about the ten virgins is clear—Rapture-ready people are those filled to overflowing with the Holy Spirit! The point of the second story is also clear—those ready for Jesus' coming are those who are faithful in using what gifts and graces God has given them.

In this second story, the master of a household departed on a journey that lasted for a long time. Prior to his departure he gave different amounts of money to his servants, each according to their ability, to be used in his absence. To one he gave five talents of money, to another two talents, and to yet another one talent. (These sums of money represented a person's whole life's earnings in the first century. One talent alone would have been twenty years of wages, equivalent to a quarter of a million dollars in today's economy.) The master's intent was that the talents that were given to each would be used by them respectively and thereby would be multiplied.

Paul understood this concept and admonished the Roman believers to use their "different gifts, according to the grace given [them]" (Rom. 12:6). To the Corinthians he wrote: "to each one the manifestation of the Spirit is given for the common good" (1 Cor. 12:7). To the Ephesians he wrote: "The whole body…grows and builds itself up in love, as each part does its work" (Eph. 4:16). To Timothy Paul wrote: "Do not neglect your gift, which was given you" (1 Tim. 4:14). And Peter, who heard this story of the talents first-hand from Jesus, likewise prophetically wrote to the saints: "The end of all things is near.…Each one should use whatever gift he has received to serve others, faithfully administering God's grace in its various forms" (1 Pet. 4:7, 10).

The story continues in Matthew 25:19–21:

> After a long time the master of those servants returned and settled accounts with them. The man who had received the five talents had earned five more. "Master," he said, "you entrusted me with five talents. See, I have gained five more." His master

replied, "Well done, good and faithful servant! You have been faithful with a few things; I will put you in charge of many things. Come and share your master's happiness!"

The same happy ending came to the two-talent servant. He had doubled what was given to him and was equally rewarded.

But things did not go well for the one-talent servant. Out of fear due largely to a misperception of his master, he hid his talent and had no gains to give the master when he came. *The Message* probably expresses the response of the one-talent person most clearly in Matthew 25:24–27:

> "Master, I know you have high standards and hate careless ways, that you demand the best and make no allowances for error. I was afraid I might disappoint you, so I found a good hiding place and secured your money. Here it is, safe and sound down to the last cent." The master was furious. "That's a terrible way to live! It's criminal to live cautiously like that! *If you knew I was after the best, why did you do less than the least?*" (emphasis added)

The outcome of this fearful servant's cautious conduct was severe: "get rid of this 'play-it-safe' who won't go out on a limb. Throw him out into utter darkness" (v. 30, THE MESSAGE)!

So the point is clear—we all have been given gifts, graces, and talents by our Lord. We are wisely to *use these resources* to expand the kingdom of God in the earth. The outcome for failing to do just that is ever so serious, but the reward for faithfulness in serving is happiness and joy when the Master comes! Especially when it comes to missions, Paul divided all believers into two classes in Romans 10:14–15. One is either *"sent"* or a *"sender,"* faithful in prayer and in support of the one that is sent! All of us have something to bring to the table!

The Sheep and the Goats

So far we have been instructed by our Lord Jesus as to how we can be ready when He comes—by being full of the Holy Spirit and by using the gifts and graces that He has given to us. In the third story in Matthew 25:31–46 we are given the third key to readiness for Jesus' return—ministering to Jesus in His deepest need.

This passage begins, "When the Son of Man comes in his glory, and all the angels with him, he will sit on his throne in heavenly glory. All the nations will be gathered before him, and he will separate the people one from another as a shepherd separates the sheep from the goats" (vv. 31–32). To the sheep on his right he will say, "Come, you who are blessed by my Father; take your inheritance, the kingdom prepared for you since the creation of the world. For I was hungry and you gave me something to eat, I was thirsty and you gave me something to drink, I was a stranger and you invited me in, I needed clothes and you clothed me, I was sick and you looked after me, I was in prison and you came to visit me" (vv. 34–36).

The sheep were stunned. When was Jesus ever hungry or thirsty or homeless or naked or sick or in prison? And when did they ever minister to *Him* in such deep need? His answer was simple— "Whatever you did for one of the least [literally, 'the littlest,' 'the youngest,' 'the smallest'] of these brothers of mine, you did it for me" (v. 40). *The Message* translates this key statement: "Whenever you did one of these things to someone overlooked or ignored, that was me—you did it to me."

When Mother Theresa opened an AIDS clinic in New York City, her reason was *to minister to Jesus in His most distressed form!* She saw Him in each dying AIDS patient. We ourselves need to see Him in the little Jewish boy whose parents were killed in a shelling. We need to see Him in the little Palestinian girl left as an orphan in the Intifada. We will be able to find Jesus in scores of different places— in the garbage dump in Guatemala City, in the Kibera slum in Nairobi, among the street kids in the Philippines and in India, and as a child in the womb threatened by death through abortion. And the list goes on. Yet the issue is always the same: "Whatever you did for one of the least of these brothers of mine, *you did for me.*"

Concerning the goats on Jesus' left hand: though goats resemble sheep in appearance, they are a very different animal. The goats in our story, unlike the compassionate sheep, had selfishly closed their hearts to those who were hungry and thirsty, homeless and naked, and sick and in prison. Jesus said, "Whatever you did not do for one of the least of these, you did not do for me" (Matt. 25:45). For that reason, "they will go away to eternal punishment, but the righteous to eternal life" (v. 46).

We might wonder at this juncture if salvation was placed by our Lord on the basis of good works. Not really. James, our Lord's half-brother who probably knew of this story of the sheep and the goats, articulated the bottom line quite clearly:

> What good is it, my brothers, if a man *claims* to have faith but has no deeds? Can *such faith* save him? Suppose a brother or sister is without clothes and daily food. If one of you says to him, "Go, I wish you well; keep warm and well fed," but *does nothing about his physical needs, what good is it?* In the same way, faith by itself, if it is not accompanied by action, is *dead.*
> —JAMES 2:14–17, EMPHASIS ADDED

"Sheep-faith" is full of good works and overflowing with acts of compassion, and this is how we are found to be ready for Jesus' return.

Keep watch, because you do not know the day or the hour.
—MATTHEW 25:13

Chapter 17

JESUS' END-TIME TEACHINGS IN MARK AND LUKE AND THE END-TIME TEACHINGS OF PETER AND JAMES

THE END-TIME TEACHINGS of our Lord Jesus on the slopes of Mount Olivet are of such importance that they are recorded in each of the Synoptic Gospels—in Matthew, Mark, and Luke. Of the three, Matthew has the fullest account, as we have just seen. Mark, in chapter thirteen, gave an almost identical, though shorter, version of what we read in Matthew. Mark was Peter's spiritual son (1 Peter 5:13) and undoubtedly recorded what he himself heard from the lips of Peter on numerous occasions. Both Matthew and Peter heard the Master's Olivet teachings personally and continued to teach them; hence the similarity between Matthew and what we read in Mark's account.

Luke, who was not personally present with Jesus on the Mount of Olives, gleaned his understanding from those who "were eyewitnesses" (Luke 1:1). Consequently, in Luke 21:5–38, Luke gave us important material that is not found *per se* in Matthew or Mark. Therefore, we will want to consider that material carefully. Luke made special mention of the outburst of persecution in Israel by the religious leaders against the elect. He wrote, "They will lay hands on you and persecute you. They will deliver you to synagogues and prisons....But make up your mind not to worry beforehand how you will defend yourselves. For I will give you words and wisdom that none of your adversaries will be able to resist or contradict" (Luke 21:12, 14–15).

All three Gospel writers also spoke of martyrdom: "You will be...put to death" (Matt. 24:9); "Children will rebel against their

111

parents and have them put to death" (Mark 13:12); "And they will put some of you to death"! (Luke 21:16). Only Luke added this most wonderful promise: "But not a hair of your head will perish. By standing firm you will gain life" (Luke 21:18–19). What a wonderful promise of deliverance for those in the last days! In Luke 21:36 Luke reiterates this thought of deliverance: "Be always on the watch, and pray that you may be able to escape all that is about to happen, and that you may be able to stand before the Son of Man." The Greek word translated "escape" is *ekpheuge,* used by Luke three times in his writings (Luke 21:36; Acts 16:27; and Acts 19:16). The word simply means "to flee," and here in Luke 21, "to flee safely." For this reason The Living Bible margin (as does the New English Bible) translates this passage, "Pray for strength to pass safely through these coming horrors." J.B. Phillips likewise translates this phrase to "come safely through" (Phillips). We as believers are consequently to be careful and watchful and prayerful (Luke 21:34–36) that we may be able to "pass safely through all that is about to happen," and "that [we] may be able to stand before the Son of Man"!

The statements in Luke 21:20–24, which are peculiar to Luke, speak of "Jerusalem being surrounded by armies" (v. 20) and that "Jerusalem will be trampled on by the Gentiles until the times of the Gentiles are fulfilled" (v. 24). This statement "until the times of the Gentiles are fulfilled" has been translated in the following ways: "until their day is over" (TCNT); "til the period of the Gentiles expires" (Moffat); "until the time granted to the Gentile nations has run out" (Knox); "until the heathen's day is over" (Phillips); "until the time of heathen domination will have come to an end" (Norlie). This statement apparently means what Daniel described in the vision of Daniel 2:44: "The God of heaven will set up a kingdom that will never be destroyed, nor will it be left to another people. It will crush all those kingdoms and bring them to an end, but it will itself endure forever."

These statements in Luke refer to the assault on Jerusalem just before the return of Jesus, prophesied by Zechariah in Zechariah 14:2–3. The first-century destruction of Jerusalem in A.D. 70 by the armies of Titus was a picture of this end-time assault on Jerusalem.

Eusebius, one of the early historians, wrote about the A.D. 70 destruction of Jerusalem:

> The people of the church in Jerusalem had been commanded by a revelation, vouchsafed to approved men...to leave the city and to dwell in a certain town of Perea call Pella. And when those that believed in Christ had come [to Pella] from Jerusalem, then, as if the royal city of the Jews and the whole land of Judea were entirely destitute of holy men, the judgment of God at length overtook those who had committed such outrages against Christ and his apostles and totally destroyed that generation of impious men.[xiii]

If the Lord preserved His elect in the devastation of A.D. 70, He will surely do it again in these last days! Jesus promised, "Not a hair of your head will perish. By standing firm you will gain life" (Luke 21:18–19). And Jesus admonishes His end-time followers, "Be always on the watch, and pray that you may be able to *safely flee* all that is about to happen, and that you may be able to stand before the Son of Man" (v. 36).

The words of Psalm 91 are so appropriate for the last days; they contain for us wonderful assurances of deliverance by the hand of our almighty God:

> He who dwells in the shelter of the Most High will rest in the shadow of the Almighty. I will say of the LORD, "He is my refuge and my fortress, my God, in whom I trust." Surely he will save you from the fowler's snare and from the deadly pestilence. He will cover you with his feathers, and under his wings you will find refuge; his faithfulness will be your shield and rampart. You will not fear the terror of night, nor the arrow that flies by day, nor the pestilence that stalks in the darkness, nor the plague that destroys at midday. A thousand may fall at your side, ten thousand at your right hand, but it will not come near you. You will only observe with your eyes and see the punishment of the wicked. If you make the Most High your dwelling—even the LORD, who is my refuge—then

---

xiii. Eusebius, as quoted in *Nicene and Post Nicene Fathers, Second Series, Volume 1,* edited by Philip Schaff (Peabody, MA: Hendrickson Publishers, 1994), 138.

no harm will befall you, no disaster will come near your tent. For he will command his angels concerning you to guard you in all your ways; they will lift you up in their hands, so that you will not strike your foot against a stone. You will tread upon the lion and the cobra; you will trample the great lion and the serpent. "Because he loves me," says the LORD, "I will rescue him; I will protect him, for he acknowledges my name. He will call upon me, and I will answer him; I will be with him in trouble, I will deliver him and honor him. With long life will I satisfy him and show him my salvation."

THE END-TIME TEACHINGS OF
PETER AND JAMES

If there were no literal end-time restoration of Israel, Jesus, before His ascension, had the perfect opportunity to tell His followers exactly that when they asked Him, "Lord, are you at this time going to restore the kingdom to Israel?" (Acts 1:6). Instead of telling them that there would be no such restoration because the church would now replace Israel in God's purposes, Jesus rather said, "It is not for you to know the times or dates the Father has set by his own authority" (v. 7). This exchange guided the thinking of the early apostles regarding the last days.

According to Acts 2:14–16, when "Peter stood up with the Eleven" on the Day of Pentecost to answer the question of the bewildered crowd, "What does this mean?" (v. 12), Peter sought to explain the Pentecostal happenings of that day from Joel's end-time prophecy: "This is what was spoken by the prophet Joel" (v. 16). Peter's wording is important. When a prophecy is actually fulfilled, that is exactly what is said about it. For example, in John 19:36 when the prophetic picture from Exodus 12:46 and Psalm 34:20 concerning the Passover lamb was actually being *fulfilled* by Jesus on the cross, these were the words John used: "These things happened so that the scripture would be fulfilled: 'Not one of his bones will be broken.'" Verse 37, the next statement, however, reads differently: "And, as another scripture says, 'They will look on the one they have pierced.'" Concerning this scripture, Zechariah 12:10, John did not say it was *fulfilled,* because it is a last-days Scripture and will only be fulfilled in the end-times when Israel looks upon the wounded Messiah and realizes what they have done. Then this prophecy will be fulfilled, and it will be noted as fulfilled. So in Acts 2:16, in giving his explanation of the events of that Day of Pentecost, Peter did not say, "That it might be fulfilled which was spoken by the prophet Joel," because that prophecy also yet awaits an end-time fulfillment. Acts 2:20 actually tells us so by referring to the future "coming of the great and glorious day of the Lord," which is eschatological, or end-time, in its scope.

As we already noted, the last days were ushered in by the first coming of Jesus, according to passages such as 1 Peter 1:20 and Hebrews 1:1–2. These last days will continue on until His second coming, with clear signs that point to the imminence of that second coming. One of those signs will be the fulfillment of Joel's prophecy. In the latter days, God will pour out His Spirit on all people—on all races and all cultures. This is not only on Israel but on the Islamic world and the Buddhist world and the Hindu world and the nominal Christian world and the animist world. The entire world has already begun to receive the beginnings of this powerful outpouring from heaven. It is believed that by the end of the first century one out of every three hundred sixty persons were confessing Christians. By the year 2000, with a world population of over 6 billion people, *one out of every six people* were confessing Christ as Lord!

Peter continued: "Your sons and daughters will prophesy" (Acts 2:17). This will be an outpouring not only on all races but on both genders, and it will also be intergenerational: "Your young men will see visions, your old men will dream dreams" (v. 17). And spiritual gifts will accompany this visitation—prophecies, visions, dreams, signs, and wonders in heaven above and on the earth below.

Also what Jesus stated in Matthew 24:29 would happen just before His return will happen in the days of this outpouring just before the great and glorious Day of the Lord: "The sun will be darkened and the moon will not give its light" (Acts 2:20). But the most wonderful part of this prophecy is the ingathering of souls that is predicted, for "everyone who calls on the name of the Lord will be saved" (Acts 2:21). The Greek wording of this statement is powerful: "It will be everyone—whoever calls on the name of the

Master, who will be saved." Consequently, John described this final harvest as "a great multitude that no one could count, from every nation, tribe, people and language" (Rev. 7:9)!

In Acts 3:17–21 Peter again painted for us a stunning picture of the last days, the time just preceding the return of Jesus. Speaking to those who had disavowed Jesus in the dark hours before His death, Peter said, "Now, brothers, I know that you acted in ignorance, as did your leaders [for he himself had done the same thing in the courtyard of Caiaphas]. But this is how God fulfilled what he had foretold through all the prophets, saying that his Christ would suffer. Repent, then, and turn to God, so that your sins may be wiped out, that times [*kairos times,* literally] of refreshing may come from the Lord" (vv. 17–19). The New King James Version translates this as "times of refreshing from the Presence of the Lord." The Greek use of the word *kairos* indicates divinely appointed visitations, *kairos* times of refreshing, that will actually mark the church age right up to the second coming of Jesus, when the Father will "send the Christ, who has been appointed for you—even Jesus. He must remain in heaven until the time comes for God to restore everything, as he promised long ago through his holy prophets" (v.20–21). And surely He will restore a sleeping church as well as a blinded Israel and an orphaned Arab world! Amazing and awesome promises! And Peter was a man who lived life in the light of the last days. That is why he would write to the saints scattered across Asia Minor, "The end of all things is near" (1 Pet. 4:7). And for us today it is nearer yet!

James, the half-brother of our Lord, penned an amazing prophetic word in James 5:7–8. He obviously had the coming of our Lord in mind, for he says: "Be patient [persevering, persistent], then, brothers, until the Lord's coming. See how the farmer waits for the land to yield its valuable crop ['the precious fruit of the earth,' NKJV] and how patient [persevering, persistent] he is for the autumn [the early] and spring [the latter] rains. You too, be patient [persevering and persistent] and stand firm, because the Lord's coming is near." James prophetically saw the Lord's coming; he also saw the great harvest that would be gathered in just before the Lord's coming, and he saw the double-strength outpouring from heaven, the early and the latter rain, that would make that great harvest possible. Also James encouraged us to a patient, persistent, persevering faith—like Elijah, who "prayed, and the heavens gave rain, and the earth produced its crops" (James 5:18). Elijah was a man just like us—with all his foibles and leaning sides—but he prayed earnestly; literally, he prayed with prayer, and God answered! And He *will* answer His Elijahs in these last days!

Chapter 18

PAUL'S UNDERSTANDING OF ISRAEL AND THE CHURCH

Paul in His Letter to the Galatians

WHEN WE TRACE the messianic promises given to the patriarchs in Genesis, we note the repeated statement "through your offspring [your seed] all nations on earth will be blessed" (Gen. 22:18). In writing to the Galatians Paul gives us a wonderful insight into this. He wrote: "The promises were spoken to Abraham and to his seed. The Scripture does not say 'and to seeds,' meaning many people, but 'and to your seed,' meaning one person, who is Christ" (Gal. 3:16)! Thus Paul made it clear that the promised Seed to whom all the covenant promises are given is *Christ!*

Paul then expanded this thought. The Seed to whom all the promises are given is Christ, but the resurrected Christ has now become a *corporate Man.* Paul wrote: "All of you...were baptized into Christ [in whom] there is neither Jew nor Greek, slave nor free, male nor female, for you are all one in Christ Jesus...[and so] you are Abraham's seed, and heirs according to the promise" (vv. 27–29). The resurrected Christ is now a many-membered Man. All who believe in Him—whether Jew or Gentile, slave or free, male or female—have been baptized into Him and by that very act have all been made part of His body, so that together they are now Abraham's seed and heirs according to His promise! Consequently, we no longer see believing Israel as separate from the believing Gentiles. Israel and the Gentiles together are now a part of God's one new man. Therefore, Israel cannot be considered a separate kingdom from the church, nor has the church replaced Israel. Believing Israel is joined with the believing Gentiles in one body, the body of Christ! And this "new creation" in Paul's concluding words to the Galatians is "the Israel of God" (Gal. 6:15–16).

Paul in His Letter to the Ephesians

What Paul began to define in his letter to the Galatians, he then continued to define in his letter to the Ephesians. He saw the Gentiles in their past as "separate from Christ, excluded from citizenship in Israel and foreigners to the covenants of the promise, without hope and without God in the world" (Eph. 2:12). Then Paul saw the miracle which Jesus wrought on the cross:

> But now in Christ Jesus you who once were far away have been *brought near* through the blood of Christ. For he himself is our peace, who has *made the two one* and has destroyed…the dividing wall of hostility…His purpose was to create in himself *one new man* out of the two, thus making peace, and in this *one body* to reconcile both of them to God through the cross, by which he put to death their hostility.…Consequently, you [Gentiles] are *no longer* foreigners and aliens, but *fellow citizens* with God's people [Israel].…Through the gospel the Gentiles are *heirs together with Israel, members together of one body,* and *sharers together in the promise in Christ Jesus.*
> —Ephesians 2:13–16, 19; 3:6, emphasis added

It is clear that Israel can *never* be a separate kingdom from the church, nor has the church replaced believing Israel in the purposes of God. Starting on a new foundation, the Gentiles have been included as fellow citizens in the commonwealth of Israel; Jew and Gentile together are now one brand new man, members together of one body and heirs together of the promises of God!

Paul in His Letter to the Romans

In Romans 9, 10, and especially chapter 11, Paul continued to unfold for us God's purposes for believing Israel, especially in the last days, and particularly in relationship to the Gentiles. Romans 9 teaches us that "not all who are descended from Israel are Israel" (v. 6). The true Israel of God has always been a divine election, and to our utter amazement that divine election now includes those whom He called "not only from the Jews but also from the Gentiles" (Rom. 9:24)! Consequently, in chapter 10 Paul declared, "There is no difference between Jew and Gentile—the same Lord is Lord of all and richly blesses all who call on him, for, 'Everyone who calls on the name of the Lord will be saved'" (vv. 12–13). Then in chapter 11, Paul addressed the subject of natural Israel in the last days. He began in verse 1 by asking the question concerning natural Israel, "Did God reject his people?" The answer was emphatic: "By no means…God did not reject his people, whom he foreknew" (vv. 1–2).

Paul then asked that question again, but in a different way: "Again I ask: Did they stumble so as to fall beyond recovery?" (Rom. 11:11). Again the answer was emphatic: "Not at all!" (v. 11). Paul continued, "Rather, because of their transgression, salvation has come to the Gentiles to make Israel envious. But if their transgression means riches for the world, and their loss means riches for the Gentiles, how much greater riches will their fullness bring!" (vv. 11–12). Inherent in that phrase "their fullness" is an apparent promise of restoration in the last days, for "how much greater riches will their fullness bring!"

Then Paul repeated this same thought using different words: "For if their rejection is the reconciliation of the world, what will their acceptance be but life from the dead?" (Rom. 11:15) The twin phrases "their fullness" and "their acceptance" are statements of hope for natural Israel in the last days. They will experience both fullness and acceptance as they turn from blindness and unbelief to the Lord Jesus Christ!

THE STORY OF TWO OLIVE TREES, ONE CULTURED AND ONE WILD

In Romans 11:16–24 a powerful figure of speech is used to illustrate the wonderful truths we are studying. The cultivated olive tree is presented to us as a symbol of Israel, and its "root is holy" (v. 16). Paul further spoke of "the nourishing sap from the olive root" (v. 17), undoubtedly referring to the life of the patriarchs who are the foundation, the root of Israel. Israel is founded on the spiritual lives of Abraham, Isaac, and Jacob and their faith walk with God. Abraham, because of his faith walk, according to Paul, is "our *individual choice matters*

Christianity

father in the sight of God in whom he believed" (Rom. 4:17). Indeed, Abraham is "is the father of us all" (Rom. 4:16).

Painfully, in the course of time, "some of the branches [natural Jews] have been broken off [of this cultured olive tree].... broken off because of unbelief," and amazingly, believing Gentiles, "though a wild olive shoot, have been grafted in among the others and now share in the nourishing sap from the olive root" (Rom. 11:17, 19).

Two things become increasingly clear to us as we walk through this chapter. First of all, Israel and the church are *not* two separate kingdoms. There is only *one* cultivated olive tree, and *both* believing Jews and believing Gentiles are branches *together* in that one cultivated tree, the true Israel of God. Secondly, the church does not replace Israel, but the church is now clearly defined as both Jews and Gentiles joined together in the cultivated olive tree, Israel. Believing Jews are the natural branches, for the olive tree was originally theirs by divine election. But now, as a further part of that divine election, believing Gentiles are "cut out of an olive tree that is wild by nature, and contrary to nature [are] grafted into a cultivated olive tree" (Rom. 11:24), the true Israel of God.

Paul used the expression "contrary to nature" to describe the grafting of the Gentiles into the cultivated olive tree, Israel. The grafting of the Gentiles is contrary to nature because in a natural grafting, a good producing branch, a scion, is grafted into a poor stock, a scrubby tree. Yet, the fruit produced is good fruit, an expression of the good, producing branch. Here, however, a useless, wild olive branch is taken from a useless, wild olive tree and, contrary to nature, is grafted into a cultivated olive tree. To our utter amazement the useless branch produces good fruit, an expression not of the scrubby branch but an expression of the cultivated tree into which the branch has been grafted! A true miracle!

Again, believing Israel and the church are not two separate kingdoms, but believing Jews and Gentiles together *are* one cultivated olive tree! And again, the church does not replace Israel; we are warned against thinking that "branches were broken off so that I could be grafted in" (Rom. 11:19). Paul rebuked that thought. "Do not be arrogant, but be afraid" (v. 20). The church does not replace Israel; rather, believing Gentiles are grafted into Israel to become

still refers to original Israel   *the Hebraic root*

one new nation comprised of both believing Jews and believing Gentiles.

But what about natural Jews who are still in unbelief—the branches that were broken off because of the blindness of unbelief? Is there any hope for these? Paul said there is! He declared, "If they do not persist in unbelief, they will be grafted in, for God is able to graft them in again" (Rom. 11:23). When Paul considered the miracle that had happened to the Gentiles, he exclaimed, "How much more readily will these, the natural branches, be grafted into their own olive tree!" (v. 24). Again, it is important for us to note that a restored Israel will not be a *separate* olive tree but rather will be regrafted into their original olive tree, the same olive tree that believing Gentiles have been grafted into by the awesome grace of God! This is God's "one new man"!

Paul's concluding thoughts in Romans 11:25–27 are eschatological in nature. His very wording indicates this: "I do not want you to be ignorant of this mystery," Paul wrote (v. 25). He saw Israel's plight as blindness and hardness, but he feared the church's plight was ignorance and conceit. And so both Israel and the church need to be healed. He continued:

> I do not want you to be ignorant of this mystery, brothers, so that you may not be conceited: Israel has experienced a hardening in part until the full number of the Gentiles has come in. And so all Israel will be saved, as it is written: "The deliverer will come from Zion; he will turn godlessness away from Jacob. And this is my covenant with them [and God has never forgotten His covenant with Israel] when I take away their sins."
> —ROMANS 11:25–27

This amazing end-time salvation of the whole believing remnant of Israel was previously discussed in our study of Zechariah 13:8–9.

Even in Israel's present blinded and hardened state as "enemies" of the gospel, they are yet "loved on account of the patriarchs, for God's gifts and His call are irrevocable" (Rom. 11:28–29)! Our God is a God who will be true to His word; He will fulfill His promises. His gifts and His call over Israel are irrevocable!

Little wonder that Paul should conclude his treatise on Israel with this amazing doxology:

> Oh, the depth of the riches of the wisdom and knowledge of God! How unsearchable his judgments, and his paths beyond tracing out! 'Who has known the mind of the Lord? Or who has been his counselor? Who has ever given to God, that God should repay him?' For from him [as the source] and through him [as the means] and to him [as the ultimate goal] are all things. To him be the glory forever! Amen"[xiv]
>
> —ROMANS 11:33–36

---

xiv. Appendix Three is an article titled "Israel and the Church," which contains an amplification of the truths explored in this chapter. Of special importance is the section titled "Nations Have a Purpose in God." This article can be downloaded from our Web site www.immanuels.org or copied from this appendix and freely distributed for use in Bible studies and discussion groups.

Chapter 19

PAUL'S UNDERSTANDING OF JESUS' SECOND COMING AND OF THE RAPTURE OF THE CHURCH

PAUL'S LETTER TO THE CORINTHIANS

THERE IS NO question that Paul is the major shaper of the basic teachings of the church, and that includes his understandings of the second coming of our Lord Jesus and of the Rapture of the church. We will discover as we study Paul's writings with an open mind that his understandings are in sync with the Matthew 24 teachings of our Lord Jesus on the Mount of Olives. What the Master taught, Paul taught. (And hopefully, what Jesus and Paul taught will be what we will teach.)

Chapter 15 of 1 Corinthians contains one of Paul's great eschatological teachings. The Corinthian issue at hand was, "How can some of you say that there is no resurrection of the dead?" (v. 12). The denial of the bodily resurrection by some was one of a number of issues Paul, as a spiritual father to the Corinthians, was compelled to correct in his first letter to them. In answer to the heretical statement, "There is no resurrection of the dead" (v. 13), Paul responded:

> But *Christ has indeed been raised from the dead*, the firstfruits of those who have fallen asleep [those who have died].... For as in Adam all die, so in Christ all will be made alive. But each in his own turn: Christ, the firstfruits; then, when he comes, those who belong to him. Then the end will come, when he hands over the kingdom to God the Father after he has destroyed all dominion, authority and power. For he must

124

reign until he has put all his enemies under his feet. The last
enemy to be destroyed is death....When he has done this,
then the Son himself will be made subject to [the Father] who
put everything under [Jesus], so that God may be all in all.

—1 CORINTHIANS 15:20, 22–26, 28, EMPHASIS ADDED

Different translations of the phrase "God...all in all" are awe
inspiring: "God utterly supreme" (TLB); "God, everything to
everyone" (AMP); "everything and everyone is finally under God's
rule...God's rule is absolutely comprehensive—a perfect ending"
(THE MESSAGE). *Peake's Commentary on the Bible* describes this
passage as "the final cord of Pauline theology."[17]

As Paul continued with his thoughts on the Resurrection, he
came to the second coming of Jesus and the Rapture of the church:

I declare to you, brothers, that flesh and blood cannot inherit
the kingdom of God, nor does the perishable inherit the
imperishable. Listen, I tell you a mystery: We will not all sleep,
but we will all be changed—in a flash, in the twinkling of an
eye, at the last trumpet. For the trumpet will sound, the dead
will be raised imperishable, and we will be changed. For the
perishable must clothe itself with the imperishable, and the
mortal with immortality...then the saying that is written will
come true: "Death has been swallowed up in victory."

—1 CORINTHIANS 15:50–54

The reference to the "last trumpet" brings us to John's Revelation,
where "the seventh [the last] angel sounded his trumpet" (Rev. 11:15).
The last trumpet in human history to sound causes the final cry to
go up: "The kingdom of the world has become the kingdom of our
Lord and of his Christ, and he will reign for ever and ever" (v. 15).
Then the heavenly elders declare, "You have taken your great power
and have begun to reign...The time has come for judging the dead
[for this is the time of the resurrection], and for rewarding your
servants the prophets and your saints and those who reverence
your name, both small and great" (Rev. 17–18). This is Paul's understanding of the second coming and of the Rapture of the church,
and his understanding is in sync with John's Patmos revelation on
the last days.

PAUL'S FIRST LETTER TO
THE THESSALONIANS

The most that Paul has to say about the second coming of our Lord Jesus Christ and the Rapture of the church is found in his two letters to the Thessalonians. From time to time I hear concerns from people who have been believers for ten or even twenty years that these end-time truths are very difficult to grasp. The amazing fact is that the former pagan, idol-worshiping Thessalonians were only *a few weeks old in the Lord* when Paul, Silas, and Timothy were driven from them. Yet, when Paul writes back to them, his words evidence that even though they were only a few weeks old in Christ, newly saved out of pagan idolatry with no previous Bible background, they were able to grasp all of these profound truths about the end times! Paul even told them, "Don't you remember that when I was with you I used to tell you these things?" (2 Thess. 2:5). That should be a great encouragement to us likewise to press into these truths for ourselves!

The eschatological section in 1 Thessalonians that deals with our Lord's return goes from 4:13 through 5:11. Paul begins in 4:13: "Brothers, we do not want you to be ignorant about those who fall asleep [those who die], or to grieve like the rest of men, who have no hope." Christians do grieve the loss of those who are so close to them, but they do not grieve like those who have no hope. Paul continues, "We believe that Jesus died and rose again and so we believe that God will bring with Jesus those who have fallen asleep in him" (1 Thess. 4:14). When a believer dies, they are spoken of as having "fallen asleep" in Jesus. In 1 Thessalonians 5:23 Paul touches in passing on the tripartite nature of mankind—spirit, soul, and body. Groups such as the Jehovah's Witnesses, the Adventists, and others extend the "sleep" spoken of by Paul to the whole person—spirit, soul, and body; hence the expression "soul sleep." The author personally does not hold that view. The Scriptures teach that the body sleeps in the earth, but the spirit and soul—the real person—is very much alive, though incomplete, awaiting the resurrection of the body. Paul wrote in 2 Corinthians 5:6, 8: "We are always confident and know that as long as we are at home in the body we are away from the Lord…We are confident, I say, and would prefer to be away from the body and at home with the Lord ['to be absent from the body and to be present with the Lord,' NKJV]." Paul's words are plain: there is a conscious existence apart from the body in the presence of the Lord!

In 2 Corinthians 5:10, Paul further writes, "For we must all appear before the judgment seat of Christ, that each one may receive what is due him for the things done while in the body, whether good or bad." We have usually thought that the Judgment Seat of Christ for all believers is a future, one-time event at the end of the age, but perhaps the Judgment Seat of Christ is really an immediate event that each one faces as he or she goes into the presence of the Lord. This would seem more reasonable than waiting for years or even centuries or millennia (for some) to clear the slate before the Judgment Seat of Christ. Does not Hebrews 9:27 teach us this, that "man is destined to die once, and after that to face judgment"?

In Philippians where Paul was facing the possibility of imminent death, he gave this revealing testimony: "What shall I choose? I do not know! I am torn between the two: I desire to depart and be with Christ, which is better by far; but it is more necessary for you that I remain in the body" (Phil. 1:22–24). If words mean anything, the departed state is one of consciousness: "with Christ, which is better by far." And so we rest the case on this issue.

Returning to 1 Thessalonians 4, Paul continued in verses 15–17:

> According to the Lord's own word [a clear reference to Jesus' Mount Olivet teachings], we tell you that we who are still alive, who are left till the coming of the Lord, will certainly not precede [go before] those who have fallen asleep. For the Lord himself will come down from heaven, with a loud command, with the voice of the archangel and with the trumpet call of God, and the dead in Christ will rise first. After that, we who are still alive and are left will be caught up together with them in the clouds to meet the Lord in the air. And so we will be with the Lord forever.

This 1 Thessalonians 4 passage parallels the 1 Corinthians 15 passage. The "last trumpet" in 1 Corinthians is "the trumpet call of God" in 1 Thessalonians. And "the dead in Christ will rise first" in

1 Thessalonians parallels "the dead will be raised imperishable" in 1 Corinthians. The reference to "we who are alive" corresponds to the statement "we will be changed." When we then compare Paul's 1 Corinthians and his 1 Thessalonians passages with Jesus' words in Matthew 24, we note again the similarities—the coming of Jesus in the presence of the angels with the divine trumpet call and the gathering of the elect "to meet the Lord in the air." The word "meet" used by Paul in 1 Thessalonians 4:17 is the exact same word used in the story told by Jesus in Matthew 25:6: "Here's the bridegroom! Come out to meet him!"

Leo Harris in an article, "The Day Christ Returns," commented on the meaning of the Greek word translated "meet":

> The word "meet" is a Greek word, *apantesin*, which…means *to meet as an escort, to meet and return with.* In Matthew 25:1, 6 the virgins were to go forth to *meet* the bridegroom. According to their customs, they would *meet* and *return as an escort* with the bridegroom to the wedding feast. In Acts 28:15, the brothers…went to *meet* Paul and *escort* him to Rome. In 1 Thessalonians 4:17, we have the only other occasion of the word *apantesin* and with precisely the same meaning. The saints will be caught up to *meet* the returning Christ, and return with Him as an *escort* to the earth. And so they shall be forever with the Lord, in glorified bodies, to live and reign with Him in His kingdom.[18]

Paul continued his instruction of the new Thessalonian believers in chapter 5 of his first letter: "Now, brothers, about times and dates ['seasons,' NKJV] we do not need to write to you." Jesus taught us that we would *not* know the "day or hour" (Matt. 24:36), but He was careful to encourage us to be ready and not ignorant of the times and the seasons. Paul reminded the Thessalonians, as Jesus taught in Matthew 24:43–44, that "the day of the Lord will come like a thief in the night," but, according to Paul, because we "are not in darkness," that day should not surprise *us* like a thief, for we "are all sons of the light and sons of the day. We do not belong to the night or to the darkness" (1 Thess. 5:2, 4–6).

First Thessalonians 5:8-9 continues on to unfold a powerful

truth: "Since we belong to the day, let us be self-controlled, putting on faith and love as a breastplate, and the hope of salvation as a helmet. For God did not appoint us to suffer wrath but to receive salvation through our Lord Jesus Christ." We know that God will not appoint His own to suffer wrath. Paul told us that Jesus "rescues us from the coming wrath" (1 Thess. 1:10). The wrath that falls on the ungodly in the earth's final hours will not fall upon God's children, for He has not appointed them to suffer wrath. Jesus rescues His people from that coming wrath. But Paul tells us our protection from the coming wrath comes as we put on the full armor of God, as we put on faith and love as a breastplate and the hope of salvation as a helmet (Eph. 6:14–17). The exact same thought is told to us in Romans 13:11–12, 14: "Understanding the present [*kairos*] time. The hour has come for you to wake up from your slumber [just as the virgins of Matthew 25:7], because our salvation is nearer now than when we first believed. The night is nearly over; the day is almost here. So let us put aside the deeds of darkness and put on the armor of light.... Clothe yourselves with the Lord Jesus Christ," our fire-retardant suit that will serve us in the fiery furnace of the last days!

This exact same thought was sounded by Paul in Ephesians 6:13. The New King James Version says it accurately: "Take up the whole armor of God, that you may be able to withstand in the evil day, and having done all, to stand." The statement "in the evil day" is eschatological, referring to the end of the age. The church is to *stand* in the evil day, clothed in the full armor of God. In the Olivet words of Jesus in Luke 21:36, the church is to "be always on the watch [a military term], and pray that [we] may be able to pass safely through all that is about to happen, and that [we] may be able to stand before the Son of Man."

Paul concluded his end-time words in 1 Thessalonians 5:11 with this admonition: "Encourage one another and build each other up, just as in fact you are doing." This is in concert with the end-time admonition given to us by the author of Hebrews: "Let us encourage one another—and all the more as you see the Day approaching" (Heb. 10:25). And to this we say, "Yes, Lord!" Amen!

Chapter 20

PAUL'S SECOND LETTER TO
THE THESSALONIANS

CONCERNING THE THEMES of our Lord's second coming and the Rapture of the church, Paul's second letter to the Thessalonians contains the most comprehensive coverage that we have, and one that most clearly mirrors Jesus' teaching in Matthew 24.

The Thessalonians had come under intense persecution for their faith, but "in spite of severe suffering, [they] welcomed the message with the joy given by the Holy Spirit" (1 Thess. 1:6). Paul wrote to them, "You suffered from your own countrymen the same things those churches [in Judea] suffered from the Jews, who killed the Lord Jesus and the prophets and also drove us out" (1 Thess. 2:14–15).

Now in his second letter to the Thessalonians, Paul spoke to them again of "all the persecutions and trials [they were] enduring" (2 Thess. 1:4). Then he assured them: "God is just: He will pay back trouble to those who trouble you and give relief to you who are troubled, and to us as well. This will happen when the Lord Jesus is revealed from heaving in blazing fire with his powerful angels" (vv. 6–7). Paul was very clear in his timeline. The rescue of the saints from persecution comes *when* Jesus is "revealed from heaven in blazing fire with his powerful angels." To Paul there was only one coming of Jesus. He did not see a secret coming. Paul saw, as Jesus so clearly taught, that there would be only one coming—a coming that will be visible to all the world! Jesus began, "After the tribulation of those days" (Matt. 24:29, NKJV), and continued, "The sign of the Son of Man will appear in the sky, and all the nations of the earth will mourn. They will see the Son of Man coming on the clouds of the sky, with power and great glory. And he will send his angels with a loud trumpet call, and they will gather his elect from the four winds, from one end of the heavens to the other" (Matt. 24:30–31). This open coming will be the hour of deliverance for the persecuted church.

Continuing in 2 Thessalonians 1:8–10, Paul wrote: "He will punish those who do not know God and do not obey the gospel of our Lord Jesus. They will be punished with everlasting destruction…from the presence of the Lord and from the majesty of his power," and this will take place, "on the day he comes to be glorified in his holy people and to be marveled at among all those who have believed." All of these statements pinpoint for us exactly when on the prophetic timeline Jesus will return and assure us that His coming is an open coming, seen by all!

In 2 Thessalonians 2 Paul then corrected an error that had begun to surface among the Thessalonians: "Concerning the coming of our Lord Jesus Christ and our being gathered ['mustered'] to him, we ask you, brothers, not to become easily unsettled or alarmed by some prophecy, report or letter supposed to have come from us, saying that the day of the Lord has already come" (vv. 1–2). First of all, it is important for us to note the statement concerning "our being gathered ['mustered'] to him." At Jesus' coming the Rapture will be a muster, a military alert, in which the army of God will be assembled to Jesus, gathered to Him "from the four winds, from one end of the heavens to the other" (Matt. 24:31). His mustered army will then follow Him as he descends to earth to overthrow His enemies and openly establish His everlasting kingdom. This same picture was also painted for us by John in Revelation 19:11–16:

> I saw heaven standing open and there before me was a white horse, whose rider is called Faithful and True…his name is the Word of God. The armies of heaven were following him, riding on white horses and dressed in fine linen, white and clean. [We note that this army is the linen-clad 'Bride who makes herself ready' (Rev. 19:7–8).] Out of his mouth comes a sharp sword with which to strike down the nations…On his robe and on his thigh he has this name written: KING OF KINGS AND LORD OF LORDS.

Paul continued his correction in 2 Thessalonians 2:3: "Don't let anyone deceive you in any way." This is the same concern that our Lord Jesus expressed in Matthew 24:4, "Watch out that no one deceives you." Deception in the last days is apparently an ever-present danger. Paul continued, "For [that day will not come] until the rebellion occurs" (2 Thess. 2:3). The New King James Version translates "the rebellion" as "the falling away," exactly what our Lord Jesus also taught: "At that time many will turn away from the faith" (Matt. 24:10).

Not only must the falling away take place first before the Day of the Lord comes, but "the man of lawlessness ['the man of sin,' NKJV] is to be revealed, the man doomed to destruction" (2 Thess. 2:3). Jesus taught the same: "When you see standing in the holy place 'the abomination that causes desolation,' let the reader understand" (Matt. 24:15). Jesus, in addressing His followers, told them that *they would see the Antichrist* standing in the temple. Paul stated the same in writing to the Thessalonians. The Day of the Lord cannot come until the falling away first takes place and "the man of sin is revealed."

Paul then described him; he is "the man doomed to destruction" (2 Thess. 2:3). Daniel, whom Jesus referred to in Matthew 24:15, described this destruction of the man of sin: "His power will be taken away and completely destroyed forever" (Dan. 7:26); "he will be destroyed, but not by human power" (Dan. 8:25); "he will set up an abomination that causes desolation, until the end that is decreed is poured out on him" (Dan. 9:27); "he will come to his end, and no one will help him" (Dan. 11:45).

The blasphemous activities of the man of sin are then described by Paul for the Thessalonians: "He will oppose and will exalt himself over everything that is called God or is worshiped, so that he sets himself up in God's temple, proclaiming himself to be God" (2 Thess. 2:4)! In Matthew 24:15 Jesus told His disciples that they will see "standing in the holy place 'the abomination that causes desolation.'" In Daniel we see clearly the man of sin's abominable actions:

He will speak against the Most High and oppress his saints.
—DANIEL 7:21–22, 25

He will cause astounding devastation and will succeed in whatever he does…He will cause deceit to prosper, and he will consider himself superior…he will destroy many and take his stand against the Prince of princes.

—DANIEL 8:24–25

He will set up an abomination that causes desolation. *3½ years*

—DANIEL 9:27

He will exalt and magnify himself above every god and will say unheard-of things against the God of gods. He will be successful until the time of wrath is completed

—DANIEL 11:36

Paul then reminded the Thessalonians in 2 Thessalonians 2:5, "Don't you remember that when I was with you I used to tell you these things?" To Paul's understanding the last-days believers will witness the revealing of the man of sin *before* "the coming of our Lord Jesus Christ and [before] our being gathered to him" (2 Thess. 2:1). And Jesus taught the same: "When you see" (Matt. 24:15). The saints will witness the Antichrist as he exalts himself above every god. They will see him set himself up in God's temple proclaiming himself to be God. What Satan has relentlessly pursued from the very beginning will at last be in his reach: "I will make myself like the Most High" (Isa. 14:14); "bow down and worship me" (Matt. 4:9). But his achievement will be only for a very brief moment, for "the Lord Jesus will overthrow [him] with the breath of his mouth and destroy [him] by the splendor of his coming" (2 Thess. 2:8). Even before the world has time to recover from the shock of his final blasphemous claim, the Antichrist will be destroyed by the radiance of Jesus' coming!

THE RESTRAINING ONE

Second Thessalonians 2:6–7 are a fascinating couple of verses. Verse 6 says, "And now you know what is holding him back ['what is restraining,' NKJV] so that he may be revealed at the proper time." The Thessalonians, just weeks old in the Lord, *knew* the identity of the restraining one! How we today should envy them as we fumble along two thousand years later trying to figure out exactly who that restraining one is! Some suggest it was the Roman Empire; others believe he is the Holy Spirit; yet others believe it is the church or the Holy Spirit in the church; yet others believe the restraining one is the mighty, warring angel spoken of in Daniel 10. Actually, the restraining one could be any of these possibilities!

The important issue for us, however, is to understand what Paul had in mind when he wrote the words, "The one who now holds [the lawlessness one] back will continue to do so till he is taken out of the way" (2 Thess. 2:7). What does "taken out of the way" mean? Different translators render that important phrase "taken out of the way" as "removed from the enemy's path" (KNOX), until "the restraining power is removed" (PHILLIPS), or "He who now restrains will be set aside" (NORLIE). The New International Version, the American Standard Version, and the New King James Version all translate the Greek phrase as "taken out of the way." And that same Greek expression was used by Paul in Colossians 2:14, speaking of how Jesus *removed* the list of accusations "that was against us and that stood opposed to us; he took it away, nailing it to the cross." Jesus took the list of accusations away. He removed them; He set them aside. Whoever the restraining one is, and he is a person, this restraining one will continue to hold the Antichrist back *until he is taken out of the way,* until he is *removed* from the enemy's path, until *he is set aside,* until *he steps aside.* Then the lawless one will be revealed, who our Lord Jesus will destroy by the brightness of His coming.

I do not wish to be unkind, but in fairness to the principles of sound biblical exegesis, it would be a real stretch to read into this passage that even if the church were the restraining one (and that may well be), the church will be *raptured out of the earth* before the man of sin can be revealed. Too much in the passage itself, even the meaning of the very words that are used, will not allow us to do that with integrity. The restraining one will simply be *removed from the enemy's path*, allowing him to emerge.[xv]

Paul concluded his thoughts on the career of the man of sin with these words: "The coming of the lawless one will be in accordance with the work of Satan displayed in all kinds of counterfeit miracles, signs and wonders" (2 Thess. 2:9). Our Lord Jesus stated the same in Matthew 24:24–26: "False Christs and false prophets will appear and perform great signs and miracles to deceive even the elect—if that were possible. See, I have told you ahead of time. So if anyone tells you, 'There he is, out in the desert,' do not go out…do not believe it." The "desert" man of sin and his miracle-working false prophet are realities that are now possible in the Mideast. That is why we are impressed to seriously ask ourselves, "Are *these* the last days?"

Paul concluded his thoughts to the Thessalonians on a very positive note:

> We…thank God for you, brothers loved by the Lord, because from the beginning God chose you to be saved through the sanctifying work of the Spirit and through belief in the truth. He called you to this through our gospel, that you might share in the glory of our Lord Jesus Christ. So then, brothers, stand firm and hold to the teachings we passed on to you, whether by word of mouth [when Paul was with them] or [now] by letter.…the Lord is faithful, and he will strengthen and protect you from the evil one.
>
> —2 Thessalonians 2:13–15; 3:3

Yes, He will "protect you from the evil one," just as He protected Israel when the plagues of judgment rained down on Egypt and just as He protected the three in the fiery furnace and just as He protected Daniel in the lion's den! "He will strengthen and protect you from the evil one"!

---

xv. Appendix Four, titled "When Will Our Lord Jesus Return? And When Is the Rapture of the Church?" is an article that more fully discusses the subject of the Rapture, especially from a historical perspective. This treatise can be downloaded from the Web site www.immanuels.org or duplicated from this book and distributed without any further permission for personal use or for group studies or group discussions.

Tracing the Restraining
One Through History

The spirit of Antichrist has long been active in the world, as far back as the first century. The apostle John wrote: "Every spirit that does not acknowledge Jesus is not from God. This is the spirit of the antichrist, which you have heard is coming and even now is already in the world" (1 John 4:3).

Many, by their blasphemous behavior, have been candidates for the role of the Antichrist, but they have not been able to emerge because "the restraining one" has held them back. Nero, in his antichrist tirade against the church, was responsible for the martyrdom of multitudes of Christians, including Peter and Paul. As such, he was surely a prime candidate to be the biblical Antichrist, but "the restraining one" held him back. The hour had not yet come; for in Nero's day most of the world's ethnic groups were still without the gospel, and Jesus said that reaching *them* was essential to "the end" (Matt. 24:14). In the Middle Ages the Reformers identified the institutional church as fallen Babylon and its leadership as the Antichrist because of the martyrdom of the tens of thousands who were put to death by them in the Inquisition. But the hour had not yet come. "The restraining one" held back these viable candidates because a world yet needed to be reached, and Israel was not yet birthed as a nation and restored to its land.

In our own times Hitler was the most viable Antichrist figure to appear. Eichmann, the architect of Hitler's Final Solution, once boasted, "I will leap into my grave laughing because the feeling that I have five million [which finally became six million] human beings on my conscience is for me a source of extraordinary satisfaction."[19] I wonder what he and his Nazi cohorts believe now in the fires of God's eternal judgments! Such irrational hatred that led to the demonic extermination of 6 million Jews and 5 million from other groups in the death camps of Europe,[20] made Hitler, surrounded by his thugs, a prime candidate for the Antichrist. But "the restraining one" held him back, and Nazi socialism was eventually crushed in a judgment that has hung over Germany for generations.

The same was true of Stalin's antichrist communism, destroying tens of millions of lives. But the Antichrist's hour had not yet come.

The church had not yet fulfilled Jesus' Great Commission, and the nation of Israel had not yet been restored. But that is changing today!

Today we look into the face of yet another formidable antichrist power emerging in the earth and casting its shadow on the eastern part of what was once the ancient Roman Empire: radical Islam, with the eschatological implications of the Mahdi, Islam's awaited lord and savior, and his deputy, Isa Al-Maseeh, the Islamic "Jesus." No current two figures fit the biblical description of the Beast and the false prophet of Revelation 13 more, but so far "the restraining one" is holding them back.

But for how long? We have seen the birth of Israel as a nation in 1948, and we are now witnessing the latter rain gently falling on Israel, bringing many thousands of Jews to faith in the Messiah. And we are hearing the cry all across the land of Israel concerning Yeshua, "Blessed is he who comes in the name of the LORD" (Ps. 118:26). Also, around the world amazing progress is being made to penetrate every unreached people group, including the whole Islamic world, with the good news of eternal salvation, establishing a witnessing church in each people group and thereby bringing to Christ "a great multitude that no one could count, from every nation, tribe, people and language" (Rev. 7:9). These are the long-awaited signs heralding our Lord's soon return!

Therefore, we ask ourselves, "Are *these* the last days?" Is *this* the hour in which "the restraining one" will step aside and the man of sin will be revealed? Is *this* the generation in which our Lord Jesus will descend from heaven with a shout and the church will be caught up to meet Him in the air, returning with Him as His triumphant army to see "the beast...and with him the false prophet...cast alive into the lake of fire" (Rev. 19:20, NKJV)? Is *this* the hour in which "the kingdoms of the world become the kingdoms of our Lord and of his Christ" (Rev. 11:15, NKJV)? And if we are that generation that will not pass away until all these things are fulfilled, how then shall we live, as we "look forward to the day of God and speed its coming" (2 Pet. 3:12)?

Chapter 21

THE RESTORED TEMPLE
OF THE LAST DAYS

ISTORICALLY, WE KNOW that the first temple, Solomon's Temple, was destroyed by the Babylonians in 586 B.C., and the second temple, the restoration temple of Zerubbabel, which had been remade by Herod, was destroyed in A.D. 70 by the armies of the Roman general Titus. We also know that there has been no temple on the temple mount for nearly two thousand years. Today on that site stands the Dome of the Rock, a Muslim sacred place.

We also know that the prophets envisioned both a third temple built *prior* to the Lord's return, followed by another, a glorious fourth temple, in the kingdom age. Of this fourth glorious kingdom-age temple Isaiah prophesied that "in the last days the mountain of the LORD's temple will be established as chief among the mountains...and all nations will stream to it" (Isa. 2:2). In Isaiah's further prophecy in chapter 60, with vast promises for the Arab world, the word was given: "All Kedar's flocks [Kedar was Ishmael's second born son] will be gathered to you, the rams of Nebaioth [Ishmael's first born son] will serve you; they will be accepted as offerings on my altar, and I will adorn my glorious temple.... The glory of Lebanon will come to you...to adorn the place of my sanctuary" (Isa. 60:7, 13). Isaiah 66:20 continues, "They will bring all your brothers, from all the nations, to my holy mountain in Jerusalem...to the temple of the LORD" (Isa. 66:20).

Ezekiel also prophesied about the glorious kingdom age fourth temple in the last days: "I will put my sanctuary among them forever. My dwelling place will be with them...Then the nations will know that I the LORD make Israel holy, when my sanctuary is among them forever" (Ezek. 37:26–28). In Ezekiel 40–47, the glorious fourth temple of the kingdom age is pictured for us, a possible "extreme makeover," if you will, of the third temple that will exist in Jerusalem when Jesus returns!

Daniel concerned himself with this rebuilt third temple that will exist *when Jesus returns.* He saw the Antichrist sitting in it, putting "an end to sacrifice and offering. And on a wing of the temple he will set up an abomination that causes desolation" (Dan. 9:27).

Joel also saw a third temple in the last days during the days of Israel's great testing. He admonished: "Let the priests, who minister before the LORD, weep between the temple porch and the altar" (Joel 2:17). Joel, however, also saw the future glorious fourth temple of the kingdom age and declared, as Ezekiel did, that "In that day... a fountain will flow out of the LORD's house" (Joel 3:18).

Amos, in Amos 8:3, prophesied, "'In that day,' declares the Sovereign LORD, 'the songs in the temple will turn to wailing. Many, many bodies—flung everywhere! Silence!'" This temple is obviously the third one that will be built before our Lord's return.

Micah saw, as did Isaiah, the glorious fourth temple. Micah 4:2 Tells us, "Many nations will come and say, 'Come, let us go up to the mountain of the LORD, to the house of the God of Jacob.'"

Haggai envisioned a third temple present when Jesus returns, but a temple which He will then fill with His glory: "'I will shake all nations, and the desired of all nations will come, and I will fill this house with glory,' says the LORD Almighty" (Hag. 2:7).

We already noted that in November 2007 a delegation from West Papua New Guinea brought a large gift of gold to Jerusalem in what they felt was obedience to the word of the Lord found in Zechariah 6:15: "Those who are far away will come and help to build the [third] temple of the LORD, and you will know that the LORD Almighty has sent me to you." In Zechariah 14:20–21 a closing reference was made to "the cooking pots in the LORD's house" being holy, and "on that day there will no longer be a Canaanite in the house of the LORD Almighty." This apparently refers to the holiness of the future fourth kingdom temple.

Finally, Malachi prophesied of that third temple to which the LORD will come: "'Then suddenly the Lord you are seeking will come to *his temple*...But who can endure the day of his coming? Who can stand when he appears?...He will sit as a refiner and purifier of silver; he will purify the Levites and refine them like gold and silver" (Mal. 3:1–3). These are some of the various last days prophecies about the temple from the Old Testament—both the third temple to which Jesus will come at His return and the following glorious fourth kingdom temple.

In the New Testament there are also several references to the third temple that will be rebuilt prior to the return of Jesus. Jesus already prophesied about the destruction of the second temple under Titus in 70 A.D. that "not one stone here will be left on another; every one will be thrown down" (Matt. 24:2). He then spoke of an end-time temple, the third temple, in which his followers will "see standing in the holy place 'the abomination that causes desolation,' spoken of through the prophet Daniel" (Matt. 24:15).

But the most pronounced reference to the third temple in Jerusalem is the one we just referenced in our study in 2 Thessalonians. Speaking of the Antichrist, Paul wrote: "He...will exalt himself over everything that is called God or is worshiped, so that he sets himself up in God's temple, proclaiming himself to be God" (2 Thess. 2:4). But "Jesus will overthrow [him] with the breath of his mouth and destroy [him] by the splendor of his coming" (v. 2:8).

In the final chapters of this book, we will be examining John's Revelation, where the tribulation temple (the third temple) is described, and where a fifth, an *eternal* temple, is further described in most unusual terms: "I did not see a temple in the city, because *the Lord God Almighty and the Lamb are its temple*" (Rev. 21:22, emphasis added)! This is the fifth and final temple!

In summary, we can see clearly from the Scriptures that these five temples are spoken of:

1. *The first temple* built by Solomon—destroyed by the Babylonians in 586 B.C.

2. *The second temple* built by Zerubbabel (and Herod)—destroyed by the Romans in A.D. 70.

3. *The Tribulation (or third) temple* built in the last days in which the Antichrist will sit, declaring himself to be God (2 Thess. 2:4).

4. *The fourth glorious kingdom (millennial) temple* envisioned by the prophets and especially by Ezekiel in chapters 40–47.

5. *The eternal temple*—the fifth and final temple— spoken of in Revelation 21:22: "I did not see a temple in the city, because the Lord God Almighty and the Lamb are its temple."

Straws Blowing in the Wind

Like proverbial straws blowing in the wind, things are presently moving toward the rebuilding of the third temple in Jerusalem. It will be *this temple* in which the man of sin will sit, proclaiming himself to be God. This temple will then be followed by the glorious kingdom temple, as seen by Ezekiel; and then we will see established the ultimate temple—the eternal temple, God Himself: "the Lord God Almighty and the Lamb." For now, let's trace some of those straws that are presently blowing in the wind, pointing toward the rebuilding of the third temple in Jerusalem.

The Reappearance of the Red Heifer

Numbers states: "This is a requirement of the law that the LORD has commanded: Tell the Israelites to bring…a red heifer without defect or blemish…it is to be taken outside the camp and slaughtered….A man who is clean shall gather up the ashes of the heifer and put them in a ceremonially clean place outside the camp. They shall be kept by the Israelite community…it is for purification from sin" (Num. 19:2–3, 9). As we read through Numbers 19 we see again and again how the ashes of the red heifer were to be used, particularly to cleanse the defilement that comes from death (vv. 11–21).

Over the years of its bloody history, the Temple Mount has been defiled repeatedly by human carnage; consequently, it is an unclean place. The only way the Temple Mount could be cleansed from its defilement, so the third temple could be rebuilt on it, is by the sprinkling of "the water of cleansing" mixed with the ashes of the red heifer (Num. 19:9). The longstanding problem has been that, just after the destruction of the second temple in A.D. 70, the red heifer completely disappeared from Israel, suddenly to reappear a few years ago for the first time in nearly two thousand years![xvi] Color photos of the red heifer show it to be a rich maroon-red in color. Consequently, the cleansing of the blood-stained temple mount is now possible, for this necessary component has been miraculously provided!

The Rebirth of the Jewish Sanhedrin After 1,600 Years

On October 13, 2004, the Jewish Sanhedrin was reestablished in Tiberias, the location where it disbanded some 1,600 years ago. Once the Sanhedrin was reinstated it was moved to its permanent home in Jerusalem. The rabbinic body is convening monthly to issue rulings on matters important to Jewish life. On December 6, 2004, the men of the council, having immersed themselves in mikvaot (ritual) baths, ascended the temple mount, many for the first time.

Preparations for the Third Temple

In this picture, taken in the spring of 2012, the author is standing before a solid gold menorah, worth millions of dollars, constructed to take its place in the third temple,[xvii] with other furnishings that have been constructed, along with the priestly garments and golden utensils required for service in the temple. The Temple Institute in Jerusalem heads up these vast and detailed preparations for the future

xvi. For more information, see http://www.pbs.org/wgbh/pages/frontline/shows/apocalypse/readings/forcing.html.

xvii. The photo can be downloaded from the Web site www.facebook.com/immanuelchurch.

building of the third temple and for the reinstitution of temple worship.

A Live Demonstration of the Passover Offering

On the tenth of Nisan (April 2), 2012, the Temple Institute, in conjunction with other temple organizations, conducted a live demonstration of the Korban Pesach (Passover offering). The reenactment involved the slaughtering of the lamb, the gathering of its blood in the vessel designed especially for this purpose, and the dashing of the blood by the priests (*Kohanim*) against the stone altar (*Mizbeach*) constructed for that special purpose. The lamb was then put on a spit and roasted in a specially prepared oven, as it had been done in prior temple days. The meat was distributed to needy families. It was stressed throughout the ceremony that this was *only a demonstration* of the future *Korban Pesach* offering that will be done at the altar which will someday stand in the precise location of the holy temple altar on the Temple Mount. Over two thousand people attended the demonstration, a number of whom cried out, "Next year in the holy temple," as the reenactment concluded.

The Dome of the Rock

For years non-Muslims have not been permitted to ascend the Temple Mount, the site of the Dome of the Rock. In February 2013, however, I and a hearty band of pilgrims were permitted to ascend the mount. The Dome of the Rock was still closed to non-Muslims, but a very curious sign had appeared on the outside of this Muslim sacred place. On the wall of the shrine was the Koranic inscription: "Allah does not beget [he is not a father], nor is he begotten [he is not a son]." And just below that inscription we saw a slab of marble, pictured here, which mysteriously had begun to "weep," creating two clear "horned" images, one of which is shown here. Two "horned" images—the image of the Antichrist and the image of the false prophet! I could scarcely believe my eyes!

These are some of the straws blowing in the wind pointing toward some of the amazing events that will be unfolding before our very eyes in the days before us, indicating to us that these are indeed the last days!

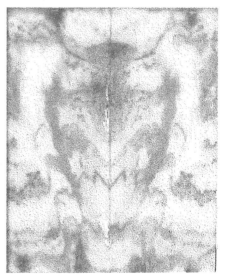

Chapter 22

THE REVELATION OF JESUS CHRIST
Chapters 1–3

THE FINAL BOOK in our Bible, Revelation, is appropriately a *prophetic* book, unfolding for us the final events of the last days. Revelation's visions abound with symbolism, some of which may be difficult to interpret, but within that symbolism we will be able to find a reality that we can readily understand. The Revelation, according to chapter 1, verse 19, came in three parts. John was told, "Write, therefore, [first] what you have seen, [then] what is now and [finally] what will take place later."

"WRITE...WHAT YOU HAVE SEEN"

What John had seen is what we find in Revelation 1:9–18, John's vision of the glorious Son of Man. John "was on the island of Patmos [a Roman penal colony] because of the word of God and the testimony of Jesus" (Rev. 1:9). From there he writes, "On the Lord's Day [literally, 'the Imperial Day'] I was in the Spirit" (v. 10), caught up, as the prophets invariably were, into the Day of the Lord. In the Spirit, in the Day of the Lord, John saw a vision of the glorious Son of Man dressed as a priest, tending the seven golden lampstands, which we are later told "are the seven churches" (v. 20).

John actually saw the glorified Jesus as Daniel saw the Ancient of Days in Daniel 7:9: "His clothing was as white as snow; the hair of his head was white like wool." Had not Jesus stated in John's hearing, "Anyone who has seen me has seen the Father...I am in the Father, and...the Father is in me" (John 14:9–10)? John was witnessing that reality of the oneness of the Father and the Son as he beheld the glorious Son of Man with "feet...like bronze glowing in a furnace, and his voice…like the sound of rushing waters…[and] His face…like the sun shining in all its brilliance" (Rev. 1:15–16). No small wonder that John "fell at his feet as though dead" (v. 17)! But Jesus reassured His beloved friend, "Do not be afraid. I am the First and the Last. I am the Living One; I was dead, and behold I am alive for ever and ever! And I hold the keys of death and Hades" (vv. 17–18). The statement, "I am the First and the Last" is found in Isaiah 44:6, where we read, "This is what the LORD [Jehovah] says— Israel's King and Redeemer, the LORD Almighty: I am the first and I am the last; apart from me there is no God."

Who, then, is Jesus? If Jehovah alone is the first and the last, and if Jesus is the first and the last, then Jesus must be that great "I AM" (John 8:58), the Jehovah of the Old Testament wrapped in human flesh who came down from heaven to be the Savior of the world! So, if apart from Jehovah "there is no God," who, then, is Jesus? In the words of John, speaking of Jesus in 1 John 5:20, "He is the true God and eternal life"! And He holds the keys of death and Hades firmly in His hands!

This comprises the first part of John's writings: "Write, therefore, *what you have seen*" (Rev. 1:19, emphasis added).

"WRITE…WHAT IS NOW"

Revelation 2–3 contain seven divinely inspired letters, each from Jesus, each given by His Spirit, and each conveyed by an angelic messenger to the respective churches—in Ephesus, in Smyrna, in Pergamum, in Thyatira, in Sardis, in Philadelphia, and in Laodicea. These are "the seven churches in the province of Asia" (Rev. 1:4), which were undoubtedly established a generation before through the labors of Paul, recorded in Acts 19:10. Five out of the seven had backslidden so grievously in one generation that they were commanded by Jesus to "repent"—Ephesus in 2:5; Pergamum in 2:16; Thyatira in 2:21–22; Sardis in 3:3; and Laodicea in 3:19. Only Smyrna and Philadelphia— two lampstands out of the seven—would not be snuffed out. Among the believers in the fallen churches, some had forsaken their first love, others had imbibed the teachings of the money-grabbing prophet Balaam, others believed the Nicolaitan error (the suppression of the laity), and yet others were drawn into the spiritually immoral ways of

Jezebel. In Sardis they had a reputation for being alive but spiritually dead, and in Laodicea they were lukewarm, about to be vomited out of the mouth of Jesus. They thought they were doing well, but they were actually "wretched, pitiful, poor, blind and naked" (Rev. 3:17). Sober warnings for us today!

To each of the seven churches Jesus revealed Himself through a different aspect of His priestly character and ministry—as the one who walks among the seven lampstands (Rev. 2:1), as the one who is "the First and the Last, who died and came to life again" (v. 8), as the one who "has the sharp, double-edged sword" proceeding from His mouth (v. 12), as the one who is "the Son of God, whose eyes are like blazing fire" (v. 18), as the one "who holds the seven spirits of God" in His hands (Rev. 3:1), as the one "who holds the key of David" and who opens doors that no one can shut and who shuts doors that no one can open (Rev. 3:7), and the one who is "the Amen, the faithful and true witness, the ruler of God's creation" (Rev. 3:14).

Finally, to those in each church who are overcomers, even though surrounded by seemingly impossible and debilitating circumstances, very special promises are given: "the right to eat from the tree of life, which is in the paradise of God" (Rev. 2:7), an assurance that they "will not be hurt at all by the second death" (v. 11), the promise of "hidden manna," and a white stone of acceptance with "a new name written on it" (v. 17). (I understand it was Charles Spurgeon who testified that it had been revealed to him what his "new name" was!) In Revelation 2:26–28, Jesus promises: "To him who overcomes and does my will to the end, I will give authority over the nations... just as I have received authority from my Father. I will also give him the morning star."

This statement about being given "the morning star" may be a reference to what Peter pointed to in 2 Peter 1:16, when he spoke about the "the power and coming of our Lord Jesus Christ." Peter had seen the majesty of Jesus on the Mount of Transfiguration when Jesus "received honor and glory from God the Father" (2 Pet. 1:17). Peter then encouraged the saints to look forward to the same glory to accompany Jesus' second coming. Then Peter introduced a very special thought. As we consider the prophetic scriptures concerning Jesus' return, something can take place in our hearts—"the day dawns and the morning star rises in your hearts" (2 Pet. 1:19)! In other words, we see by clear inner revelation what the prophets are speaking about, and we experience by revelation in our hearts the reality of Jesus' coming, *even before it takes place!* The morning star rising in our hearts! Oh, how we should covet this!

In Revelation 3:5, Jesus promised that the overcomer "will walk with me, dressed in white...I will never blot out his name from the book of life, but will acknowledge his name before my Father and his angels." In verse 12 Jesus promised that the one who over-comes will be "a pillar in the temple of my God" and will bear the inscribed name of God, the name of the city of God, and Jesus' new name! Finally, in verse 21 Jesus gave to the overcomer the right to sit with Him on His throne, as He overcame and sat down with His Father on His throne! In all of these messages we want to clearly "hear what the Spirit says to the churches" (v. 22)! We want to learn from the rebukes, we want to be quick to repent, and we want to cherish in faith the promises given to the overcomers! This section, Revelation 2 and 3, is *"what is now."*

"WRITE...WHAT WILL TAKE PLACE LATER"

Revelation 4:1 is the start of the third and longest part of the Revelation. John wrote, "After this I looked, and there before me was a door standing open in heaven. And the voice I had first heard speaking to me like a trumpet said, 'Come up here, and I will show you what must take place after this.'" Some see in these words, "Come up here," the Rapture of the church. We note, how-ever, that John *personally* was told, "Come up here." There was no reference to the whole church, and the purpose for the coming up into heaven was clearly spelled out: "I will show you *what must take place* after this." "What must take place after this" begins the third section of the Revelation.

Immediately John again "was in the Spirit" (Rev. 4:1) trans-ported into heaven, where he beheld a most beautiful sight, out of which the first future prophetic vision came. The prophetic part of Revelation, from chapter 4 through 22, is similar to the prophetic part of Daniel. Both Daniel and Revelation each contain five dis-tinct visions. The five visions of Revelation each end, as did the five visions of Daniel, with the second coming of Jesus and the triumph of righteousness over evil. The five visions of Revelation run concurrently, or simultaneously, with each other, just as did the five visions of Daniel, so we see marked similarities between these two prophetic books.

THE FIVE VISIONS OF REVELATION

The five visions of Revelation begin with *the vision of the seven-sealed book* in Revelation 4–7. Then, the second vision was given—*the vision of the seven trumpets*, which covers the section of Revelation 8–11. The third vision is described in chapters 12-14 and is *the vision of the great conflict of the ages*. This vision focuses on seven main end-time players: the sun-clothed woman, her man-child son, the dragon (Satan), the archangel Michael, the Beast (the Antichrist), the second Beast (the false prophet), and the firstfruits to God. The fourth vision, *the seven last plagues*, is the subject of Revelation 15–20 and includes the earthshaking fall of Babylon the Great and the Marriage Supper of the Lamb. After this the final and last of John's visions extends from Revelation 21–22:7 and is *the vision of a fresh heaven and a fresh earth*—a most awesome climax to the whole book!

The last verse in our New Testament ends with the promise of grace—"The grace of the Lord Jesus be with God's people. Amen" (Rev. 22:21). Malachi was the last prophet to speak in the Old Testament and ended his prophecies with the word *curse*—"I will come and strike the land with a curse" (Mal. 4:6). How wonderful that the curse is now broken because of Calvary, and the new covenant grace of God has been released upon the people of God in its place!

Chapter 23

THE VISION OF THE SEVEN-SEALED BOOK
Chapters 4–7

A s JOHN WAS caught up in the Spirit into heaven to receive from Jesus "what must take place" in the future, he immediately saw "a throne in heaven with someone sitting on it" (Rev. 4:1–2)—a radiant Being gleaming as with the brilliance of precious gems. Before the throne was seated the heavenly presbytery, the "twenty-four elders" (v. 4), who represent both the old covenant people of God, the twelve tribes of Israel, and the new covenant people of God, the followers of the twelve apostles of the Lamb. Before the throne, seen as seven blazing lamps, was the sevenfold Spirit of God (v. 5). Looking back to Isaiah 11:2 we remember the description of the sevenfold Spirit of God that rested upon the Messiah: "the Spirit of the LORD...the Spirit of wisdom and of understanding, the Spirit of counsel and of power, the Spirit of knowledge and of the fear of the LORD." And "from the throne came flashes of lightning, rumblings and peals of thunder" (Rev. 4:5)—just as on Mount Sinai when Jehovah came down to visit His people.

Close in, surrounding the throne, were four living creatures, the personal guardians of the throne. The first looked like a lion, the second like an ox, the third like a man, and the fourth like a flying eagle, reminiscent of the four living creatures of Ezekiel 1, where they also were the guardians of the throne of Jehovah, each reflecting different characteristics of our heavenly Lord.

All that is happening around the throne is centered in worship and adoration. The four seraphim, as in Isaiah 6:3, day and night never stop declaring, "Holy, holy, holy is the LORD God Almighty, who was, and is, and is to come" (Rev. 4:8). As the four living creatures "give glory, honor and thanks to him who sits on the

150

throne and who lives forever and ever, the twenty-four elders fall down before him who sits on the throne, and worship him who lives forever and ever," casting their crowns before the throne and exclaiming, "You are worthy, our Lord and God" (vv. 9–11).

I remember attending a funeral some years ago in which we were assured that our departed brother was now enjoying himself playing golf. I have often thought of how much we in the body of Christ need fresh insights from Revelation 4 on our true heavenly occupation—to worship and to adore Him!

Chapter 5 continues on with the heavenly vision. John saw a scroll in the right hand of the Holy One on the throne. It had been written on both sides and sealed with seven seals, the yet-untold story of the last days. And then a crisis erupted. A cry went up, "Who is worthy to break the seals and open the scroll?" (Rev. 5:2). But no one was found worthy. No one in heaven, on earth, or under the earth was found worthy to open the scroll or even to look inside it! John immediately burst into tears, but one of the elders said to him, "Do not weep! See, the Lion of the tribe of Judah, the Root of David, has triumphed. *He is able* to open the scroll and its seven seals" (v. 5).

The next five verses focus on the Lion of Judah's tribe, but as John wiped the tears from his eyes he saw not a lion but a lamb. The Greek word is diminutive—"a little lamb." The little Lamb looked as if it had just been freshly slain. The Greek word is strong; the picture is of a little lamb, looking as if it had just been *freshly slaughtered* or *freshly butchered*. And the little, freshly butchered Lamb was standing in the center of the throne, surrounded by the presbytery and the four living creatures, who reflect His character.

The church fathers saw in these living creatures four reflections of Jesus, as presented in the four gospels—Jesus, the King of Israel, the lion, as presented in Matthew; Jesus, the faithful servant of Jehovah, the ox, as presented in Mark; Jesus, the Son of Man, the Man, as presented in Luke; and Jesus, the Son of God, the eagle, as presented in John. The little slaughtered Lamb was seen as all-powerful, having *seven* horns, and as all-knowing, with *seven* eyes.

He is the one who took the scroll from the hand of the one who sits on the throne, for He is worthy! He alone is worthy! He alone in heaven above and earth below is worthy! And with bowls full of prayers and harps of praises, they sang a new song to the little freshly slain Lamb: "You are worthy to take the scroll and to open its seals, because you were slain [slaughtered, butchered], and with your blood you purchased men for God from every tribe and language and people and nation. You have made them to be a kingdom and priests to serve our God, and they will reign on the earth" (Rev. 5:9–10). From their praises it seemed as if the church has at last completed its assigned task—to preach the gospel of the kingdom in the whole world as a testimony to all nations—"every tribe and language and people"! And now the end is able to come!

And then, as if with a wide-angle zoom lens, John saw around the throne and the living creatures and the twenty-four elders 100 million angels (ten thousand times ten thousand angelic beings) singing, "Worthy is the [little] Lamb, who was [slaughtered], to receive power and wealth and wisdom and strength and honor and glory and praise" (Rev. 5:12)! And then the lens widened even more, and John saw "every creature in heaven and on earth and under the earth and on the sea, and all that is in them, singing: 'To him who sits on the throne and to the [little Lamb] be praise and honor and glory and power, forever and ever'" (v. 13)! Paul surely envisioned this moment in time in his amazing words to the Philippians, "God exalted him to the highest place and gave him the name that is above every name, that at the name of Jesus every knee should bow, in heaven and on earth and under the earth, and every tongue confess that Jesus Christ is Lord, to the glory of God the Father" (Phil. 2:9–11). Little wonder that at this majestic sight all of heaven fell down and worshiped! The Lamb is indeed worthy!

The Lamb Opens the Seven Seals

REVELATION CHAPTER SIX

The opening of the first four seals of the scroll by the Lamb released, one by one, the four horsemen of the apocalypse.

John wrote, "I watched as the Lamb opened the first of the seven seals. Then I heard one of the four living creatures say in a voice like thunder, 'Come!' I looked, and there before me was a white horse! Its rider held a bow, and he was given a crown, and he rode out as a conqueror bent on conquest" (Rev. 6:1–2). Different opinions exist as to who this horseman is. Some say he is Christ; others say he is Antichrist. The text simply says he is "a conqueror bent on conquest." (The author personally doubts this horseman is Christ, because of the company in which he rides!)

> When the Lamb opened the second seal…another horse came out, a fiery red one. Its rider was given power to *take peace from the earth and to make men slay each other.*
> —REVELATION 6:3–4, EMPHASIS ADDED

"When the Lamb opened the third seal," John wrote, "there before me was a black horse! Its rider was holding a pair of scales in his hand…'A quart of wheat [barely enough to feed an individual] for a day's wages, and three quarts of barley [enough for a family—more filling but less nutritious] for a day's wages, and do not damage the oil and the wine'" (Rev. 6:5–6).

The first horseman brings conquest in the earth. The second horseman brings a murderous turmoil in the earth, and the third horseman brings famine in the earth. The reference to "the oil and the wine" not being damaged may be a coded message that, even in the midst of these disasters and shortfalls, the presence and power of the Holy Spirit—"the oil and the wine"—will be *plentiful* for all those who hunger and thirst after God!

The opening of the fourth seal brings with it the fourth and final horseman, "a pale [actually, a *green*] horse! Its rider was named Death, and Hades was following close behind him. They were given power over a fourth of the earth [well over 1.5 billion people] to kill by sword, famine and plague, and by the wild beasts of the earth" (Rev. 6:8).

It is possible for us to see a reference to radical Islam in these verses. The Islamic jihadists hold sway over a fourth of humanity (over 1.5 billion souls), and death by the sword is their method of execution. In their wake comes famine and plague, all the way from Syria's chemical weapons to Iran's nuclear arsenal, and on their heels come the ravaging beasts of the earth! (It is important at this juncture to underscore again that not every Muslim is a radical jihadist. There are many peace-loving Muslims who have turned away from terrorism and seek the way of peace. And many have given their lives to Jesus Christ, the Prince of peace, as He has revealed Himself to them!)

When the Lamb opened the fifth seal, John said:

> I saw under the altar the souls of those who had been slain because of the word of God and the testimony they had maintained [the host of martyrs for the Lamb]. They called out in a loud voice [a clear evidence of the conscious existence of the departed], "How long, Sovereign Lord, holy and true, until you judge the inhabitants of the earth and avenge our blood?"
>
> —REVELATION 6:9–10

They were encouraged and told "to wait a little longer," until the full number of martyrs had been completed (v. 11).

In the opening of the sixth seal by the Lamb, the heavens and the earth were visibly shaken. Revelation 6:12–13 is identical to the signs given by Jesus in Matthew 24:29 to occur just before His second coming:

> The sun turned black like sackcloth made of goat hair, the whole moon turned blood red, and the stars in the sky fell to earth, as late figs drop from a fig tree when shaken by a strong wind.
>
> —REVELATION 6:12–13

> The sun will be darkened, and the moon will not give its light; the stars will fall from the sky, and the heavenly bodies will be shaken.
>
> —MATTHEW 24:29

These are also the same signs given in Joel's prophecy to signal the end: "The sun will be turned to darkness and the moon to blood before the coming of the great and glorious day of the Lord" (Acts 2:20). And soon we shall see in the vast harvest of Revelation 7, the fulfillment of the great promise that "everyone who calls on the name of the Lord will be saved" (Acts 2:21)!

In Revelation 6:16–17, following the opening of the sixth seal, the world falls into chaos, with people of high and low estate calling on the mountains and rocks: "Fall on us and hide us from the face of him who sits on the throne and from the wrath of the Lamb! For the great day of their wrath has come, and who can stand?" It may be hard for us to comprehend a *wrathful* Lamb, but the Scriptures are clear. The little Lamb, gentle and meek, now arises to be the wrathful Lamb, for He is also the Lion of the tribe of Judah, the King of all kings and the Lord of all lords! And this signals the end of all things. The great day of God's wrath has come—yet this is also the appointed season of great revival and spiritual awakening. A grand harvest is being reaped in all the earth, as seen in the next chapter!

THE SALVATION OF THE REMNANT OF ISRAEL AND THE GENTILE NATIONS: REVELATION 7

In Revelation 7:1–8, the redemption of the remnant of Israel is pictured for us. One hundred forty-four thousand from the twelve tribes of Israel are sealed: "Put a seal on the foreheads of the servants of our God" (Rev. 7:3). Among those who believe the church has already been raptured into heaven, a theory has been built around these one hundred forty-four thousand Jews. They suddenly realize the church has been taken, they, consequently, give themselves to Christ and are saved, and they become the flaming evangelists that bring about the greatest harvest of souls of any generation. Unfortunately, all this is supposition, lacking supporting biblical evidence.

In the listing of the twelve tribes who are sealed, we notice that Dan is missing. When we recently visited the excavations of the pagan cult center at Dan in northern Israel, we could understand why. So grievous was their apostasy from the living God, they apparently were disinherited from the recovery of Israel in the last days. Sobering! As to the number of those sealed, one hundred forty-four thousand, we may be looking at a symbolic number rather than at an actual number. (We will pick up the three symbolic numbers of 12, 144, and 12,000 again further on in Revelation.)

In Revelation 7:9–17, the scope of the end-time revival widens. Not only is there a harvest from the twelve tribes of the nation of

Israel, there is an unbelievable harvest: "A great multitude that no one could count, from every nation, tribe, people and language" (v. 9)! The Great Commission of Matthew 28:18–20 has at last been fulfilled! This gospel of the kingdom has finally been preached in the whole world as a testimony to every ethnic group (Matt. 24:14)! And now the promised end has come!

John saw this mass of humanity "standing before the throne and in front of the Lamb. They were wearing white robes and were holding palm branches in their hands" (Rev. 7:9). They were apparently celebrating the Feast of Tabernacles, the festival especially dedicated to the Gentile nations. Their shout went up: "Salvation belongs to our God, who sits on the throne, and to the Lamb," for "these are they who have come out of the great tribulation; they have washed their robes and made them white in the blood of the Lamb. Therefore, 'they are before the throne of God and serve him day and night in his temple...the Lamb at the center of the throne will be their shepherd...and God will wipe away every tear from their eyes'" (Rev. 7:10, 14–17). What an awesome scene! What an amazing harvest! And all because of the slain Lamb!

The Lamb then opens the seventh seal, and in the light of all that has happened—the judgments on the earth and the vast increase in the kingdom of God—it is only proper that all of heaven should be hushed in awe. Consequently, "there was silence in heaven for about half an hour" (Rev. 8:1). Indeed, worthy is the Lamb that was slain!

Chapter 24

THE VISION OF THE SEVEN TRUMPETS
Chapters 8–11

T HE SEVEN SEALS ended with the appearance of our great God and Savior Jesus Christ, at which His enemies cried out in anguish in Revelation 6:16–17: "Hide us from the face of him who sits on the throne and from the wrath of the Lamb! For the great day of their wrath has come, and who can stand?" The last days are days of great judgment for the unrepentant, but they are also days of great redemption for the repentant, as Revelation 7 reveals—a great redemption in Israel and a great redemption among the Gentile nations of the earth!

Now a new set of judgments unfolds in Revelation 8–11 running concurrently with the seals and ending with the same powerful event, the final overthrow of evil and the final triumph of righteousness in the second coming of Jesus.

The seven trumpets are about to be blown. But an interesting and instructive happening first takes place in Revelation 8:3–5—"much incense" (v. 3), a picture of praise and adoration, coupled with the "the prayers of all the saints," faithfully stored up in heaven for this very hour, are offered by one of the angels on the golden altar before the throne of God. As "the smoke of the incense, together with the prayers of the saints, went up before God from the angel's hand" (v. 4), something was *released in heaven*. Worship and intercession does exactly that! Filling the golden censer with fire from the altar, the angel "hurled it on the earth," and "the seven angels who had the seven trumpets prepared to sound them" (vv. 5–6).

At the sound of the first trumpet "hail and fire mixed with blood…was hurled down upon the earth," possibly flaming meteorites, causing massive destruction, as "a third of the earth [with its trees and grass] was burned up" (Rev. 8:7).

157

At the sound of the second trumpet "a huge mountain, all ablaze, was thrown into the sea," possibly a giant asteroid impacting one of the earth's oceans, causing massive devastation, as "a third of the sea turned into blood," killing a third of the marine life and destroying a third of the marine vessels (Rev. 8:8).

At the sound of the third trumpet, "a great star, blazing like a torch, fell from the sky," polluting a third of the earth's fresh water as, "a third of the waters turned bitter, and many people died from the waters that had become bitter" (Rev. 8:10–11). "Wormwood," the name of the star (v. 11), is *Chernobyl* in the Russian language! We may be looking at destructive fallout from a massive nuclear explosion in the earth!

At the sound of the fourth trumpet, foreboding darkening of the sun and the moon and the stars took place, possibly as a result of the massive explosion in the days just prior, filling the atmosphere with a blanket of dust and debris. At this juncture, an eagle flying in midair screeches, "Woe! Woe! Woe to the inhabitants of the earth" (Rev. 8:13), because of the remaining trumpet blasts!

At the sound of the fifth trumpet, a star—an angel—fell from heaven with "the key to the shaft of the Abyss" in his hand (Rev. 9:1). As the fallen angel opened the Abyss, a blanket of smoke billowed out of it, and out of the smoke came demonic powers in the form of hideous locusts (described in Revelation 9:7–10), who were permitted to harm "only those people who did not have the seal of God on their foreheads" (Rev. 9:4). In chapter 7 we saw this protective seal of God being placed on the foreheads of the saved remnant of Israel; here that seal is evident upon a wider group—the tribulation saints are now "sheltered on the day of the LORD's anger," as promised in Zephaniah 2:3. The torment caused to the "unsealed" people by the demonic hoards from the Abyss is so intense that "during those days men will seek death, but will not find it; they will long to die, but death will elude them" (Rev. 9:6). Over the demonic hoards is a king "whose name in Hebrew is Abaddon, and in Greek, Apollyon ["Destroyer"]" (v. 11). John already knew from the words of Jesus who the destroyer was: "The thief comes only to steal and kill and destroy" (John 10:10); Satan is his name. He is the fallen angel of the Abyss, the king over its demonic hoard! This is the first woe, or "doom," as *The Message* reads in Revelation 9:12.

At the sound of the sixth trumpet, a mounted army of 200 million is released under the command of "the four angels, who are bound at the great river Euphrates," whose mission is "to kill a third of mankind" (Rev. 9:14–15). This is now global war! From the description given of the 200 million mounted riders, we can conclude that they are a destructive, demonically inspired horde. They ride horses whose "tails were like snakes, having heads with which they inflict injury" (v. 19). We will consider this 200-million-man army again in Chapter 26.

In concluding the outpouring of devastation that came with the blowing of this sixth trumpet, a very sober assessment was given: "The rest of mankind that were not killed by these plagues still did not repent…worshiping demons, and idols of gold, silver, bronze, stone and wood…Nor did they repent of their murders, their magic arts, their sexual immorality or their thefts" (Rev. 9:20–21). Consequently, we are not surprised when the final announcement is made in the last part of Revelation: "But the cowardly, the unbelieving, the vile, the murderers, the sexually immoral, those who practice magic arts, the idolaters and all liars—their place will be in the fiery lake of burning sulfur. This is the second death" (Rev. 21:8). The judgment of these in the ages to come was shaped by their refusal to repent as they witnessed the Tribulation judgments from God against human rebellion in this age.

The seventh—and last—trumpet is now about to be blown, and "in the days when the seventh angel is about to sound his trumpet, the mystery of God will be accomplished, just as he announced to his servants the prophets" (Rev. 10:7). What is that "mystery of God that will be accomplished" in the days of the blowing of the seventh trumpet? Paul referred to this mystery as Jesus' second coming when the church is "raised imperishable" at the sound of the last, the seventh trumpet (1 Cor. 15:52). He wrote, "Listen, I tell you a mystery: We will not all sleep, but we will all be changed—in a flash, in the twinkling of an eye, at the last trumpet" (1 Cor. 15: 51–52).

This last-days mystery also includes the mystery of the completion of the body of Christ, which is called a "mystery" by Paul in

Ephesians 3:16, and this mystery further includes the regrafting of Israel into their own olive tree, which Paul also called a "mystery" in Romans 11:25–26! Thus, the mystery of God is accomplished in the days of the blowing of the seventh trumpet.

However, before the seventh trumpet could sound, two major events needed to take place. First of all, there appeared a "mighty angel coming down from heaven…robed in a cloud, with a rainbow above his head; [with] his face…like the sun, and his legs…like fiery pillars," straddling land and sea, roaring like a lion, and declaring, "There will be no more delay!" (Rev. 10:1–2, 6). Verse 2 Tells us "he was holding a little scroll, which lay open in his hand." Some believe the mighty angel to be Jesus; others believe the mighty angel is simply "a mighty angel."

That little scroll was then given to John to eat. Initially it tasted sweet as honey, but soon turned sour in his stomach. The explanation was, "You must prophesy again about many peoples, nations, languages and kings" (Rev. 10:11). The prophetic word is often just like that. It is initially sweet in our mouths, but as the word is delivered it can become regrettably bitter in our stomachs. We see this reflected in Jeremiah's experiences: "When your words came, I ate them; they were my joy and my heart's delight" (Jer. 15:16). But then in the aftermath, we see the bitter results in Jeremiah 15:17–18: "I sat alone because your hand was on me and you had filled me with indignation. Why is my pain unending and my wound grievous and incurable?"

The second major event that needed to happen before the blowing of the last, the seventh, trumpet concerned the "two witnesses" of Revelation 11:1–13, who would bring about the second "woe," or doom.

Revelation 11:1–2 makes it clear that the temple will be rebuilt in the city of Jerusalem; it will be in this temple that the man of sin will sit. That the old city of Jerusalem should here be called "Sodom and Egypt, where also [the] Lord was crucified" (Rev. 11:8), is paving the way for the extreme makeover in the final chapters of Revelation where "the Holy City, the new Jerusalem" (literally, the "*fresh* Jerusalem") comes "down out of heaven from God, prepared as a bride beautifully dressed for her husband." (Rev. 21:2). The "the old order of things" will indeed completely pass away (v. 4)! Then in the place of the temple described in Revelation 11:1–2 will be the eternal temple of God Himself, as revealed in Revelation 21:22. But here, just before the blowing of the seventh trumpet, we are introduced to the Tribulation temple (the third temple): "Go and measure the temple of God and the altar…But exclude the outer court; do not measure it, because it has been given to the Gentiles. They will trample on the holy city for 42 months [three and a half years; the latter half of Daniel's seventieth 'seven']" (Rev. 11:1–2). Jesus had prophesied similarly, "Jerusalem will be trampled on by the Gentiles until the times of the Gentiles are fulfilled" (Luke 21:24).

Here we have an artist's rendition of how the third temple could be rebuilt on the Temple Mount, leaving the Dome of the Rock in the court of the Gentiles. We note how this proposed temple site lines up perfectly with the eastern gate, previously touched on in our Ezekiel study. It is easy to see how the Antichrist could bring peace to the troubled Middle East, peace between Jews and Muslims, by proposing such a daring possibility of a Temple Mount on which sits both the third temple sacred to the Jews and the Dome of the Rock sacred to the Muslims. This "man of peace" could indeed be the Mahdi spoken of by President Ahmadinejad in his speech to the United Nations on September 26, 2012, and the one prophesied by Muhammad as the "man of peace," who would broker "a peace agreement" that "will be upheld for seven years."

The prophet Daniel, however, saw him violating that covenant of peace in the middle of the seven years (Dan. 9:27), taking over the third temple for his own blasphemous ends (2 Thess. 2:4). Then "while people are saying, 'Peace and safety,' destruction will come on them suddenly…and they will not escape" (1 Thess. 5:3)! Interestingly, another alternative to this scenario happened in the spring of 2013 when missiles from Gaza actually landed in Jerusalem close to the Temple Mount and the Dome of the Rock! The Islamic jihadists *themselves* could destroy *their own* holy site, thus totally clearing the mount for the third temple to be built!

Consequently, during the forty-two months, or three and a half years, the last half of the final seven years of the Great Tribulation, the Lord said, "'I will give power to my two witnesses, and they will prophesy for 1,260 days [three and a half years], clothed in sackcloth [a symbol of repentance].' These are 'the two olive trees' [a figure taken from Zechariah's vision in Zech. 4:2–3, 11–14] and the two lampstands...[that] stand before the Lord of the earth" (Rev. 11:3–4). The reference to the *two* lampstands may be a reference to the two churches, the two "lampstands"—Smyrna and Philadelphia—who alone out of the seven did not need to repent. To these two overcoming churches, these two lampstands, special end-time promises had been given: "Be faithful, even to the point of death, and I will give you the crown of life" (Rev. 2:10), and, "Since you have kept my command to endure patiently, I will also keep you [in][xviii] the hour of trial that is going to come upon the whole world to test those who live on the earth. I am coming soon. Hold on to what you have, so that no one will take your crown" (Rev. 3:10–11).

The two witnesses will move in the spirit and power of Elijah, able to "shut up the sky so that it will not rain during the time they are prophesying," and the power of Moses, able to "turn the waters into blood and to strike the earth with every kind of plague as often as they want" (Rev. 11:6). Some believe the two witnesses actually are Moses and Elijah.[xix] This author leans more in favor of seeing the two witnesses as faithful martyrs from the last-days church, over-coming martyrs from the two lampstands alluded to in Revelation 2 and 3. To this holy company the promise was given, "Do not be afraid of what you are about to suffer...Be faithful, even to the point of death, and I will give you the crown of life" (Rev. 2:10).

Revelation 11:7–10 tell us:

---

xviii. The Greek preposition used here permits the translation "in". *The Living Bible* in its footnote of Revelation 3:10 states "The inference is not clear in the Greek as to whether this means 'kept from' or 'kept through' the coming horror."

xix. One leader of an internationally known sect actually declared that he and his father were the two witnesses!

> When [the two witnesses] "finished their testimony, the beast that comes up from the Abyss will attack them, and overpower and kill them. Their bodies will lie in the street of the great city [Jerusalem, and] for three and a half days men from every people, tribe, language and nation will gaze on their bodies... [our modern global media will make this possible]. The inhabitants of the earth [will refuse them burial and] will gloat over them and will celebrate by sending each other gifts, because these two prophets had tormented those who live on the earth.

Yet, faithful to His word to give them "the crown of life," God will breathe life back into them, and they will be raised and then caught up to heaven, "while their enemies [look] on" (Rev. 11:12). They will be the firstfruits of the very Rapture of the whole church that now begins at the last trumpet.

Revelation 11:13 continues, "At that very hour there was a severe earthquake and a tenth of the city [of Jerusalem] collapsed. Seven thousand people were killed in the earthquake, and the survivors were terrified and gave glory to the God of heaven." And *in that very hour* "the seventh angel sounded his trumpet," the last trumpet, spoken of by Paul in 1 Corinthians 15:51–52, and the cry went up: "The kingdom of the world has become the kingdom of our Lord and of his Christ, and he will reign for ever and ever" (Rev. 11:15). God has now "taken [His] great power and [has] begun to reign... The time has come for judging the dead [for this is the first resurrection], and for rewarding your servants the prophets and your saints and those who reverence your name, both small and great" (Rev. 11:17–18), for this is the gathering of God's "elect from the four winds, from one end of the heavens to the other" (Matt. 24:31)!

At this juncture, "God's temple in heaven was opened [the blueprint temple which became the pattern for the earthly temples that would be built], and within his temple was seen the ark of his covenant" (Rev. 11:19), and in the midst of lightning and thunder, an earthquake, and a great hailstorm, the vision of the seven trumpets dramatically closes! "The kingdom of the world has [now] become the kingdom of our Lord and of his Christ, and he will reign forever and ever" (v. 15). Amen!

Chapter 25

THE VISION OF THE GREAT CONFLICT
Chapters 12–14

R EVELATION 12 BEGINS with the announcement, "A great and wondrous sign appeared in heaven." And so begins vision number three of John's five visions: the *vision of the great conflict.* In this vision there are seven main players: the sun-clothed woman, her man-child son, the dragon (Satan), the archangel Michael, the Antichrist Beast, the false prophet, and the firstfruits company.

Revelation 12:1–6 and then verses 13–17 introduce us to the first three of the seven players: the sun-clothed woman, her man-child son, and the dragon. The first of these is the "woman clothed with the sun, with the moon under her feet and a crown of twelve stars on her head" (v. 1). This woman has already been interpreted for us in Scripture as Israel, since the symbolism of the sun, the moon, and the twelve stars was given by God to Joseph in a prophetic dream to indicate the clan of Israel (Gen. 37:9–10). This woman of Revelation 12 "was pregnant and cried out in pain as she was about to give birth.... She gave birth to a son, a male child, who will rule all the nations with an iron scepter. And her child was snatched up ['caught up,' NKJV] to God and to his throne" (Rev. 12:2, 5).

In Revelation 19:15–16 Jesus is pictured in His second coming as that one who will "rule [the nations] with an iron scepter," a messianic quote from Psalm 2:7–15 describing the Son of God. It is, therefore, reasonable to see the man-child as Jesus birthed out of Israel, who was then caught up to God and to His throne in ascension glory.

We would be remiss not to mention that along with Jesus, the

164

overcomers are also described in the exact same words: "To him who overcomes and does my will to the end, I will give authority over the nations—that one 'will rule them with an iron scepter and will dash them to pieces like pottery'—just as I have received authority from my Father" (Rev. 2:26–27).

If the overcomers are the man-child of Revelation 12, then the sun-clad woman would be the church that brought them forth. The catching up to the throne of God would be their ascension to kingdom authority. We will want to keep that option open. The possibility of the sun-clad woman being Mary, the mother of our Lord, is probably least likely, mainly because that stature is not given to Mary in the apostolic writings and only appears centuries later in the history of the institutional church.

As the woman is about to give birth to the man-child:

> Another sign appeared in heaven: an enormous red dragon [identified for us in verse nine as Satan] with seven heads and ten horns and seven crowns on his heads. His tail swept a third of the stars [angels] out of the sky and flung them to the earth [which may have happened at the time of his defection, recorded in Isaiah 14:12–15]. The dragon stood in front of the woman who was about to give birth, so that he might devour her child the moment he was born. She gave birth to a son, a male child, who will rule all the nations with an iron scepter. And her child was snatched up [caught up] to God and to his throne.
>
> —Revelation 12:3–5

War in Heaven

Revelation 12:7–9 then describes war in heaven:

> Michael and his angels fought against the dragon, and the dragon and his angels fought back. But he was not strong enough, and they lost their place in heaven. The great dragon was hurled down—that ancient serpent [of Genesis 3] called the devil [from the Greek word *diabolos*, "the accuser"], or Satan [from the Hebrew and Greek, also meaning "the accuser"], who leads the whole world astray. He was hurled to the earth, and his angels with him.

This "accuser" is "the accuser of our brothers, who accuses them before our God day and night" (Rev. 12:10). That is why John in 1 John 2:1 Presents Jesus Christ, the Righteous, as the "one who speaks to the Father in our defense"! The New King James Version translates these words as "we have an Advocate with the Father," a *lawyer, an attorney,* who, with His blood, ever pleads our case before the Father! So, the accused "overcame [the accuser] by the blood of the Lamb [our perfect, righteous plea] and by the word of their testimony [testifying on the witness stand to the efficacy of that blood]; they did not love their lives so much as to shrink from death" (Rev. 12:11)! They were willing to embrace martyrdom for Jesus' sake! And Satan indeed was thrown down, knowing "that his time is short" (v. 12).

THE WOMAN IN THE WILDERNESS

"The woman [meanwhile] fled into the ["wilderness," NKJV] to a place prepared for her by God, where she might be taken care of for 1,260 days [three and a half years]"
—REVELATION 12:6

These three and a half years are the crisis years of the Great Tribulation, during which God's people will be kept safe. We are again reminded of Eusebius' account of how the Lord prepared a safe haven for His own "in a certain town of Perea called Pella," and how God led His people out of harm's way by a supernatural revelation given through His prophets just before the destruction of Jerusalem by the Roman general Titus in A.D. 70. John, the author of Revelation, had been spared by that very prophecy as he fled Jerusalem for Ephesus. Revelation 12:13–17 describes the accuser's futile attempts to destroy the woman, all to no avail. Whether the woman is natural Israel and/or the church, she is divinely protected, and the enraged dragon cannot destroy her!

THE BEAST OUT OF THE SEA

Revelation 13 presents us with the next two players: the Antichrist and the false prophet. The "beast coming out of the sea… [very much like the dragon of 12:3] had ten horns and seven heads, with ten crowns on his horns, and on each head a blasphemous name" (v. 1). This beast "resembled a leopard, but had feet like those of a bear and a mouth like that of a lion" (v. 2)—a composite of all the evil empires of Daniel 7: the Babylonian Empire (the lion), the Medo-Persian Empire (the bear), and the Grecian Empire (the leopard).

When the Antichrist beast was described in Daniel 8:24, we were told that "he will become very strong, but not by his own power." In Revelation 13:2 we are given the key to the beast's amazing power: "The dragon gave the beast his power and his throne and great authority." The beast is empowered by the dragon himself! John continues, "One of the heads of the beast seemed to have had a fatal wound, but the fatal wound had been healed. The whole world was astonished and followed the beast" (v. 3). Author Joel Richardson raises the possibility that the healing of the fatal wound of one of the heads of the beast is the restoration of the Islamic Caliphate.[21] The collapse of the Ottoman Empire in the 1920s ended the Islamic Caliphate. But the present passion of radical Islam has been to see the Caliphate restored under the Mahdi. Such a restoration would indeed be *astonishing,* as John predicted in Revelation 13:3–4: "The whole world was astonished and followed the beast. Men worshiped the dragon…and they also worshiped the beast" (Rev. 13:2–4). Worship by the world, that which has long been sought after by Satan, will now be gained, but Satan's tether is limited. The beast will only be able to "exercise his authority for forty-two months [three and a half years]" (Rev. 13:5)!

As with the same beast described in Daniel 7, the beast here "was given power to make war against the saints and to conquer them…All inhabitants of the earth will worship the beast—all whose names have not been written in the book of life belonging to the Lamb that was slain from the creation of the world" (Rev. 13:7–8).

The overcoming church, with names written in the Book of Life, will stand victorious in these days. They will say, as the three Hebrew sons said to Nebuchadnezzar in Daniel 3:18, "We want you to know...that we will not serve your gods or worship the image of gold you have set up"!

Then a sober note is sounded: "If anyone is to go into captivity, into captivity he will go. If anyone is to be killed with the sword, with the sword he will be killed. [We note again that the people who execute by the sword are radical Islamists.] This calls for patient endurance and faithfulness on the part of the saints" (Rev. 13:10).

THE BEAST OUT OF THE EARTH

Throughout the Book of Revelation the Lamb is the ultimate symbol of our Lord Jesus Christ—the slain Lamb. It is, therefore, a shock for us to note that when the false prophet emerges in Revelation 13:11–18 as deputy to the Antichrist he appears "like a lamb." He is the beast coming out of the earth, speaking like a dragon, but he has "two horns *like a lamb*...He exercised all the authority of the first beast *on his behalf*" (Rev. 13:11–12, emphasis added); he is the public relations man for the Antichrist, and as such he makes "the earth and its inhabitants worship the first beast, whose fatal wound had been healed. And he performed great and miraculous signs...[by which] he deceived the inhabitants of the earth" (vv. 12–14), setting up an image that appears to speak in honor of the beast and requiring that "all who refused to worship the image [should] be killed" (v. 15).

As we read over these sobering scriptures, we remember the remarks of Iran's President Ahmadinejad in his September 2012 Speech before the United Nations, in which he pictured Jesus Christ as the deputy to the Mahdi, Islam's awaited savior.

According to Islamic teachings about Isa Al-Maseeh, the Islamic Jesus: "Jesus (peace be upon him) will come and perform the obligatory prayers behind the Mahdi and follow him."[22] "Jesus will descend from heaven and espouse the cause of the Mahdi. The Christians and the Jews will see him and recognize his true status. The Christians will abandon their faith in his godhead."[23]

Muhammad himself had prophesied: "Jesus...will...descend...

He will break the cross...Allah will [cause to] perish all religions except Islam"[24] It has been conjectured about Muhammad's prediction that "Jesus...will *break the cross*," that Jesus, the Islamic Isa, will go from church building to church building throughout the whole world tearing down the cross, testifying that He never died on that cross!

What the future may unfold, we do not know, but at this present time there are not two more viable candidates for the Beast and the false prophet than the Islamic Mahdi and the Islamic Jesus!

THE MARK OF THE BEAST

> He also forced everyone, small and great, rich and poor, free and slave, to receive a mark on his right hand or on his forehead, so that no one could buy or sell unless he had the mark, which is the name of the beast or the number of his name. This calls for wisdom. If anyone has insight, let him calculate the number of the beast, for it is man's number. His number is 666.
>
> —REVELATION 13:16–18

Much has been written by many seeking to clarify the Mark of the Beast. We know from the inspired text that "the mark...is the name of the beast or the number of his name" and that "the number of the beast...is man's number. His number is 666." Six is the biblical number for man, which falls short of seven—the biblical number for completion and perfection. Man's incompleteness and imperfection is thereby testified to by the number six. Seven is the number of completeness and perfection. Eight is the number of *newness,* such as the eighth day, which is also the first day of the week; it is associated with the resurrection of our Lord Jesus. The number of the name of Jesus, consequently, is 888. Greek, as well as Hebrew and Latin, use their alphabet letters to signify their numbers, unlike our system, in which we have both alphabet and numbers. Each letter in the name of Jesus has a numerical value *I* (10), *E* (8), *S* (200), *O* (70), *U* (400), *S* (200), which when added up totals 888, the number of Jesus' name. It is *that* name that the firstfruits of chapter 14 will bear on *their* foreheads (Rev. 14:1).

On the grim observation that "no one could buy or sell unless he had the mark" (Rev. 13:17), we are made aware of modern technology that is making that grave happening a possibility. Nearly every human being in the civilized world has now been assigned a number. In the past few years we have seen this number extended to newborns. A child without a Social Security number cannot be declared as a dependent on an income tax return. Radio Frequency Identification (RFID) technology has also come on the scene, making possible the tracking of any object anywhere with a transponder—a microchip and an antenna. Then we add to that the Global Positioning System (GPS), which enables anyone to be located anywhere they are. I remember our experience as a family when we returned to visit our friends in northern Minnesota a few years ago. We were driving a rental vehicle and had accidentally gotten lost on the back roads. Fortunately, the vehicle came equipped with a GPS, so we turned it on. It showed *us* on the screen, and then showed an approaching vehicle on the same dirt road—all on a remote wilderness back road in northern Minnesota! You and I can be found anywhere!

One of the current hot-button issues has been the national ID. The deadline for the enforcement of a national ID card in America was set for January 15, 2013, but that deadline has been deferred because many states have simply *refused to comply*! Over thirty years ago, in 1981, a national ID was proposed during a cabinet meeting of the Reagan administration. Journalist Stephen Moore writes of this meeting:

> Then-Attorney General William French Smith argued that a perfectly harmless ID card system would be necessary to reduce illegal immigration. A second cabinet member asked: Why not tattoo a number on each American's forearm? According to Martin Anderson, the White House domestic policy advisor at the time, Reagan blurted out, "My God, that's the Mark of the Beast." As Anderson wrote, "That was the end of the national identification card during the Reagan years."[25]

We have already seen a system of world government taking shape before our very eyes, all the way from the International Monetary

Fund, the World Bank, the World Trade Organization, to the World Court, the World Health Organization, and the United Nations itself. Globalization is a key word in this hour – exactly as predicted in the Holy Scriptures by God regarding the last days! [26]

If a refusal to submit to the antichrist system means "no one could buy or sell unless he had the mark" (Rev. 13:17), the question arises, How then shall true believers survive in these days? The same way Israel survived as Egypt lay devastated under the wrath of God. Israel survived by a miraculous daily supply from heaven (Exod. 16–17). Our God is our Jehovah Jireh provider! Amen!

THE FIRSTFRUITS TO GOD AND THE LAMB

In Revelation 14:1, 3–5, the final players in the vision of the great conflict appear:

> Then I looked, and there before me was the Lamb [the true Jesus], standing on Mount Zion, and with him *144,000* [more than likely a symbolic number] *who had his name and his Father's name written on their foreheads* [in deep contrast with those who had the name of the beast inscribed on *their* foreheads] ... And they sang a new song before the throne and before the four living creatures and the elders. No one could learn the song except the 144,000 who had been redeemed from the earth ... they kept themselves pure. They follow the Lamb wherever he goes. They were purchased from among men and offered as firstfruits to God and the Lamb. No lie was found in their mouths; they are blameless.

These 144,000 are "offered as firstfruits to God and the Lamb." Before the chapter ends, we will be introduced to the full harvest, and these are the firstfruits of that harvest. These are exemplary in their consecration, in their radical pursuit of the Lamb, in their sterling lives. They kept themselves pure from the defilements of the fallen woman, Babylon. They follow the Lamb wherever he goes; they are blameless. What longing should fill our own hearts to be like them, the "firstfruits to God and the Lamb"!

In Revelation 14:6–13, three angels appear front and center. The first "had the eternal gospel to proclaim to those who live on the earth—to every nation, tribe, language and people" (v. 6). Many of us had been taught that only *people* can share the gospel, for only they can know the despair of sin and the joys of salvation. But apparently God has a better idea. Most of us have already heard of miraculous conversions to Christ, especially in Islamic lands, as a result of angelic visitations!

The second angel heralds the fall of Babylon the Great, a subject so important that it will cover several chapters in the next section of Revelation—the vision of the seven last plagues.

The third angel brings a very severe warning that "if anyone worships the beast and his image and receives his mark on the forehead or on the hand... He will be tormented with burning sulfur in the presence of the holy angels and of the Lamb" (Rev. 14:9–10)! Most of us were taught that eternity for those who are lost will be *separation* from God; but here the exact opposite is true—these will be tormented "in the presence of the holy angels and of the Lamb"!

Finally, a word of encouragement is given to God's faithful saints, especially the martyrs of the Lamb: "Blessed are the dead who die in the Lord from now on... they will rest from their labor, for their deeds will follow them" (Rev. 14:13).

THE HARVEST OF THE EARTH

All five visions in Revelation conclude with the coming of Jesus and the gathering of the saints to be with Him. Consequently, John wrote, "I looked, and there before me was a white cloud, and seated on the cloud was one 'like a son of man' ['One like the Son of Man,' NKJV] with a crown of gold on his head and a sharp sickle in his hand... he who was seated on the cloud swung his sickle over the earth, and the earth was harvested" (Rev. 14:14–16). This is our Lord in His return and the gathering of His elect to Him!

However, before this vision concludes, there is one more harvest, a harvest of a vastly different kind. An angel from the temple in heaven came with a sharp sickle and "swung his sickle on the earth, gathered its grapes and threw them into the great winepress of God's wrath. They were trampled in the winepress outside the city, [Jerusalem] and blood flowed out of the press, rising as high as the horses' bridles for a distance of 1,600 stadia [about one hundred eighty miles]" (Rev. 14:19–20)!

This vision is borrowed from Isaiah 63:1–4:

> Who is this coming from Edom [Israel's bitterest Arab rival], from Bozrah [Edom's capital], with his garments stained crimson? Who is this, robed in splendor, striding forward in the greatness of his strength? "It is I, speaking in righteousness, mighty to save [answers Jesus]." Why are your garments red, like those of one treading the winepress? "I have trodden the winepress alone [Jesus answers]; from the nations no one was with me. I trampled them in my anger and trod them down in my wrath; their blood spattered my garments, and I stained all my clothing. For the day of vengeance was in my heart, and the year of my redemption has come."

Revelation 19:15–16 plainly reveals this one to be Jesus, the "King of kings and Lord of lords"! Praise God that the *vengeance* of our God lasts but a day ("the day of vengeance"), but the *redemption* of our God lasts a year ("the year of my redemption"). Just as Isaiah wrote in Isaiah 61:1–2: "He has sent me…to proclaim the year of the LORD's favor and the day of vengeance of our God"! Amen!

Chapter 26

THE VISION OF THE SEVEN LAST PLAGUES
Chapters 15–19

JOHN WROTE, "I saw in heaven another great and marvelous sign: seven angels with the seven last plagues" (Rev. 15:1). The New King James Version ends John's statement, "for in them the wrath of God is complete" (v. 1). Standing beside "what looked like a sea of glass mixed with fire" were "those who had been victorious over the beast and his image and over the number of his name" (v. 2, NIV). From these statements it is obvious that we are seeing the final days of the Great Tribulation, for what was begun in the opening of the seals and the blowing of the trumpets is now to be completed.

When the first angel poured out his bowl on the land, "ugly and painful sores broke out on the people who had the mark of the beast and worshiped his image" (Rev. 16:2). When "the second angel poured out his bowl on the sea…it turned into blood…and every living thing in the sea died" (v. 3). When the third angel poured out his bowl on the rivers and springs of water "they became blood" (v. 4). When the fourth angel "poured out his bowl on the sun," intense flares from the sun or a gamma ray burst, depleting the earth's protective ozone layer, which caused people to be "seared by the intense heat and they cursed the name of God, who had control over these plagues, but they refused to repent and glorify him" (vv. 8–9). This was a response similar to the one in Revelation 9:20–21. Then when the fifth angel poured out his bowl, the kingdom of the beast was "plunged into darkness," and "men gnawed their tongues in agony and cursed the God of heaven" but "refused to repent of what they had done" (vv. 10–11). Then the sixth angel poured out his bowl on the great river Euphrates causing it to run dry.

Endtime Magazine reports:

> On January 13, 1990, the *Indianapolis Star* carried the head-
> line 'Turkey will cut off flow of Euphrates for one month.' The
> article stated that a huge reservoir had been built by Turkey.
> While filling up the reservoir, the flow of the Euphrates would
> be stopped for one month and a concrete diversion channel
> built. These things have now been done. With this newly built
> dam, Turkey has the ability to stop the Euphrates River at will.
> The conditions for fulfilling this 1900 year-old prophecy are
> now in place.[27]

The drying up of the Euphrates will be "to prepare the way for the
kings from the East" (Rev. 16:12). This coming from the East may
be a possible reference to China, with its 200-million-man army
(possibly referred to in Revelation 9:16) or to the Islamic nations
that will be converging on Israel. An Islamic prophecy declares
that "armies carrying black flags [the sign of *jihad*] will come from
Khurusan [Iran and the nations to the east]. No power will be able
to stop them, and they will finally reach Eela [the temple mount in
Jerusalem] where they will erect their flags...The last hour would
not come unless the Muslims will fight against the Jews and the
Muslims would kill them."[28]

Next John wrote, "I saw three evil spirits that looked like frogs"
that "came out of the mouth of the dragon, out of the mouth of
the beast and out of the mouth of the false prophet [that evil and
unholy trinity]...performing miraculous signs, and they go out to
the kings of the whole world, to gather them for the battle on the
great day of God Almighty...to the place that in Hebrew is called
Armageddon" (Rev. 16:12-14, 16). This reference to Armageddon,
or Har Mageddon, may refer to a rallying point on the actual
vast plains of Megiddo in northern Israel, or the reference to Har
Mageddon may be symbolic. In Joel 3:2 The Lord says, "I will gather
all nations and bring them down to the Valley of Jehoshaphat,"
the Valley of Judgment. This also may be actual or symbolic. But
if the staging place for these nations is literally on the plains of
Meggido, then the actual final battle may well take place in the
Valley of Jehoshaphat in Jerusalem. William Smith, the author of

Bible Dictionary notes, "Both Muslims and Jews believe that the last judgment is to take place there."[29]

Then came a word from Jesus, similar to His word in Matthew 24:42–44, a word both to encourage and to warn His elect: "Behold, I come like a thief! Blessed is he who stays awake and keeps his clothes with him, so that he may not go naked and be shamefully exposed" (Rev. 16:15). We recall again that the blood, the frogs, the hail, and the darkness are all reminiscent of the plagues that fell on Egypt as Israel prepared for the Exodus; but during these plagues *God's people were kept safe in the hollow of His hand!* And so, He is able to keep His elect in the last days as they prepare for their exodus! As Revelation 16:15 reminds us, "Blessed is he who stays awake and keeps his clothes with him, so that he may not go naked and be shamefully exposed."

When the seventh angel poured out his bowl in Revelation 16:17, a word from the throne of God declared: "It is done!" Then in the aftermath of the most powerful earthquake ever recorded in human history, "The great city [Jerusalem] split into three parts, and the cities of the nations collapsed" (v. 19). Massive hailstones fell from heaven, and men cursed God because of the hail, for the plague was so terrible!

And "God remembered Babylon the Great and gave her the cup filled with the wine of the fury of his wrath" (Rev. 16:19).

BABYLON, THE WOMAN ON THE SCARLET BEAST

John wrote, "The angel carried me away in the Spirit into a desert. There I saw a woman sitting on a scarlet beast that was covered with blasphemous names and had seven heads and ten horns…She held a golden cup in her hand, filled with abominable things and the filth of her adulteries…written on her forehead: MYSTERY, BABYLON THE GREAT THE MOTHER OF PROSTITUTES AND OF THE ABOMINATIONS OF THE EARTH. I saw that the woman was drunk with the blood of the saints, the blood of those who bore testimony to Jesus" (Rev. 17:3–6).

The immediate questions before us are: Who is this woman, and who is the beast that she is riding?

First of all, the key to understanding the identity of the woman lies in remembering the antithetical parallels that we have discovered so far:

1. First of all, there is the unholy trinity of the dragon (the *father* of lies), the Antichrist (the *son* of perdition), and the false prophet (the false *spirit* of prophecy)— the antithesis of the true and holy Trinity of the Father, the Son, and the Holy Spirit, the true Spirit of prophecy.

2. Second, there is the mark placed on the foreheads of those who worship the Beast, "the mark, which is the name of the beast or the *number of his name*...His number is 666" (Rev. 13:16–18). This is the antithesis of those "who had his name and his Father's name written on their foreheads" (Rev. 14:1). And the number of Jesus' name we know to be 888.

3. Third, there is the fallen city Babylon (Rev. 18:2), which is in deep contrast with the "Holy City, the new Jerusalem" (Rev. 21:2). We will focus more clearly on that city shortly.

4. Finally, there is the fallen woman, Babylon (Rev. 17:5), which is the antithesis of the pure bride of the Lamb (Rev. 19:7).

The woman, fallen Babylon, the great prostitute, stands in stark contrast to the virgin bride of Christ. That contrast is made clear in Revelation 19:1–3:

> "Hallelujah! Salvation and glory and power belong to our God, for true and just are his judgments. He has condemned *the great prostitute* who corrupted the earth by her adulteries. He has avenged on her the blood of his servants." And again they shouted: "Hallelujah! The smoke from her goes up forever and ever." (emphasis added)

Then we see the antithesis, the exact opposite of the fallen woman, in Revelation 19:6–8:

Hallelujah! For our Lord God Almighty reigns. Let us rejoice and be glad and give him glory! For the wedding of the Lamb has come, and *his bride* has made herself ready. Fine linen, bright and clean, was given her to wear [fine linen stands for the righteous acts of the saints]. (emphasis added).

If the bride of Christ, the wife of the Lamb, is the true church in all of her awesome beauty and holy purity, then fallen Babylon is the exact opposite—the world's fallen religions, with their horrific record: "The woman was drunk with the blood of the saints, the blood of those who bore testimony to Jesus" (Rev. 17:6). The multitudes, including Peter and Paul, betrayed by dead Judaism and martyred by the Roman Empire, are among the martyrs. The tens of thousands tortured and killed by the Catholic Church of the Middle Ages in the Inquisition are also in that holy number of martyrs. The multiple Anabaptists who were "tortured terribly on the rack, so that they were torn apart and died"[30] at the hands of both the Catholic Church *and the Reform-minded Protestants* as well, are in that holy number of martyrs. Theirs is "the blood of those who bore testimony to Jesus" (Rev. 17:6). This is a picture of a fallen mother church with her fallen daughters committing abominable acts in the earth!

Included as part of that fallen woman and her fallen daughters is radical Hinduism with its fallen daughter, Buddhism, both with the blood of the saints *on their hands*. Also high on the list is radical Islam, causing tens of millions to be martyred in the past century, primarily in the 10/40 Window, slain by the sword of radical Islam. All these fallen and false religions and others besides them will ultimately be overthrown because God will judge "the great prostitute who corrupted the earth by her adulteries." He will avenge "on her the blood of his servants" (Rev. 19:2)!

BABYLON, THE GREAT CITY

Babylon is not only "the woman"; Babylon is "the great city," according to Revelation 17:18: "The woman you saw is the great city that rules over the kings of the earth." We note the same parallel in Revelation 21:9–10: "The bride, the wife of the Lamb... [is] the Holy

City, Jerusalem, coming down out of heaven from God." In both cases the woman is the city.

If the woman, fallen Babylon, is the *religious* scourge in the earth, then the city, fallen Babylon, is the controlling *political and economic power* in the earth: "The kings of the earth committed adultery with her [politically], and the merchants of the earth grew rich [economically] from her excessive luxuries" (Rev. 18:3). In the divine overthrow of this vast political and economic system, "The merchants of the earth will weep and mourn over her because no one buys their cargoes any more....The merchants who...gained their wealth from her will stand far off, terrified at her torment" (Rev. 18:11, 15). This will precipitate the greatest worldwide depression.

> In one hour she has been brought to ruin! Rejoice over her, O heaven! Rejoice, saints and apostles and prophets! God has judged her for the way she treated you....In her was found the blood of prophets and of the saints, and of all who have been killed on the earth.
>
> —REVELATION 18:19–20, 24

The Roman Empire, in its day was both the fallen woman and the fallen city. The revived Roman Empire, in our day, with both the western leg and the eastern leg of the great statue of Daniel 2, is the fallen woman and the fallen city in the last days. We find in the eastern leg, which is the Middle East, the irrational rage of radical Islam against both Israel and the church. Plus, we find in the Islamic prophecies about Mahdi Al-Muntadhar, the Mahdi, the possibility of the final world antichrist ruler, and in the prophecies about Isa Al-Maseeh, the Islamic Jesus, the Mahdi's deputy, a viable candidate for the false prophet of Revelation 13. We also find in the western leg, the European theater, the makings of a powerful economic and political world power—the European Community of Nations! The symbolism of the following pictures may be purely coincidental, but more than likely they are prophetic signs of the times, signs to which we must pay close attention.

This is the present flag of the European Union (EU), seemingly borrowing the twelve stars on its field of blue from the twelve stars of Revelation 12!

This is a stamp of the EU picturing the twelve stars surrounding the woman riding the beast, exactly as portrayed in Revelation 17! The German inscription reads: "ECU, the way of the future."

This is a painting of the ancient tower of Babel.

This is the EU Parliament building in Strasbourg, opened in December 2000. It was deliberately built as a replica of the Tower of Babel. It has been reported that when a secular journalist living in Strasbourg asked EU officials the question, "Why the Tower of Babel?" the officials answered that they would finish what others failed to complete 3,000 years earlier. (Actually, the Genesis Tower of Babel dates back to 2,250 B.C. or 4,250 years ago!)

Are these just coincidences? As students of Bible prophecy we must weigh them in the light of the prophetic Scriptures, and our conclusion may well be that *these are indeed the last days!* On July 18, 2013, the European Union issued orders bidding all twenty-eight member states to cease transferring funds or giving scholarships or research grants to organizations or individuals based in Judea and Samaria, eastern Jerusalem, and even the Golan Heights, thus redrawing Israel's borders back to the 1949 lines. The restrictions are for the years 2014–2020. The decision also states that any future agreement signed with Israel must include a section that says the "settlements" are *not* part of sovereign Israel. And so the true nature of the European Union is emerging, and the hostility of both legs of Daniel's vision against Israel is becoming increasingly clear!

THE SCARLET BEAST

John wrote, "I saw a woman [Babylon] sitting on a scarlet beast that was covered [with blood, and] with blasphemous names and had seven heads and ten horns" (Rev. 17:3). This scarlet beast most likely is the Beast, the Antichrist, of Revelation 13:1: the "beast coming out of the sea [who] had ten horns and seven heads, with ten crowns on his horns, and on each head a blasphemous name." It is not unreasonable then to see the fallen woman who rides on him as his evil woman, Babylon, the prostitute!

The following words regarding the scarlet beast remain a mystery to us at this time, though many have sought to interpret them in different, and often contradictory, ways: "The beast, which you saw, once was, now is not, and will come up out of the Abyss and go to his destruction...he once was, now is not, and yet will come" (Rev. 17:8). As for the scarlet beast's seven heads: "The seven heads are seven hills on which the woman sits" (v. 9). This may be a veiled reference to the ancient City of Rome built upon seven hills; others actually feel it may refer to Old Jerusalem, which is built on seven hills. Convinced that Rome is that city built on seven hills, various scholars of biblical prophecy see the Roman Church in the prophetic words regarding the fallen woman, Babylon. It is true that the history of the Roman Church, especially in the Middle Ages, is the history of an apostate church. However, it is also true that probably over 180 million evangelical Catholics have now been touched by the movement of the Holy Spirit within the Catholic Church and that many of these are, therefore, now a part of Jesus' spotless bride! This is a marvel of God's amazing grace!

An interesting prophecy is ascribed to Malachy (pronounced "*Malachi*"), an Irish saint who in 1139 set out on a pilgrimage to Rome. On seeing the city he fell to the ground and began to prophesy in Latin. To those who study his words, 90 percent of his prophecies are believed to have come true. In his prophetic utterances, he predicted that there would be one hundred and twelve more popes. The recent pope, Benedict, was number one hundred eleven on the list. Malachy, if he is being properly understood by those who study his words, declared that the pope following him will be *the last* pope. On February 11, 2013, Benedict XVI resigned his office. A new supreme pontiff was then elected by the conclave of Cardinals on March 13, 2013—Pope Francis I. These are Malachy's prophetic words concerning the last pope:

> In extreme persecution, the seat of the Holy Roman Church will be occupied by Petrus Romanus [which may be the last pope's code name], who will lead his sheep through many tribulations, at the end of which the city of seven hills shall be destroyed, and the dreadful Judge shall judge the people.[31]

Could this prophecy be valid? Could Francis I be Petrus Romanus? Something more for us to consider, as we ponder the question, *Are these the last days?*

John continues regarding the seven heads, which are the seven hills, that "they are also seven kings. Five have fallen, one is, the other has not yet come; but when he does come, he must remain for a little while. The beast who once was, and now is not, is an eighth king. He belongs to the seven and is going to his destruction" (Rev. 17:10–11). As stated before, many have sought to interpret these bewildering statements in different and often contradictory ways. We are perhaps wisest to let them remain a mystery to us at this time, for "now [we] know in part," but as the day draws near we will "know fully, even as [we are] fully known" (1 Cor. 13:12)!

THE ACTIVITIES OF THE SCARLET BEAST

The activities of the blood-red beast, recorded in Revelation 17:12–17, are clear for us to understand.

> The ten horns [of the beast that] you saw are ten kings who have not yet received a kingdom, but who for one hour will receive authority as kings along with the beast. They have one purpose [to exalt the beast in all the earth, and to that end they] and will give their power and authority to the beast. They will make war against the Lamb, but the Lamb will overcome them because he is Lord of lords and King of kings— and with him will be his called, chosen and faithful followers.

Then the plot will thicken even more: "The beast and the ten horns you saw will hate the prostitute. They will bring her to ruin and leave her naked; they will eat her flesh and burn her with fire" (Rev. 17:16). What a cruel way for this antichrist to treat his bride, but before him who demands universal worship, all religions—as false as they may be—must fall! (How unlike the way Jesus treats *His* bride!) This bizarre behavior is all because "God has put it into their hearts to accomplish his purpose by agreeing to give the beast their power to rule, until God's words are fulfilled" (v. 17). But the Beast, as with Babylon, will soon come to his end!

THE WEDDING SUPPER OF THE LAMB

We already noted the contrast between the fallen woman Babylon of Revelation 19:2 and the pure bride of Christ in Revelation 19:7–8. The church, the bride of Christ, "has made herself ready. Fine linen, bright and clean was given her to wear" (Rev. 19:7–8). This is the church without spot or wrinkle! Then, in Revelation 19:9 comes the Wedding Supper of the Lamb. The Bridegroom appears out of heaven:

> I saw heaven standing open and there before me was a white horse, whose rider is called Faithful and True. With justice he judges and makes war. His eyes are like blazing fire, and on his head are many crowns...He is dressed in a robe dipped in blood, and his name is the Word of God. The armies of heaven

were following him, riding on white horses and dressed in fine linen, white and clean.

—REVELATION 19:11–14

These armies, by the very description given them, are the bride of verse 8 to whom "fine linen, bright and clean, was given...to wear." These are also the ones already mentioned in the war between the Lamb and the Beast and his kings in Revelation 17:14: "And with him [the Lord of lords and King of kings] will be his called, chosen and faithful followers."

> Out of [the Lamb's] mouth comes a sharp sword with which to strike down the nations...He treads the winepress of the fury of the wrath of God Almighty. On his robe and on his thigh he has this name written: KING OF KINGS AND LORD OF LORDS.
> —REVELATION 19:15–16

Revelation 19:17 then seemingly refers back to the Wedding Supper of the Lamb of Revelation 19:9: "And I saw an angel standing in the sun, who cried in a loud voice to all the birds flying in midair, 'Come, gather together for the great supper of God.'" It may seem strange that these carrion birds would be among those on the invitation list to the great supper of God! But this is no stranger than the menu for that supper, which includes in its different courses "the flesh of kings, generals, and mighty men, of horses and their riders, and the flesh of all people, free and slave, small and great" (Rev. 19:18). Perhaps at this juncture we need to remind ourselves again that these symbolisms were never intended to be taken *literally*, but rather *figuratively*, conveying in their symbolism a deep reality—the triumph of Jesus in His coming to judge and punish all evil and injustice!

THE FINAL OVERTHROW OF THE BEAST AND THE FALSE PROPHET

John wrote:

> I saw the beast and the kings of the earth and their armies gathered together to make war against the rider on the horse

> [Jesus] and his army [His raptured church]. But the beast was captured, and with him the false prophet who had performed the miraculous signs on his behalf. With these signs he had deluded those who had received the mark of the beast and worshiped his image. The two of them were thrown alive into the fiery lake of burning sulfur.
> —REVELATION 19:19–20

It is just as described by Daniel regarding the Antichrist: "The beast was slain and its body destroyed and thrown into the blazing fire" (Dan. 7:11). Paul's description of the demise of the Antichrist beast is a bit more concise: "Whom the Lord Jesus will overthrow with the breath of his mouth and destroy by the splendor of his coming" (2 Thess. 2:8).

This vision in Revelation closes with these sober words: "The rest of them [the armies 'gathered together to make war' against the Lamb] were killed with the sword that came out of the mouth of the rider on the horse, and all the birds gorged themselves on their flesh" (Rev. 19:21).

This vision concludes, as do the others that preceded it, with the coming of our Lord Jesus Christ and the mustering of the church, His army, and the final defeat of evil and the triumph of God's kingdom, for Jesus is indeed "KING OF KINGS AND LORD OF LORDS" (Rev. 19:16). Amen!

Chapter 27

THE FINAL VISION OF THE KINGDOM AND THE HOLY CITY
Chapters 20–22

R EVELATION 20 BEGINS with John's declaration:

> I saw an angel coming down out of heaven, having the key
> to the Abyss and holding in his hand a great chain. He
> seized the dragon, that ancient serpent, who is the devil, or
> Satan, and bound him for *a thousand years*. He threw him
> into the Abyss, and locked and sealed it over him, to keep him
> from deceiving the nations anymore until *the thousand years*
> were ended. After that, he must be set free for a short time.
>
> —REVELATION 20:1–3 [EMPHASIS ADDED]

For the first time, not only in Revelation but in the Scriptures as
a whole, we are introduced to the term "the thousand years," or *the
millennium* (which literally means thousand [*mille*] years [*ennium*]).
The issue of the kingdom-reign of our Lord is well established in
the whole of the Scriptures, but that this kingdom-reign should
extend for *one thousand years* appears only in Revelation 20, where
the phrase "thousand years" appears six times. Needless to say,
there has been much discussion among Christians as to whether
the "thousand years" are literal or figurative.

The second-century Fathers, those closest to the apostles, were
pre-millennial in their eschatology, believing that the literal coming
of our Lord Jesus would come before (*pre*) the millennium. They
also apparently believed that the millennium was *literally a thousand years in duration*. Papias, in *Fragments, VI*, wrote: "There will
be a millennium after the resurrection from the dead, when the

personal reign of Christ will be established on this earth." Barnabas, in chapter 13 of the book that bears his name, wrote:

> God made in six days the work of his hands; and he finished them on the seventh day and he rested…Consider, my children, what that signifies…that in six thousand years the Lord God will bring all things to an end. For with him one day is as a thousand years…Therefore, children, in six days, that is, in six thousand years, shall all things be accomplished…when His Son shall come and abolish the season of the wicked one, and judge the ungodly…then He shall rest in that seventh day [the final thousand years, the millennium].

Irenaeus, who was discipled by Polycarp, who himself was discipled by the apostle John, writing in the mid-second century, made the same statements as Barnabas regarding the six days of creation being a picture of the six thousand years of human history in *Against Heresies,* Book IV, 28:3. Many Bible students place the beginning of biblical human history at 4,000 B.C. That would make Barnabas's and Irenaeus's "six thousand years" end at approximately A.D. 2,000 (a further signpost, indicating that these are the last days)! Most evangelicals today are pre-millennial, as were the early church fathers, and most believe the thousand years to be literal.

The amillennial view, a view articulated by the Catholic theologian Augustine in the fourth century, declares that there is no actual, literal kingdom of God on earth over which Christ will rule; the kingdom of God is rather in the hearts of faithful men.

Augustine's views have come down to us through the Reformation as Reformed or Covenant Theology. Reformed Theology on Israel and the church is also known as Replacement Theology, in that the church now replaces Israel. Most evangelicals, however, as noted before, are premillennial and believe the millennium to be literal, as did the early church fathers, those closest in time to the original apostles.

In Revelation 20:3 John declared that Satan would be bound for the thousand years, but "after that, he must be set free for a short time." The "setting free" occurs in verses 7–10 of this chapter.

First, however, we are introduced to the saints who will reign with Christ for the thousand years, those who are "blessed and holy…who share in the first resurrection. The second death has no power over them, but they will be priests of God and of Christ and will reign with him for a thousand years" (Rev. 20:6).

We note that special attention is given to a particular group of martyrs within this wider number of saints, "those who had been beheaded" for their faith (Rev. 20:4). Foreshadows of these martyrs are seen in the June 23, 2013, murder of a Franciscan priest publicly beheaded by Syrian rebels. Francois Murad, age forty-nine, was executed with two others in the countryside of northern Syria by Islamic jihadists. In graphic video footage circulated online, Francois Murad is seen tied up and pushed to the ground as a man slowly cuts his head off from behind with a long knife. Several dozen onlookers, including children, can be heard chanting, "*Allah Akhbar*" ("Allah is great"), as the beheading takes place.[32]

On July 11, 2013, the decapitated body of sixty-year-old Magdy Habashi was also found in a cemetery in Northern Sinai after being abducted by Islamist radicals. He was the second Christian to be killed in northern Sinai in less than a week.[33]

John wrote:

> And I saw the souls of those who had been beheaded [and today, primarily radical Islam practices beheading as their method of execution. These martyrs were beheaded] because of their testimony about Jesus and because of the word of God. They had not worshiped the beast or his image and had not received his mark on their foreheads or their hands. They came to life and reigned with Christ a thousand years. (The rest of the dead did not come to life until the thousand years were ended.) *This is the first resurrection.*
> —REVELATION 20:4–5, EMPHASIS ADDED

Since "this is the first resurrection," and the *first* resurrection can only take place at the Rapture of the church at the second coming of our Lord Jesus Christ (1 Thess. 4:16–17), the time of Jesus' second coming and the gathering of His elect is identified here for us by the statement that these martyrs "had not worshiped the beast or its image and had not received its mark on their foreheads or their hands" (Rev. 20:4), obviously at the end and not before the Great

Tribulation. Jesus' return and the Rapture of the church is, therefore, exactly when Jesus taught it would be in Matthew 24:29–31: not
before, but "immediately after ['the tribulation,' NKJV] of those days."
We note that there can be no resurrection *before the first*; otherwise,
the first would not be the first! And in this first resurrection, the
saints—including those who were martyred rather than worship the
beast or receive his mark—will rise to be *priests of God and of Christ*
and *will reign with him* for a thousand years (Rev. 20:6). Here we see
the church mediating as priests and reigning as kings with Christ
over a new society, a new world in which righteousness dwells.

Unfortunately, the peace of this beautiful age will suddenly be
disrupted by the announcement that when "the thousand years
are over, Satan will be released from his prison and will go out to
deceive the nations in the four corners of the earth…to gather them
for battle" (Rev. 20:7–8). "Gog and Magog," from a thousand years
before (Ezek. 38–39), are here mentioned again by name, undoubtedly because they have now become the symbol of all human rebellion against the kingdom of God. For one last time the deceived
people of the earth will march across the breadth of the earth and
surround the camp of God's people, Jerusalem, the city He loves.
But fire will come down from heaven and devour them (Rev. 20:9).
Then after this one final dramatic sputter, "the devil, who deceived
them, was thrown into the lake of burning sulfur, where the beast
and the false prophet had been thrown. They will be tormented day
and night forever and ever" (v. 10).

Why this one, final dramatic sputter? Why should the age-lasting
peace of God's righteous kingdom be allowed to be broken yet
again by releasing Satan for one last try? That mystery ultimately
lies locked in the counsels of God, but perhaps He allows this one
last sputter because for an age people have known only righteousness *with no alternatives*. The very reason God allowed the peace
of the original Eden to be broken by the intrusion of that ancient
serpent, the devil, was because of the desire of His heart to have a
people who love Him passionately *not because they have no other
choice* but because *they have chosen Him in the face of the pressure
of opposing choices!*

The unholy and evil trinity of the underworld is now together in the lake of fire, where "they will be tormented day and night for ever and ever" (Rev. 20:10). In John's Revelation the statement "for ever and ever" appears some twelve times, and three of these times this phrase is used to describe the punishment of the wicked (Rev. 14:11; 19:3; and 20:10). The Greek phrase translated "for ever and ever" in Revelation 14:11, *eis aionas aionon*, literally means "to ages of ages"; but an apparently stronger Greek phrase used in Revelation 19:3 and 20:10, *eis tous aionas ton aionon*, meaning literally, "to *the ages* of *the ages*." Such are the descriptive words for those who have risen up in rebellion against a holy God! And the judgments of God continue.

THE GREAT WHITE THRONE

John then sees "a great white throne and him who was seated on it…the dead, great and small [were] standing before the throne, and books were opened…If anyone's name was not found written in the book of life, he was thrown into the lake of fire" (Rev. 20:11–12, 15).

In this fearful imagery we witness the judgment of those whose names were not found recorded in the Lamb's Book of Life. The imagery is similar to what Daniel saw in Daniel 7:10: "The court was seated, and the books were opened"; and in Daniel 12:1: "Everyone whose name is written in the book—will be delivered." In Revelation the expression "the book of life" is used multiple times (Rev. 3:5; 13:8; 17:8; 20:12; 20:15; and 21:27, where the book is called "the Lamb's book of life"). From these passages we see the extreme importance of our own individual response in faith to the call of the Spirit to "'Come!' Whoever is thirsty, let him come; and whoever wishes, let him take the free gift of the water of life" (Rev. 22:17).

I would ask you, my fellow student of the end times, do you know with *assurance* that *your name* is written in the Lamb's Book of Life? John has already written in his first epistle: "God has given us eternal life, and this life is in his Son.…I write these things…so that you may know that you have eternal life" (1 John 5:11, 13). The provision for our salvation is complete and sufficient in Jesus, God's Son, and it is for us with sincere God-given repentance and faith to gladly receive this great salvation so we may indeed *know* that we have eternal life!

The New Heaven and the New Earth

We are now at the conclusion of John's vision; we are peering past the Tribulation and past the millennial kingdom into eternity. As he writes in Revelation 21:4, "The old order of things has passed away," and we behold with awe a *new*, literally, a *fresh* heaven and a *fresh* earth, "for the first heaven and the first earth had passed away" (Rev. 21:1). We also see a new, *fresh* Jerusalem "coming down out of heaven from God, prepared as a bride beautifully dressed for her husband" (v. 2). Later, in Revelation 21:9–10, John was told, "'Come, I will show you the bride, the wife of the Lamb.' And he...showed me the Holy City, Jerusalem, coming down out of heaven from God." As with the fallen woman, Babylon, *the woman is the city.* Here the bride, the wife of the Lamb, *is* the holy city, Jerusalem.

We are witnessing the most *extreme makeover* that this world has ever seen. The old order has completely passed away. The heavens are fresh. The earth is fresh. The holy city, Jerusalem, is fresh. The old earth is gone. The old heavens are gone. The old city of Jerusalem is no more. The holy city is now the Bride, the wife of the Lamb. The corrupted Tribulation temple, in which the Beast sat, is gone, and even the millennial temple, in which the Lamb was continually celebrated, is gone, for now the Father Himself and the Lamb Himself are the eternal temple! The old has passed away; everything has become fresh and new!

> He who was seated on the throne said, "I am making every-thing new [fresh]!" Then he said, "Write this down, for these words are trustworthy and true."
> R<small>EVELATION</small> 21:5

The overcomer "will inherit all this," God promises, "and I will be his God and he will be my son" (Rev. 21:7). As for the unrepentant, ungodly, "their place will be in the fiery lake of burning sulfur. This is the second death" (v. 8). The expression "burning sulfur" brings to mind God's awful judgment on Sodom and Gomorrah: "Then the L<small>ORD</small> rained down burning sulfur on Sodom and Gomorrah—from the L<small>ORD</small> out of the heavens" (Gen. 19:24). As surely as there is a heaven to gain, there is a judgment to flee from, just as Lot fled from Sodom and its perverted lifestyle! This is a grave warning for us today, especially in view of the brazen moral deviance of our western civilization!

The holy city, the city foursquare, rises mystically in the earth as a perfect cube, like the holy of holies in the ancient sanctuary, but now immense in size—fourteen hundred miles in length and width and height—sizable enough to fit just over twice into the land mass of the United States of America! This golden city has twelve gates of pearl, inscribed with the names of the twelve tribes of Israel. It also has twelve foundations of precious stones, stones similar to the stones in the breastplate of the High Priest of Exodus 39, inscribed with the names of the twelve apostles of the Lamb. The city shines in brilliance as transparent as glass, and "the great street of the city was of pure gold, like transparent glass" (Rev. 21:21). This is a city awesome in beauty and majesty! It will remain yet to be seen the degree to which these awesome descriptions are literal or figurative of a grander beauty and transparency than we could ever imagine!

The very glory of God gives the city its light, "and the Lamb is its lamp" (Rev. 21:23). And amazingly:

> The nations will walk by its light, and the kings of the earth will bring their splendor into it. On no day will its gates ever be shut…[as] the glory and honor of the nations will be brought into it. [The only restriction will be that] Nothing impure will ever enter it, nor will anyone who does what is shameful or deceitful, but only those whose names are written in the Lamb's book of life.
>
> —REVELATION 21:24–27

As we make the final transition to the climax of this vision in Revelation 22:1–5, we see "the river of the water of life, as clear as crystal, flowing from the throne of God and of the Lamb," similar to—but greater than—the kingdom river pictured in Ezekiel 47. And rather than Ezekiel's "fruit trees of all kinds," there will be but one tree—"the tree of life…And the leaves of the tree are for the healing of the nations" (Rev. 21:1). So, even in eternity, if words mean anything, God stands as the continued healer of the broken nations of earth. Had not John previously prophesied: "All nations will come and worship before you, for your righteous acts have been revealed" (Rev. 15:4)! Oh, our amazing, redemptive God![xx]

Eternity has indeed begun. "No longer will there be any curse" (Rev. 22:3). The enthroned God and the Lamb will be reigning supreme. God's servants who bear His name on their foreheads will serve Him and forever gaze upon His awesome face. "And they will reign for ever and ever"; "unto the ages of the ages," literally. Revelation 22:6 assures us, "These words are trustworthy and true. The Lord, the God of the spirits of the prophets [the God who inspired the prophets], sent his angel to show his servants the things that must soon take place." Jesus is indeed *coming soon!* That statement is repeated three times. And, therefore, unlike Daniel's visions, these visions are *not sealed up,* "because the time is near" (v. 10). Yes, Jesus is coming soon (Rev. 22:7, 12, 20). Amen! Maranatha! Come, Lord Jesus! And may your *grace,* Lord Jesus Christ, powerfully rest upon us as your church until that blessed day. Amen!

---

xx. In Appendix Six you will find the brief treatise, "Now is the Time to Worship," a balanced presentation on the state of the lost. This study is able to be downloaded from www.immanuels.org, and it can be freely distributed and used by study groups and for personal study.

Chapter 28

WHAT KIND OF PEOPLE
OUGHT YOU TO BE?

W E HAVE COME to the end of our prophetic overview of both the Old and New Testaments. In the light of the things we have seen, our question now must be, How then shall we live? In other words, How does this study *impact my life*? What *adjustments do I need to make in my own life* in the light of Jesus' near return? In the words of 2 Peter 3:11, because these are the last days, "What kind of people ought you to be?"

I believe 2 Peter 3—which answers this very question—is one of the most challenging chapters in the whole of Scripture. I want Peter's answer to this question, "What kind of people ought you to be?" to become our challenge as we conclude this study.

In 2 Peter 3:3-4, Peter raises a very real concern: "First of all, you must understand that in the last days scoffers will come, scoffing and following their own evil desires. They will say, 'Where is this coming he promised? Ever since our ancestors died, everything goes on as it has since the beginning of creation.'" Then in verse 8 Peter provides a most unique response to this scoffing: "But do not forget this one thing, dear friends: With the Lord a day is like a thousand years, and a thousand years are like a day." We previously discussed this prophetic "thousand years are like a day" benchmark from Moses' Psalm 90:4. We then saw how Moses' understanding helps us to interpret the prophetic statement in Hosea 6:2: "After two days [that is, after two thousand years of being gone] he will [come and] revive us; on the third day [in the kingdom age] he will restore us that we may live in his presence." Here in 2 Peter we have yet another similar exercise. The time that elapsed since Jesus promised He would return is met with the observation, especially meaningful to us today, that Jesus has really only been gone for two days by Moses' divine reckoning of time!

Peter, in verse 9, then launches out into the first of three great challenges that the imminent return of Jesus brings to us: "The Lord is not slow [that is, *slack*] in keeping his promise [to return, but]...he is patient [that is, persistent] with you [the church], [because He is] not wanting anyone [in the world] to perish, but everyone [everywhere] to come to repentance." In other words, Jesus has not yet returned as He promised He would because He is patiently and persistently *waiting* for the church to do the one thing that He commissioned them to do when He left—to evangelize the whole world (Matt. 28:18–20)! His very return, as we also noted in Matthew 24:14, can *only* take place *when* the church has fulfilled that Great Commission that He gave to us when He left us, for our Lord Jesus is "not wanting anyone to perish, but everyone to come to repentance"!

Peter then announces in verses 10 through 13 the passing away of the whole old order of things and the coming of "a new heaven and a new earth, the home of righteousness." Next, in verse 14, Peter raises the second challenge we must accept if we are to properly respond to Jesus' soon return: "Since everything will be destroyed in this way, what kind of people ought you to be?" (2 Pet. 3:11). The answer is given: "You ought to live holy and godly lives" (v. 11), for Jesus is returning not only for a people who have completed the task of world evangelism but for a bride who has "made herself ready" (Rev. 19:7–8.) Paul also sounded that very same note in Ephesians 5:27—Jesus' intent at His coming is to "present [the church] to himself as a radiant [glorious] church, without stain [spot] or wrinkle or any other blemish, but holy and blameless." Consequently, Peter, borrowing from these very words of Paul, admonishes us to "make every effort to be found spotless, blameless and at peace with him" (2 Pet. 3:14).

Peter then tells us that we "ought to live holy and godly lives as [we] look forward to the day of God and speed its coming" (2 Pet. 3:11–12). What an awesome responsibility that we can actually *hurry and speed along* the coming of the day of God by our obedience!

The third and final challenge to us is found in the phrase that Peter uses three times in this passage—"looking forward"—looking forward to the day of God. We are to be a *watchtower* people, actually, the *true watchtower* people! We are to be a people on prophetic watch, "looking forward" to the day of God! That day is not to catch us unawares. We are to be those who discern the signs of the times! (This very issue of our being an *alert* people became one of the main reasons for the writing of this book!) It appears that every city in Israel had a *watchtower*—whether on the city wall itself or on an elevated platform outside the city. Prophetic watchmen are described in both Psalm 127:1 and Psalm 130:6; they were to "stand guard" against the enemy, and were "to wait for the morning," to look forward to the rising of the daystar from on High! Isaiah touched on this same theme:

> I have posted *watchmen on your walls,* O, Jerusalem; they will never be silent day or night. You who call on the LORD, give yourselves no rest and give him no rest till he establishes Jerusalem and makes her the praise of the earth.
> —ISAIAH 62:6–7, EMPHASIS ADDED

These are the people of the prophetic watchtower.

How then shall we live? We shall live with the evangelization of the world high on our agenda! We shall live as the bride who makes herself ready, perfecting holiness in the fear of God! We shall live, hurrying and speeding along the coming of the day of God! Finally, we shall thus live as a people on prophetic watch[xxi], so that this day will not surprise us like a thief! In the light of these challenges, we cry out, "Maranatha. Come, Lord Jesus. Come!"

MY PERSONAL CONSECRATION

Lord Jesus Christ, in the light of Your soon return, I consecrate myself afresh to You, to be Your passionate servant in these last days! Take over my life, my destiny, my treasures, my time! I devote myself afresh to You—for bridal preparation, for world evangelism, and for prophetic watchfulness! In your dear name, amen!

_____ *(my name)*

_____ *(date)*

---

xxi. See Appendix Seven for a sample copy of the prophetic-watch periodical *"A Midnight Cry!" An Alert From Current Events on the Signs of the Times,* available free of charge at www.immanuels.org.

Appendix One

DIFFERENT ESCHATOLOGICAL UNDERSTANDINGS

1. Eschatological: End-time, relating to the last days (from the Greek *eschatos,* "last")

2. Covenant Theology: Also known as Reformed Theology or Replacement Theology, which holds that the church has *replaced* Israel in God's plan, that the Jews are no longer God's chosen people, and that God does not have future plans for the nation of Israel

3. Dispensational Theology: A system of theology teaching different stewardships (or *dispensations)* of God's dealings with man. Dispensational Theology makes a clear distinction between Israel and what is call the "parenthesis" of the church. It teaches that after the church has been raptured from the earth, God will restore the kingdom to Israel and all the promises of God to Israel will be literally fulfilled

4. Amillennialism: The belief that there will be no actual, literal kingdom of God on the earth over which Christ will rule; the kingdom of God will rather be in the hearts of faithful men

5. Premillennialism: The belief that Jesus will literally return to the earth before (pre) the millennium (the thousand-year kingdom age) and that He Himself will inaugurate and rule over it

6. Postmillennialism: The belief that the gospel, like leaven, will permeate the entire world, and eventually men, through the effect of the gospel, will bring in the kingdom. Then, when everything is set right, after a thousand years of man's progressive improvement,

Christ will return after (post) the millennium. Also known as Dominion Theology

7. Pre-Tribulation Rapture: The belief that Christ will rapture true believers before the Tribulation begins

8. Mid-Tribulation Rapture: The belief that the Rapture of the church will occur three and one-half years into the Tribulation period, before the final bowls of wrath, described in Revelation 16

9. Post-Tribulation Rapture: The belief that the church will go through the Tribulation, assured that God will keep His own in the hour of trial

10. Four Methods of Interpreting Biblical Prophecy:
    - Preterism: interpreting biblical prophecies in terms of historical events that have already taken place
    - Historicism: interpreting biblical prophecies as events that are historically being fulfilled right up until the end of history
    - Futurism: interpreting biblical prophecies primarily as events that will happen in the last days
    - Idealism: interpreting biblical prophecies as symbolic pictures of timeless truths, such as the victory of good over evil

—Compiled by Charles P. Schmitt

Appendix Two
A COMMENTARY ON DANIEL 11

T O HELP US understand this extraordinary chapter (Daniel
11), I created the following commentary. Daniel's final vision
traces the stormy history of the Persian and the Greek
empires down to the reign of the Antichrist in the last days.

[2] Now then, I tell you the truth: Three more kings will
appear in Persia [Cambyses (Cyrus' eldest son), Pseudo-
Smerdis, and Darius I], and then a fourth [Xerxes I], who will
be far richer than all the others. When he has gained power
by his wealth, he will stir up everyone against the kingdom of
Greece [his attempts to conquer Greece in 480 B.C.—the battle
of Thermopylae and the destruction of Athens; in the final
battle at Platea in 479, Persia lost over a quarter of a million
men, while the Greeks lost only one hundred and fifty-four!].

[3] Then a mighty king will appear [Alexander the Great (336–
323)], who will rule with great power and do as he pleases.

[4] After he has appeared, his empire will be broken up and parceled out toward the four winds of heaven [upon Alexander's
untimely death in 323 B.C.]. It will not go to his descendants
[for Alexander's young son, Alexander IV, was murdered in
310 B.C.], nor will it have the power he exercised, because his
empire will be uprooted and given to others [Macedonia and
Greece to Antipater and his son Cassander; Thrace and Asia
Minor to Lysimachus; Syria to Seleucus I; Palestine and Egypt
to Ptolemy I].

[5] The king of the South [Ptolemy I] will become strong [he
actually built the first lighthouse ever—four hundred feet high

in the harbor of Alexandria; Ptolemy also studied geometry under Euclid], but one of his commanders [Seleucus I Nicator] will become even stronger than he and will rule his own kingdom with great power [the northern Syrian kingdom].

[6] After some years, they will become allies. The daughter of the king of the South [Berenice, daughter of Ptolemy II of Egypt, who himself ordered the Septuagint translation of the Hebrew Scriptures] will go to the king of the North [Antiochus II Theos of Syria] to make an alliance [a treaty cemented by the marriage of Berenice to Antiochus], but she will not retain her power, and he [Antiochus II] and his power will not last [because Laodice, Antiochus' former wife, conspired to put Berenice and Antiochus II to death]. In those days she [Berenice] will be handed over, together with her royal escort [Berenice and her newborn were decapitated, and Antiochus II was poisoned to death] and her father [Ptolemy II] and the one who supported her.

[7] One from her family line [Berenice's brother, Ptolemy III of Egypt] will arise to take her place [Ptolemy III brought Alexandrian learning to its height; for instance, he proved the earth was a globe with a twenty-five-thousand-mile circumference]. He will attack [from 246 to 241 B.C.] the forces of the king of the North [Seleucus II of Syria] and enter his fortress [the cities of Antioch and Seleucia]; he will fight against them and be victorious.

[8] He will also seize their gods [Syrian idols], their metal images and their valuable articles of silver and gold and carry them off to Egypt [and for this he was hailed as "Benefactor"]. For some years he will leave the king of the North [Seleucus II] alone [due to a peace treaty with Seleucus II in 240 B.C.].

[9] Then the king of the North [Seleucus II] will invade the realm of the king of the South [in the 230s, regaining control of northern Syria and Phoenicia, several conquered possessions of Egypt] but will retreat to his own country.

[10] [Seleucus II's] sons [Seleucus III and Antiochus the Great] will prepare for war and assemble a great army, which will

sweep on like an irresistible flood and carry the battle as far as his fortress [Ptolemy's fortress at Raphia in southern Palestine].

[11] Then the king of the South [Ptolemy IV of Egypt] will march out in a rage and fight against the king of the North [Antiochus the Great], who will raise a large army, but it will be defeated [at Raphia in 217 B.C.].

[12] When the army is carried off, the king of the South [Ptolemy IV] will be filled with pride and will slaughter many thousands [Antiochus the Great lost nearly ten thousand men at Raphia], yet he will not remain triumphant.

[13] For the king of the North [Antiochus the Great] will muster another army, larger than the first; and after several years, he will advance with a huge army fully equipped.

[14] In those times many will rise against the king of the South [Ptolemy V, who was crowned at age four; the Rosetta Stone details the "many" that rose up against the boy-king, Ptolemy V]. The violent men among your own people [Jews who joined the forces of Antiochus III] will rebel in fulfillment of the vision [this vision now being given to Daniel], but without success [Ptolemy's General Scopus crushed this rebellion at Gaza in 200 B.C.].

[15] Then the king of the North [Antiochus III] will come and build up siege ramps and will capture a fortified city [the seaport of Sidon]. The forces of the South [Ptolemy V's forces] will be powerless to resist; even their best troops will not have the strength to stand. [General Scopus surrendered to Antiochus III at Sidon.]

[16] The invader [Antiochus III] will do as he pleases; no one will be able to stand against him. [Antiochus III] will establish himself in the Beautiful Land [he gained control of Palestine in 197 B.C.] and will have the power to destroy it [especially the pro-Egyptian resistance in Israel].

[17] He will determine to come with the might of his entire kingdom and will make an alliance with the king of the South [Ptolemy V of Egypt]. And [Antiochus III] will give [Ptolemy V, now 10] a daughter [Cleopatra I] in marriage [in 195 B.C.] in order to [infiltrate and] overthrow the [Ptolemic] kingdom, but his plans [to control Egypt] will not succeed or help him. [Cleopatra eventually embraced the Egyptian cause, much to the disappointment of her father, Antiochus III.]

[18] Then [Antiochus III, the Great] will turn his attention to the coastlands [of the Aegean] and will take many of them, but a commander [Lucius Cornelius Scipio Asiaticus of Rome] will put an end to his insolence [Antiochus was defeated by Lucius at Magnesia in Asia Minor, 190 B.C.] and will turn his insolence back upon him [the humiliating Treaty of Apamea, 188 B.C.].

[19] After this, [Antiochus III, the Great] will turn back toward the fortresses of his own country [Syria] but will stumble and fall, to be seen no more [he was slain, plundering the temple of Bel in 187 B.C.].

[20] His successor [the eldest son of Antiochus III, Seleucus IV] will send out a tax collector [Heliodorus] to maintain the royal splendor. In a few years, however, [Seleucus IV] will be destroyed, yet not in anger or in battle [he was actually poisoned by Heliodorus].

[21] [Seleucus IV] will be succeeded by a contemptible person [Seleucus' younger brother, Antiochus IV Epiphanes, who claimed himself to be "God-Manifest"] who has not been given the honor of royalty [Antiochus IV Epiphanes seized the throne from Seleucus's son, Demetrius I]. [Antiochus] will invade the kingdom [Syro-Palestine] when its people feel secure, and he will seize it through intrigue [he was called "the Nero of Jewish history"].

[22] Then an overwhelming army will be swept away before him; both it and a prince of the covenant [the High Priest Onias III] will be destroyed [murdered in 170 B.C.].

[23] After coming to an agreement with [Onias], [Antiochus IV] will act deceitfully, and with only a few people he will rise to power.

[24] When the richest provinces [of Syro-Palestine] feel secure, [Antiochus IV] will invade them and will achieve what neither his fathers nor his forefathers did. He will distribute plunder, loot and wealth among his followers. He will plot the over-throw of fortresses [in Egypt]—but only for a time.

[25] With a large army [Antiochus IV] will stir up his strength and courage against the king of the South [Ptolemy]. The king of the South [Ptolemy] will wage war with a large and very powerful army, but he will not be able to stand because of the plots devised against him.

[26] Those who eat from [Ptolemy's] provisions will try to destroy him; [Ptolemy's] army will be swept away, and many will fall in battle.

[27] The two kings [Antiochus IV and Ptolemy], with their hearts bent on evil, will sit at the same table and lie to each other, but to no avail, because an end will still come at the appointed time.

[28] The king of the North [Antiochus IV] will return to his own country [Syria] with great wealth, but his heart will be set against the holy covenant. He will take action against it [plundering the Temple in Jerusalem in 169 B.C., when thou-sands were massacred] and then return to his own country [Syria].

[29] At the appointed time [168 B.C.], [Antiochus Epiphanes] will invade the South [Egypt] again, but this time the out-come will be different from what it was before.

[30] Ships [Roman vessels] of the western coastlands [under Popilius Laenas] will oppose him [at Alexandria, Egypt], and he will lose heart. Then he will turn back [withdrawing from Egypt] and vent his fury against the holy covenant [Jerusalem, its Temple, and the people of God]. [Antiochus] will return

and show favor to those who forsake the holy covenant [apostate Jews under the corrupt priest Menelaus].

[31] [Antiochus Epiphanes'] armed forces will rise up to desecrate the temple fortress and will abolish the daily sacrifice [in December 168 B.C.]. Then they will set up the abomination that causes desolation [the altar to the god Zeus Olympus, ordered to be placed in the temple by Antiochus].

[32] With flattery [glowing promises, Antiochus] will corrupt those who have violated the covenant [the apostate Jews], but the people who know their God will firmly resist him. [This is the Jewish resistance movement, the Maccabees. In December of 165 B.C., the temple was captured in Israel by them from Antiochus and rededicated to God. This would become known as the Festival of Hanukkah.]

[33] Those who are wise [the Hasidim] will instruct many [in the Holy Law], though for a time they will fall by the sword or be burned or captured or plundered.

[34] When they fall, they will receive a little help [from the successful guerrilla warriors in 168 B.C. who began in Modein, seventeen miles northwest of Jerusalem under Mattathias and his son Judas Maccabeus (the "Hammer")], and many who are not sincere [insincere followers who attached themselves to the cause] will join them.

[35] Some of the wise [the teachers] will stumble, so that they may be refined, purified and made spotless until the time of the end [Daniel now focuses, as he did in his previous visions, on the end times and the "abomination of desolation" spoken of by Jesus in Matthew 24:15], for it will still come at the appointed time.

For the commentary on Daniel 11:36–12:4, please see Chapter 9 of the book.

—Compiled by Charles P. Schmitt

Appendix Three

ISRAEL AND THE CHURCH

T HERE ARE CURRENTLY two main points of view on Israel and the church. The first of these is the view that the church has *replaced* Israel in God's plan, that the Jews are no longer God's chosen people, and that God does not have future plans for the nation of Israel.

The second point of view on Israel and the church makes a clear distinction between Israel and what is called the "parenthesis" of the church. This belief indicates that after the church has been raptured from the earth, God will restore the kingdom to Israel, and all the promises of God to Israel will be literally fulfilled.

A BIBLICAL RESPONSE

Paul's understanding of the church is not that it is a parenthetical thought in the purposes of God, nor that the church is a replacement of Israel; rather the church, made up of Jew and Gentile, is the very heart of God's "eternal purpose which he accomplished in Christ Jesus our Lord" (Eph. 3:11), and it has always been so. In other words, the church is the *center* of God's divine intent. The church is "the mystery of Christ which was not made known to men in other generations as it has now been revealed by the Spirit of God" (Eph. 3:4–5). In other words, it is not as if men in previous generations saw *nothing* regarding the church; they simply did not see the church *as clearly as it has now been revealed* by the Spirit of God to His holy apostles and prophets. For example, Isaiah, when he spoke of believers from Gentile nations in union with Israel, was actually describing the church, though through a glass darkly (Isa. 45:22, 25; 49:5–6; 51:4–5; 56:6–8; etc.).

The church is consequently now *clearly defined* by Paul in these words: "through the gospel the Gentiles are heirs together with Israel, members together of one body, and sharers together in the promise in Christ Jesus" (Eph. 3:6). God has taken the Gentiles, who were at one time "excluded from citizenship in Israel," and now "in Christ Jesus…[they] have been brought near through the blood of Christ" (Eph. 2:12–13). The excluded are now the included!

The biblical understanding lies in seeing the church as God's "one new man." Jesus did not *replace* Israel with the church but "made the two one," creating "in himself one new man out of the two" (Eph. 2:14–15). In order to effect this our Lord destroyed "the dividing wall of hostility, by abolishing in his flesh the law [the old covenant] with its commandments and regulations" (v. 15), leaving the "one new man" not lawless but under a new covenant, the "law of the Spirit of life" (Rom. 8:2). In one body Jesus has reconciled both Jew and Gentile to God through the Cross! Consequently, "[Gentiles] are no longer foreigners and aliens, but fellow citizens with God's people [Israel] and members of God's household" (Eph. 2: 19).

Indeed, the church is not *a parenthetical thought* in God's plan either; the church, as God's "one new man," is His eternal intent, His eternal purpose from the very start. Also, as previously stated, the church does not *replace* Israel, but as God's "one new man," the church is a glorious union of Israel and the Gentiles, brought together by the power of the blood of Jesus Christ! And there is only one way of salvation for both Jew and Gentile—only through the blood of Jesus Christ! Those who teach a separate and different covenant of salvation for Israel are clearly in grave error (Acts 4:12).

When Jesus warned the unbelieving Jews, "The kingdom of God shall be taken from you, and given to a nation bringing forth the fruits thereof" (Matt. 21:43, AKJV), He was envisioning the "one new man" spoken of in Ephesians 2:15; the "Israel of God" spoken of in Galatians 6:16; and "the chosen people", the "royal priesthood", the "holy nation" described in 1 Peter 2:9.

The church consequently is *the new covenant* people of God, for the old covenant, "the law with its commandments and regulations" (Eph. 2:15), has been abolished by Jesus in His sacrifice on the cross. The *new covenant*, however, had long before been promised to Israel in Jeremiah 31:31–34: "I will make a new covenant with the house of Israel and with the house of Judah," and because God has now included believing Gentiles in "citizenship in Israel," as "fellow citizens with God's people," this "one new man," this "one body," this holy nation, the church, is now the *new covenant people of God*.

The analogy of the olive tree in Romans 11, clearly underscores this divine purpose. God has not rejected his people, Israel (Rom. 11:1–2); Israel consequently did not "fall beyond recovery" (v. 11). Yes, many of the natural (Jewish) branches of the olive tree were broken off because of unbelief. But, praise God, wild, believing (Gentile) olive branches have, "contrary to nature" (v. 24), been grafted in "among the others" (v. 17)—believing Gentiles grafted into the olive tree, *right among* the natural olive branches of believing Israel, sharing "in the nourishing sap from the olive root" (v. 17). And then a glorious promise is held forth for natural Israel. Not that a kingdom separate from the church has been prepared for them, but as Jews come to faith in Jesus, "They will be grafted in, for God is able to graft them in again" (v. 23) Yes, "how much more readily will these, the natural branches, be grafted into their own olive tree" (v. 24). The message in this passage is eschatological, or end-time, for "Israel has experienced a hardening in part until the full number of the Gentiles has come in. And so all Israel will be saved" (vv. 25–26).

Zechariah 13:8–9 describes exactly how this remnant nation will all be brought to faith in Jesus. In purging trials they will find the Lord Himself! And this is in keeping with Paul's vision for a restored Israel—"How much greater riches will their fullness bring.... What will their acceptance be but life from the dead?" (Rom. 11:12, 15). Worldwide shock waves of revival will accompany the end-time spiritual restoration of Israel! And this is exactly what we are beginning to see in the earth today—a third of a million messianic Jewish believers worldwide with probably close to twenty thousand messianic believers in several hundred messianic congregations in Israel itself! We are presently seeing the greatest number of Jews coming to faith in Jesus ever, probably even exceeding the number of messianic believers in the first century. They are not being grafted into a separate olive tree, and they are not being replaced by the church.

They are a vital part of the church, God's "one new man," the "one body of Christ," the true "Israel of God," God's "holy nation," to which believing, though undeserving, Gentiles have also been joined by grace, amazing grace!

NATIONS HAVE A PURPOSE IN GOD

Apart from the spiritual component regarding Israel that we find in the apostolic writings, there is a natural component as well that is unfolding before our very eyes. Nations have a divine purpose in God; there are *kairos* (prophetic) times set for each of them, as we read in Acts. 17:26, "He made every nation of men, that they should inhabit the whole earth; and he determined the [*kairos*] times (literally) set for them and the exact places where they should live."

In the fifth century, Patrick brought the Irish, as a people, to "the *kairos* times set for them." The Irish "swarmed like bees into the dark places of heathen Europe,"[34] as Celtic Ireland became the instrument of redemption for western civilization in its darkest hour.

The discovery of the New World by Columbus in 1492 was part of God's sovereign intent for America. Columbus wrote, "It was the Lord who put it into my mind. I could feel his hand upon me....There was no question that the inspiration was from the Holy Spirit, because He comforted me with rays of marvelous inspiration from the Holy Scriptures."[35,xxii] *Operation World* describes the foundation that the Pilgrim Fathers then laid in America: "On that foundation developed *one of the largest and most dynamic Christian movements in history*,"[36] currently leading the world in apostolic missionary outreach as a beacon of hope for all humanity!

And then there were the states of Germany used by God so powerfully in the Reformation of the 1500s and the United Kingdom, used by God in worldwide revivals in the 1600s, 1700s, 1800s, and early 1900s, literally transforming the world! The torch was then passed to the United States, from where the Pentecostal worldwide revivals of the twentieth century originated.

Then there is South Korea, a current prayer and mission powerhouse in the world, and China with the "Back to Jerusalem"

---

xxii. Although Columbus' landing on an island in the Caribbean was God's plan, the slavery and genocide that resulted was not.

movement. Nigeria is impacting much of Africa, and Brazil, a missions leader, and other nations are fulfilling their national destinies in God!

Consequently, after two thousand years, for Israel suddenly to be birthed *as a nation* in May of 1948 is no insignificant coincidence. Many are the undeniable promises made concerning Israel as a nation in the Holy Scriptures by *a God who cannot lie*. Let us consider just a few of them.

In Jeremiah this promise is given by God:

> This is what the LORD says, he who appoints the sun to shine by day, who *decrees* the moon and stars to shine by night…"Only if these *decrees* vanish from my sight," declares the LORD, "will the descendants of Israel ever *cease to be a nation before me.*" This is what the LORD says: "Only if the heavens above can be measured and the foundations of the earth below be searched out *will I reject all the descendants of Israel because of all they have done,*" declares the LORD.
>
> —JEREMIAH 31:35–37, EMPHASIS ADDED

This promise is clear. Then concerning Jerusalem, the promise is further given by God: "'The days are coming,' declares the LORD, 'when this city will be rebuilt for me…The city will never again be uprooted or demolished'" (Jer. 31:38, 40). The city that was rebuilt under Nehemiah and Ezra after the Babylonian captivity could not have been the fulfillment of this promise, for that rebuilt city and temple were then demolished yet again by the Roman legions in A.D. 70. But the promise we are looking at here declares: "The city will never again be uprooted or demolished." This awaits a further end-time fulfillment.

In Ezekiel 36:24–28, this promise is given:

> I will take you out of the nations; *I will gather you from all the countries and bring you back into your own land.* I will sprinkle clean water on you, and you will be clean…I will give you a new heart and put a new spirit in you; I will remove from you your heart of stone and give you a heart of flesh. And I will put my Spirit in you and move you to follow my decrees and be careful to keep my laws. *You will live in the*

land I gave your forefathers; you will be my people and I will
be your God. (emphasis added)

The present return of Jews to the land and the amazing parallel
conversion rate to the Messiah points toward the fulfillment of this
powerful word before our very eyes!

In Hosea 3:5, this promise is also given: "Afterward the Israelites
will return and seek the LORD their God and David their king.
They will come trembling to the LORD and to his blessings in the
last days." In the tremendous turning to Jesus that we are seeing,
these words are now taking on fresh, new meaning!

In Joel and in Amos the Lord promises:

> "Then you will know that I, the LORD your God, dwell in
> Zion, my holy hill. Jerusalem will be holy; *never again will
> foreigners invade her*....Judah will be *inhabited forever* and
> Jerusalem *through all generations*. Their bloodguilt, which I
> have not pardoned, *I will pardon*. The LORD dwells in Zion!"
> —JOEL 3:17, 20–21, EMPHASIS ADDED

> I will *bring back my exiled people Israel;* then they will *rebuild
> the ruined cities and live in them*...I will plant Israel in their
> own land, *never again* to be uprooted from the land I have
> given them,' says the LORD your God.
> —AMOS 9:14–15, EMPHASIS ADDED

These "never again" words from Joel and Amos require a return
from exile far beyond the return from Babylon in 536 B.C. In Micah,
the LORD promises:

> You will again have compassion on us; you will tread our sins
> underfoot and hurl all our iniquities into the depths of the sea.
> *You will be true to Jacob,* and show mercy to Abraham, *as you
> pledged on oath to our fathers in days long ago.*
> —MICAH 7:19–20, EMPHASIS ADDED

In this promise we can see the basic issue in all of this: God
pledged an oath to Abraham, Isaac, and Jacob and to their children
after them. And so we see God's faithfulness to His pledged oath to
Israel as a nation. Consequently:

"At that time *I will gather you;* at that time *I will bring you home.* I will give you honor and praise among all the peoples of the earth when I restore your fortunes before your very eyes," says the Lord.

—Zephaniah 3:20, emphasis added

Perhaps the most profound prophecies concerning Israel as a nation in the last days are found in Zechariah:

On that day, when all the nations of the earth are gathered against her, I will make Jerusalem an immovable rock for all the nations. All who try to move it will injure themselves....On that day I will set out to destroy all the nations that attack Jerusalem. And I will pour out on the house of David and the inhabitants of Jerusalem the Spirit of grace and supplication. They will look on me, the one they have pierced and they will mourn for him as one mourns for an only child, and grieve bitterly for him as one grieves for a firstborn son....On that day a fountain will be opened to the house of David and the inhabitants of Jerusalem, to cleanse them from sin and impurity....On that day his feet will stand on the Mount of Olives, east of Jerusalem, and the Mount of Olives will be split in two from east to west...The Lord my God will come, and all the holy ones with him....On that day living water will flow out from Jerusalem...The Lord will be king over the whole earth....[Jerusalem] will be inhabited; *never again* will it be destroyed. *Jerusalem will be secure.*

—Zechariah 12:3, 9–10; 13:1; 14:4–5, 8–9, 11,

EMPHASIS ADDED

All of these promises taken one after another remain yet to be fulfilled, and *they shall all come to pass* "on that day," the great and notable Day of the Lord! Israel, as a nation shall be fully restored; Israel as a people will be redeemed through faith in the Pierced One; Jesus the Messiah shall return, as He left, to the Mount of Olives; and the Lord Himself shall reign supreme over all the earth, King of all kings and Lord of all lords! Amen!

CONCLUSION

In this brief study we have seen something of God's plan for Israel and the church: one "holy nation," made up of Jew and Gentile; "one new man"; the true "Israel of God"; "one body" in Christ! The church is neither a replacement of Israel nor a parenthetical thought in God's plan of things, exclusive of Israel. The church is the very heart of God's eternal purposes, and the church includes both Jew and Gentile.

And there are yet-unfulfilled promises and a prophetic destiny that rests upon Israel as a physical nation. Even as America, as a physical nation, has a destiny, as do other nations, so Israel as a nation has even a greater destiny as God fulfills the scriptural promises to them that He has sworn on oath. The vehement hatred expressed against the existence of Israel as a nation by Jihadist Islam is but further and clearer proof of Satan's hatred against the purposes and the promises of God. But we have read the final chapters of the book. Satan loses; God wins! God's promises are fulfilled! His word of oath remains unbroken! He will have done all He said He would!

> To him be glory in the church in Christ Jesus throughout all generations, forever and ever! Amen.
> —EPHESIANS 3:21

—CHARLES P. SCHMITT

Appendix Four

WHEN WILL OUR LORD JESUS RETURN, AND WHEN IS THE RAPTURE OF THE CHURCH?

P AUL, APOSTLE OF Jesus Christ, tells the Thessalonians of the great reunion of all believers, dead and alive, when together they meet Christ as He descends from heaven:

> The dead in Christ shall rise first: then we which are alive and remain shall be caught up together with them in the clouds, to meet the Lord in the air; and so shall we ever be with the Lord.
> —1 THESSALONIANS 4:16–17, KJV

This will be the triumphant climax of Christian history. In glorified, immortal bodies, released from the pull of gravity that has long bound man to this sin-cursed planet, believers of all generations will rise to meet the Christ they have loved, served, and followed—and for whose sake tens of millions have gladly laid down their lives. This is our blessed hope—the second coming of our Lord Jesus Christ and the Rapture of the church to meet Him!

Many evangelicals, for reasons that we will examine shortly, believe that seven years *before* the glorious return of our Lord Jesus Christ faithful Christians will be raptured, translated, caught up to heaven. This understanding has become known as the pre-Tribulation Rapture. A major legitimate concern about the pre-Tribulation Rapture is that, historically, it found its way into the evangelical mainstream only in the mid 1800s. Millions of godly, evangelical believers for almost eighteen hundred years did not believe in a pre-Tribulation Rapture. Among these are men of apostolic stature such as John and Charles Wesley, Charles Spurgeon, Matthew

Henry, John Knox, John Hus, William Carey, John Calvin, Isaac Newton, George Whitfield, A. B. Simpson, John Newton, Jonathan Edwards, John Wycliffe, John Bunyan, George Mueller, and many others. George Mueller, who lived in the mid-1800s, is reported to have stated, "If you can show me a trumpet *after the last* [1 Cor. 15:52] and a resurrection *before the first* [Rev. 20:4–5], then I can believe this new doctrine." And as far as the post-apostolic, early church fathers go, they apparently did not believe in a pre-Tribulation Rapture either. They write:

> Then shall the race of men come into the fire of proving trial and many be made to stumble and fall. But *those who remain established in their faith* shall be saved *under the very curse.*
> —DIDACHE, 16:5, EMPHASIS ADDED

> Happy ye who *endure the great tribulation* that is coming on.
> —THE SHEPHERD OF HERMAS, CHAPTER II, VISION II,
>   EMPHASIS ADDED

Irenaeus (a disciple of Polycarp, who was a disciple of John the Beloved) comments in his *Against Heresies* (5.25.3) concerning the reign of the Antichrist, that "this tyranny shall last, during which *the saints* shall be put to flight." And Augustine, commenting on Daniel 7:21, states, "He who reads this passage, even half asleep, cannot fail to see that the kingdom of Antichrist shall fiercely, though for a short time, *assail the Church.*"[37]

Gerhard Pfandi, Ph.D., associate director of the *Biblical Research Institute*, in an excellent article titled "The Rapture: Why It Cannot Occur Before the Second Coming," traces some of the roots of the pre-Tribulation Rapture teaching:

> John Nelson (J. N.) Darby (1800–1882) is regarded as the father of dispensationalism. Darby developed an elaborate philosophy in which he divided history into eight eras or dispensations, "each of which contained a different order by which God worked out His redemptive plan." Furthermore, Darby asserted that Christ's coming would occur in two stages. The first, an invisible "secret rapture" of the believers, which would end the great "parenthesis," or Church age which

began when the Jews rejected Christ. Following the Rapture, the Old Testament prophecies concerning Israel would be literally fulfilled, leading to the great tribulation, which would end with the Second Coming of Christ in glory. The doctrine of the pre-Tribulation Rapture was disseminated around the world, primarily through J.N. Darby...and men of God such as Arno Gabelein, Harry Ironside, James Gray, and also the Scofield Reference Bible. Untold multitudes became pre-Tribulationists as a result of Scofield's notes, which, because attached to his reference *Bible*, became highly authoritative in the minds of many. In the twentieth century the theory was taught in schools like Moody Bible Institute and Dallas Theological Seminary. Hal Lindsey's *Late Great Planet Earth* and many books of a similar nature further propagated the secret Rapture theory.[38]

Other scholars also cite the 1820s Irvingite charismatic visionary, Margaret MacDonald, as another of the sources of the modern-day pre-Tribulation Rapture.

BUT WHAT DID OUR LORD JESUS TEACH?

Jesus' final teaching on His second coming, given on the slopes of the Mount of Olives and recorded in Matthew 24 and 25, Mark 13, and Luke 21 is extremely clear. It was the teachings of Matthew 24 that changed my own thinking a number of years ago. I was impressed that if anyone should know the times and seasons of His return, Jesus surely would. In Matthew 24, there is *no* Second Coming and *no* Rapture until "after the tribulation of those days...[for] then shall appear the sign of the Son of Man in the clouds of heaven with power and great glory. And He shall send His angels with a great sound of a trumpet, and they shall gather together His elect from the four winds, from one end of heaven to the other" (Matt. 24:29–31, KJV). Mark 13:24–27 and Luke 21:25–28 teach the same. Luke, in 21:36, gives one additional charge: "Be always on the watch, and pray that you may be able to escape [translated as "pass safely through," in The Living Bible margin and in the New English Bible, and translated by J. B. Phillips as "come safely through"] all that is about to happen, and that you may be able to stand before the Son of Man." Our Lord sought to prepare His disciples for His coming, and in the process told them *exactly when* He was coming ("after the tribulation of those days") and how not to be caught unawares, that they might "come safely through" all these things to stand before Him.

Dispensational teaching, which appears to rebuild the dividing wall between Israel and the church (that very wall that Jesus died to destroy according to Ephesians 2:11–22), relegates these words of Jesus in Matthew 24 as pertinent only for the Jews. But Paul, in Ephesians 2:15, pointedly declared concerning Jews and Gentiles that Jesus' "purpose was to create in himself *one new man* out of the two," and that now "Gentiles are *heirs together* with Israel, *members together* of one body, and *sharers together* in the promise in Christ Jesus" (Eph. 3:6). Because of this we simply *cannot* relegate the truth of Matthew 24 only to the Jews. We are one body with them and they with us!

What Were the Apostles' Understandings?

Paul, in 1 Corinthians 15:51–52 places the Rapture of the church "at the last trumpet," as does John in Revelation 11:15, 18: "The seventh angel sounded his trumpet [and this is the last one], and there were loud voices in heaven, which said: 'The kingdom of the world has become the kingdom of our Lord and of His Christ and He will reign forever and ever.'... 'The time has come for judging the dead, and for rewarding your servants the prophets and your saints and those who reverence your Name, both small and great.'" Obviously all of this takes place at the Rapture at the end of the Tribulation period, after the blowing of the seven trumpets of judgment. A close study of Revelation records that the seven seals and the seven trumpets and the seven bowls, for the most part, run concurrently and end in the second coming of Jesus. Concurrent visions are not new to the prophetic Scriptures. The visions of Daniel all run concurrently, each ending in the second coming as well.

In Revelation 3:10 Jesus had already promised, "I will keep you from [which preposition is also translated "through"] the hour of trial that is going to come on the whole world to test those who live on the earth." (The Greek preposition used here according to

the NIV Study Bible footnote on Revelation 3:10 "can mean either
'keep you *from* undergoing' or 'keep you *through* the hour of trial.'"
The Living Bible (paraphrased) footnote on Revelation 3:10 reads:
"I will keep you from failing in the hour of testing." The weight of
New Testament teaching leans in favor of the translation: "keep you
through the hour of trial.")

In the midst of the bowls of wrath, just before the final bowl, this
word is given to John in Revelation 16:15, obviously for the saints:
"Behold I come like a thief! Blessed is he who stays awake and keeps
his clothes with him, so that he may not go naked and be shamefully exposed."

In Revelation 20:4–6, the *first* resurrection is clearly described.
And we need to remember (as George Mueller allegedly pointed
out) that there *cannot* be a resurrection seven years *before* the *first*
resurrection, or the first resurrection would not be the *first*. In this
first resurrection are found "those who had been beheaded because
of their testimony of Jesus…They had not worshipped the beast
[the Antichrist] or his image" (v. 4); so the Rapture and the first
resurrection apparently are at the *end* of the Great Tribulation, after
the reign of the Antichrist and *not* seven years *before*!

From the Book of Revelation, an argument for a pre-Tribulation
Rapture has been advanced by some because the word "church" *per
se* is not used by John between chapters 4 and 21, their reasoning
being that the church is not present in the earth during these chapters. The facts are that chapters 4 through 21 are *highly symbolic
chapters*, abounding with figures of speech for both Jesus and His
church, and that the church *does* appear in the symbolism of these
chapters as the "saints," the "kingdom of priests," the "great multitude," the "candlesticks," the "firstfruits," God's "people," the
"bride," the "armies of heaven," the "new Jerusalem," etc., even as
Jesus Himself appears with numerous symbolic names also (e.g.,
the Lamb, the Lion, the Man-Child, the Word of God, the Alpha
and Omega, etc.). And the suggestion that the "saints" of Revelation
4–21 are the Jews, rather than the many-membered, Jewish-Gentile
body of Christ again violates the revelation of God's "one new man"
(Eph. 2:15) and undercuts Paul's understanding of *Israel's reinclu-
sion* into that "one new man" in these last days. We are to note

carefully Romans 11:17, 23–27, where restored Israel in the last days is not raised up as an entity *separate* from the church but rather grafted back into their olive tree, which the mainly Gentile church has been already graciously grafted into by God. Once a serious student of the Scriptures understands the issue of Israel's restoration to the body of Christ as "one new man," *all* the seeming arguments for both dispensationalism and the pre-Tribulation Rapture completely fall apart.

Paul, in 2 Thessalonians 2:1–8, also clearly taught that the coming of our Lord Jesus Christ and the Rapture (the gathering, or "mustering," literally) of the saints to Jesus cannot take place until the great apostasy has *first* happened and the man of sin (the antichrist) is *first* revealed (v. 3). Paul also taught that the church will get "relief" from persecution and tribulation only "when [and not seven years before] the Lord Jesus is revealed from heaven in blazing fire with His powerful angels. He will punish those who do not know God and do not obey the gospel" (2 Thess. 1:7–8).

On the subject of the Antichrist being revealed, much discussion has centered in the statement of Paul in 2 Thessalonians 2:6–8:

> And now you know what is holding [the man of lawlessness, the Antichrist] back, so that he may be revealed at the proper time. For the secret power of lawlessness is already at work; but the one who now holds it back will continue to do so till he is taken out of the way. And then the lawless one will be revealed, whom the Lord Jesus will overthrow with the breath of his mouth and destroy by the splendor of his coming.

Paul thus states that there is a restraining one. According to verse 6 the Thessalonians knew the identity of that one, but unfortunately we today do not. Some suggest it is the Holy Spirit, others suggest it is the church or the Holy Spirit in the church, and yet others believe the restraining one is the archangel spoken of in Daniel 10, and so on. Actually, the restraining one could be any one of these possibilities.

Those who believe that the restraining one is the church see the Rapture of the church in the statement about the restraining one being "taken out of the way" (2 Thess. 2:7). But we need to inquire what Paul's statement means: "the one who now holds [the secret power of lawlessness] back will continue to do so *till he is taken out of the way*"? "Taken out of the way" is how the King James Version and the New International Version translate the Greek phrase that Paul used. Knox translates that phrase, "until he [the restraining one] is removed from the enemy's path." Phillips translates that phrase, "until the restraining power is removed." Norlie translates that phrase, "he who now restrains will be set aside." The Greek expression used here is also used by Paul himself in Colossians 2:14: "Having canceled the written code...that was against us and stood opposed to us; he took it away, nailing it to the cross." Here in Colossians the phrase "he took it away" obviously does *not* mean that he raptured it into heaven; it simply means "he took it away, out of the way." He took away the written code that was against us. And for us, consequently, to try to read a Rapture of the church into the Thessalonian passage, "taken out of the way," would have to be done at the expense of reasonable exegesis. The restraining one— whoever he is—is simply *taken out of the way, removed from the enemy's path, set aside,* but not raptured into heaven *per se.* And with his removal, the lawless one is revealed or made manifest.

One of the main concerns among those who hold to a pre-Tribulation rapture is a valid biblical concern—that the church will not endure the wrath of God in the closing days of time. And indeed it will *not*, for "God did not appoint us to suffer wrath but to receive salvation through our Lord Jesus Christ" (1 Thess. 5:9). This salvation from wrath, however, according to verse 8 of 1 Thessalonians 5, comes through the saints *putting on the armor of God*, that they might stand "in the evil day" (see Eph. 6:13). Powerful examples are given to us in the Holy Scriptures of how God was able to keep His own in the hour of His outpoured wrath. For example, the children of Israel were preserved in the plagues that fell on Egypt. Many of those plagues are identical to the ones that will yet fall in the Great Tribulation—but God's ancient people were safely "kept by the power of God" (1 Pet. 1:5; see Exodus 8:22; 9:4–7, 25–26; 10:23; 12:12–13). And God's promise is as true for us today as it was for them back then: "No destructive plague will touch you when I strike Egypt" (Exod. 12:13). Further examples of God's keeping power in the midst of great tribulation are Daniel being kept safely in the lion's den and the three Hebrew sons kept safely in the fiery furnace. Indeed, the promises of God were valid for them as they will be for us—"when you pass through the waters, I will be with you; and when you pass through the rivers, they will not sweep over you. When you walk through the fire, you will not be burned; the flames will not set you ablaze" (Isa. 43:2).

But Exactly Why Should We Be Here?

The question, *Why* should we be here? has a most wonderful answer. First of all, only a pampered, effete western Christianity can afford to believe in an end time that is tribulation free. The millions who suffered tribulation even unto death under atheistic communism and increasingly under radical Islam did not have that luxury! And should the saints suffer at the hands of godless men in these last days, it will only be out of love for our Lord Jesus that they will endure, willing to lay down their very lives for Him. The real reason for being here—the real reason for our actually *wanting* to be here—is that these last days are ordained by God to be days of unparalleled outpouring of the Holy Spirit and days of unprecedented harvest among the nations. And, simply stated, God has promised to take care of us in these days if we will but give ourselves to carry out His purposes of worldwide apostolic evangelism!

Scripturally, God has not relegated this harvest solely to Jews who are left behind but rather to His total Jewish–Gentile bride, the body of Messiah! Just note the implications of these precious promises: "In the last days, God says, I will pour out my Spirit on all people.... The sun will be turned to darkness and the moon to blood before the coming of the great and glorious day of the Lord. And everyone who calls on the name of the Lord will be saved" (Acts 2:17, 20–21) What a harvest is implicit in that "everyone" statement!

> Repent, then, and turn to God, so that your sins may be wiped out, that *times of refreshing may come from the presence of the* Lord, and that he may send the Christ, who has been appointed before you—even Jesus. He must remain in

heaven *until the time comes for God to restore everything,* as
He promised long ago through His holy prophets.

—ACTS 3:19–21, EMPHASIS ADDED

And what a glorious restoration that will be!

Also, "Israel has experienced a hardening in part until the full
number of Gentiles has come in. And so all Israel will be saved"
(Rom. 11:25–26). What a harvest that will be!

> Be patient, then, brothers, until the Lord's coming. See how
> the farmer waits for the land to yield its valuable crop and
> how patient he is for the autumn [early] and spring [latter]
> rains. You, too, be patient and stand firm because the Lord's
> coming is near.
>
> —JAMES 5:7–8

A grand end-time harvest just prior to Jesus' coming is clearly
promised. And as a result of the outpouring of the Spirit from
heaven, John could testify: "I looked and there before me was *a
great multitude that no one could count,* from every nation, tribe,
people and language.... These are they who have *come out of the
great tribulation*; they have washed their robes and made them
white in the blood of the Lamb" (Rev. 7:9, 14). Who would not want
to participate in such a glorious outpouring and harvest, right in
the midst of the Great Tribulation?

Scripturally, God's plans for the climax of the ages are clear: an
unparalleled end-time outpouring of His Holy Spirit, accompanied
by an unprecedented harvest of souls, including a restoration of
Israel to Himself. All of this will be accompanied by the protection of God's people from His falling wrath on the ungodly and
finally Jesus' glorious second coming! And Jesus' return includes
our mustering, our gathering together, to meet the Lord (literally,
to "greet the Lord in the air," 1 Thess. 4:17) and then, as His gathered and assembled army, to return with Him to reign over all the
earth (Rev. 19:14)! In that mustering, or gathering together, which is
the real *purpose* of the Rapture, the unprepared will be left behind
for judgment, but the prepared people of God will be wedded to our
Lord Jesus Christ forever at the glorious Wedding Supper of the

Lamb (Rev. 19:7, 9, 17). I can think of nothing more awesome for us to give ourselves to than these great and wide purposes of God in these last days! Amen!

—CHARLES P. SCHMITT

Appendix Five

"OTHER CHRISTS"

I N MARCH OF 2013 the author engaged in dialogue with a member of the Islamic sect, the Ahmadiyya, who believe that the second coming of Christ *has already come* in the person of their prophet Mirza Ghulam Ahmad. The following is the Ahmadiyya statement and then my response (which I trust was clear but gracious).

THE AHMADIYYA STATEMENT

I am a member of the Ahmadiyya Muslim Community. This community believes that there will be one Jesus/Messiah [POH] who will return, complete God's mission in the latter days, unite mankind, establish the Kingdom of God, and bring peace/justice to everyone. The time for the coming of the Messiah was more than a hundred years ago. In Qadian, India, Mirza Ghulam Ahmad[POH] claimed he was the Messiah of the latter days, he was Jesus [POH] in spirit. Why did he choose to spread Islam to the whole world? God says in the Holy Quran: "I have completed your teaching and named it Islam, which will remain with you forever." In the latter days, he gave this task to the Ahmadiyya Muslim Community, thus repeating the history of the first Messiah, Jesus. [POH]

MY RESPONSE

Thank you for your e-mails on the second coming of our Lord Jesus Christ. The return of our Lord Jesus Christ will be seen by all nations and they will mourn over their rejection of Him— "*all the nations* of the earth will mourn. *They will* see the Son of Man coming on the clouds of the sky, with power and great glory.*" True believers will know that Jesus has returned as

He taught us, *not* because people are saying "look, here is the Christ!" Or, "there he is!" We are told by Jesus: "Do not believe it. For false Christs and false prophets will appear" (Matt. 24:23–24). True believers will know that the true Jesus has returned *because* they will be caught up to meet Him in the air—"He will send His angels with a loud trumpet call, and they will gather his elect from the four winds, from one end of the heavens to the other" (Matt. 24:31). Paul describes this gathering in his first letter to the Thessalonians: "The Lord himself will come down from heaven, with a loud command, with the voice of the archangel and with the trumpet call of God, and…we will be caught up…in the clouds to meet the Lord in the air. And so we will be with the Lord forever" (1 Thess. 4:16–17).

John also similarly describes Jesus' second coming in Revelation 1:7: "Look, he is coming with the clouds, and every eye will see him, even those [Israel] who pierced him; and all the peoples of the earth will mourn because of him. So shall it be!" The prophet Zechariah also describes the second coming of the Messiah: "They will look on me, the one they have pierced, and they will mourn for Him as one who mourns for an only child" (Zech. 12:10). The prophet Zechariah carries this theme of the "Pierced One" forward in his statements in Zechariah 13:6–7: "If someone asks Him, 'What are these wounds in your hands?' He will answer, 'The wounds I was given at the house of my friends.' 'Awake, O sword, against my shepherd, against the man who is my companion!' declares the Lord Almighty. 'Strike the shepherd, and the sheep will be scattered.'"

The One whose return we are awaiting will come *openly;* He will be *seen by all nations;* He will come *with power and glory;* the nations, and especially Israel, will see Him as the One they pierced (with spear and thorns and nails); we, His saints, will be *caught up to meet Him* in the clouds of heaven and so we will be *with Him forever!* This is the second coming of our Lord Jesus Christ which we are waiting for.

When our Lord Jesus ascended into heaven after the resurrection, His followers were told explicitly: "This same Jesus, who has been taken from you into heaven, will come back in the same way you have seen him go into heaven" (Acts 1:10–11). It is for this soon coming of this same Jesus that we are waiting!

—CHARLES P. SCHMITT

Appendix Six

NOW IS THE TIME TO WORSHIP

As I have ministered in churches across the land, I have noticed the beautiful lyrics to the song "Now Is the Time to Worship" being sung by different congregations. Brian Doerksen, this song's author, has captured a powerful New Testament truth, dealing both with *the present* (the song is called "*Now Is the Time to Worship*") and also with *the future*.

The New Testament is very clear in its teachings concerning *the present* that "now is the day of salvation" (2 Cor. 6:2) and that "today, if you hear His voice, do not harden your hearts" (Heb. 3:7, 15). Salvation is God's offer for *today!* However, though the Scriptures insist that "now is the day of salvation" and that "today" is the day we are to respond to God, the Scriptures also declare the awesome truth that *one day* every tongue will confess Jesus as Lord. These are Paul's words in Philippians 2:8–9 concerning the overwhelming victory toward which our God is marching in the person of our Lord Christ Jesus! Just listen to Paul's exultation in this Scripture:

> [Jesus] "humbled himself and became obedient to death—even death on a cross! Therefore, God exalted him to the highest place and gave him the name that is above every name, that at the name of Jesus *every knee should bow*, in heaven and on earth and under the earth [in the underworld] and *every tongue confess that Jesus Christ is Lord, to the glory of God the Father.*
> —Philippians 2:8–11, emphasis added

What a marvelous declaration!

Unfortunately, we in evangelical circles, out of an unwarranted fear that these words could be a prelude to the unscriptural and extreme concept of universalism, have leaned away from rejoicing in this bold proclamation, or at least we have tried to minimize it by declaring that this universal acclaim of Jesus will be a "forced one," with vengeful hearts yet hating and resisting our Lord, or at best that these words will be fulfilled by the people in the Millennium or in eternity by a select group of people called "the elect." Other Scriptures, however, help clarify for us that our Lord's universal acclaim shall indeed be both *genuine* and *all-encompassing,* as it rises from *the whole of creation to the glory of God the Father!* Just listen to John's words in that marvelous statement in Revelation 5:13-14: "Then I heard *every* creature in heaven and on earth and under the earth [in the realms below] and on the sea, and *all* that is in them, singing: To Him who sits on the throne and to the Lamb be praise and honor and glory and power forever and ever!" What a marvelous finale to the whole of human history! This is a universal confession, if words mean anything, to the greatness of our Father and our Lord Jesus Christ!

Paul had already declared in 1 Corinthians 15:20–24 that this is the ultimate intent of our God in all of human history. Just listen to his words: "As in Adam all die, so in Christ all will be made alive. But each in his own turn: Christ, the firstfruits, then, when He comes, those who belong to Him." Obviously, those who "belong to Him" are those who have been born again; they are His. But we must then ask at this juncture, what about the *rest* of humanity? Just listen to Paul as he continues on: "Then the end will come, when He has destroyed all dominion, authority, and power." The Greek word for "destroy" is *katargeo,* which means "to make thoroughly inactive, to render powerless; to bring to an end; to destroy; to render inoperative; to do away entirely; to make of none effect."[39] Thus He shall destroy *all* opposing dominion and authority and power everywhere!

First Corinthians 5:25–28 continues: "For He must reign until He has put *all* His enemies under His feet. The last enemy to be destroyed is death. For He 'has put *everything* under His feet'... When He has done this, then the Son Himself will be made subject to Him [the Father] who put *everything* under Him [the Son], so that God may be *all in all*" (emphasis added). The Revised Standard Version translates this last phrase "that God may be everything to every one." What a marvelous consummation to human history! *Peake's Commentary on the Bible* describes this passage as "the final chord of Pauline theology."[40]

Paul in Ephesians 1:10 articulated the very heart of this central apostolic revelation when he spoke of "the mystery of [God's] will...which He purposed in Christ, to be put into effect when the times will have reached their fulfillment to bring all things in heaven and on earth together under one head, even Christ." C. B. Williams translates this arresting passage: "That at the coming of the climax of the ages, everything in heaven and on earth should be unified through Christ."[41] Greek scholar B. F. Westcott in his work, *Saint Paul's Epistle to the Ephesians,* comments concerning this verse: "This consummation lies beyond the unity of the Church, the Body of Christ...[and] it is altogether arbitrary to introduce any limitation into the interpretation of all things [Greek: ta panta]. The truth transcends our comprehension, but we see that it answers to the fact and purpose of creation."[42]

Finis Dake, in "Notes on Genesis" in his famed *Dake's Annotated Reference Bible,* apparently caught just such a vision. He comments: "In each dispensation, God has a definite and different immediate purpose, all working toward the ultimate purpose of ridding the universe of all rebellion, so that all free moral agents will be willingly and eternally subject to God, Christ, and the Holy Ghost, as originally planned, with God all in all forever."[43]

The same Book of Hebrews that pointedly declares that "today" is the day of salvation (Heb. 2:3; 4:7, 15) also declares of Christ that "in putting everything under Him, God left nothing that is not subject to Him" (Heb. 2:8).

Watchman Nee, in a thought-provoking treatise *God's Plan and the Overcomers,* a compilation of his teachings at a conference in Shanghai in 1943, collected together some of these profound New Testament thoughts in words similar to B. F. Westscott's and Finis Dake's. Nee declared:

> God works with a definite goal in mind...The purpose of God is centered on His Son, that in all things He might have the preeminence...that Christ might be 'all in all'....Today

believers are manifesting a little something of Christ. But one day all things shall manifest Christ because the whole universe shall be filled with Him....Before the creation of the world, God had a plan...to sum up in Christ all things which are in the heavens and on the earth....We are shown that the aim and purpose in whatever God does from eternity to eternity is to give the Son the preeminence in all things. For the purpose of God is to make his Son the Lord of all....We [the saved] are the firstfruits of all creation (cf. James 1:18). After we are in subjection to Christ, all other things will follow in subjection.[44]

If Scripture means anything, our God—and not Satan—is clearly destined to have the allegiance of the whole creation. Our Lord shall be glorified in His church, which is His body. But He—and not His enemies—shall be further renowned in the whole of His moral universe!

In conclusion, I wish to add that we cannot find a greater present impetus for seeking God's revival presence than this, for in times of revival *multitudes are thus drawn to Jesus—a fulfillment of our Lord's vision of Calvary's purposes* (John 12:31–33). Also, we cannot find a grander motivation for worldwide evangelism than this, that "He shall see of the travail of his soul, and shall be satisfied" (Isa. 53:11, KJV). Yes, we are able to go forth, impassioned for lost souls, not only to save them from the consuming fires of God's eternal judgments (from the loss spoken of by Jesus in Matthew 16:26 and from the destruction spoken of by Paul in 2 Thessalonians 1:7–10) but also—and of greatest importance—to contribute to that blessed hour in which our Lord Jesus shall have "put everything under His feet" (1 Cor. 15:27) and handed over the kingdom to our God and His Father, "so that God may be all in all" (1 Cor. 15:28), glorified and honored everywhere and among all, forever and ever! Of this great outcome, Paul exclaims with utter amazement: "Oh, the depth of the riches of the wisdom and knowledge of God! How unsearchable His judgments, and His paths beyond tracing out!...For from Him and through Him and to Him are all things. To Him be the glory forever! Amen!" (Rom. 11:33, 36).

—CHARLES P. SCHMITT

Appendix 7

A free periodical prophetic newsletter by Charles P. Schmitt,
available from www.immanuels.org

A MIDNIGHT CRY: AN ALERT
FROM CURRENT EVENTS ON
THE SIGNS OF THE TIMES
"The Two Faces of the Muslim World"

I RECENTLY FOUND MYSELF reading two books at the same time (which is unusual for me), only to realize that these two books complemented each other, clearly presenting the two faces of the Muslim world, a subject that has greatly exercised me in recent days.

The first book was Erick Stakelbeck's *The Brotherhood: America's Next Great Enemy*. Erick, with almost unbelievable documentation, unmasks the face of the jihadist world and its serious present threat to the United States from within. Erick, in his first chapter, "Islamist Winter Is Coming," begins his book with the motto of the Muslim Brotherhood: "Allah is our objective. The Prophet is our leader. Qur'an is our law. Jihad is our way. Dying in the way of Allah is our highest hope."

Erick then notes that whereas Al-Qaeda seeks to bring about Sharia states rapidly through violence, the Muslim Brotherhood favors a gradual, termite-like approach, burrowing deeply into a host society and eating away at it slowly from within. "They'll acquire positions of influence...They'll start Islamic organizations at the grassroots level...then, when they have the numbers and the influence...the final phase can begin."[45] This is what we have recently seen in North Africa, especially in Egypt, and according to Erick this is what is currently happening all across the United States, aided and abetted by some of our own government policies!

One example out of probably a hundred in the book stands out to me. Erick notes, "As far back as the early 1980s the Muslim

230

Brotherhood—an organization which declares jihad its way and martyrdom its highest hope—was engaging in *weapons training inside the United States*. This should have been front page news from coast to coast—but it wasn't" (emphasis added). Erick then wryly comments, "Wouldn't it be nice if the Department of Homeland Security, rather than drawing up memos warning about Tea Partiers and pro-life activists, devoted resources to investigating the Muslim Brotherhood's 'military work' on American soil?" Erick then observes that "liberals tell us talk of a Muslim Brotherhood plan to undermine America is just right-wing, racist paranoia." He adds, "If only [that] were so."[46]

I recommend reading Erick's book; we owe it to ourselves to examine his documentation. The Muslim Brotherhood, under its many pseudonyms, may be operative in our own city; as a matter of fact, according to Erick, it would be surprising if it were not!

The other book I was reading, *Muslims, Christians and Jesus* by Carl Medearis presents the other face of the Muslim world—the face turned toward God, seeking Him! Carl observes about the Quran, Islam's holy book, that "despite [the] theological differences, there is a gold mine running through the Qur'an: His name is Jesus (Isa). The Qur'an mentions Jesus about one hundred times, all with great reverence." Carl sets out to meet seeking Muslims on grounds familiar to them with the sole objective of leading them to Jesus. Carl recounted his time with a Saudi princess from the House of Saud. She was very well educated but also very much embittered against the West, America in particular. The fascinating dialogue between them concluded on this note as the princess joined Carl in prayer: "As we prayed, the Spirit of God entered the room. Within moments we were all in tears. She then prayed for God's Kingdom to enter into her heart through the anointed one—Jesus"![47]

Among the many other experiences born out of Carl's twelve years in the Middle East, the following one grabbed my heart the most. Carl was sitting in a hotel lobby in a small, southern Iraqi town when three young staff members walked over from the front desk and sat down to talk with him. In the course of the conversation Carl began to recount for them the story that Jesus told about the prodigal son. At one juncture Carl wrote:

I could sense the presence of the Holy Spirit. God was in that lobby. Just then, one of the young guys spoke up. "When I was ten, a German man gave my daddy a cassette of stories about Jesus. We gathered at our table and listened to that cassette every night for almost a year. Then it broke. That German man told my father that Jesus had a book out, but he didn't have one to give us. He told us to look for it and someday we'd get one. Do you know about the book Jesus has?"[48]

Carl responded, "Actually, I have one in my room. Can I get it for you?" Carl then writes:

I nearly tripped on the way [to my room] since I couldn't see through my tears...I brought it and handed it to him. His eyes widened as he clutched the copy and read the title..."the Gospel of Jesus Christ"...He [then] burst into tears, put it to his forehead, and then kissed it. Next, he surprised us all by running toward the front door. He yelled back, "I have to go show my father. He'll be so excited!"[49]

I heartily recommend Carl's book along with Erick's! Between these two books we can clearly see the two faces of the Muslim world. Jerry Trousdale, in *Miraculous Movements,* sums it up clearly:

When most Christians look at Muslims, they see a monolithic mass of humanity, staunch in their beliefs, ready to fight for their religion, and aggressively seeking to extend the role of Sharia law into all the world...[But] the Church of Jesus Christ is largely not aware that God Himself is working inside Islam, orchestrating events that are even now beginning to crack the foundations of Islam and prepare hearts to discover the loving God who sacrificed His Son that they might know Him.[50]

These are the two faces of the Muslim world: the jihadist antichrist face, bent on the destruction of Israel and the West; and then there is the face of the seeking Muslim world, seeking God, and by the hundreds of thousands finding Him through Jesus Christ our Savior! Let us both watch and pray, as Jesus asked us to do, for these *are* the last days!

NOTES

1.   Rambam, in Article 12 of the Thirteen Principles of Faith (Commentary to the Mishnah, Sanhedrin II); as quoted in *Tehillim* (Brooklyn, NY: Mesorah Publications, Ltd., 1985), 67.

2.   Joel Rosenberg, "Exclusive: Ahmadinejad's End Times Speech to the UN: Gives most detailed explanation of Twelfth Imam to date; tells UN leaders Madhi will "soon" reign over world," *Joel C. Rosenberg's Blog*, September 26, 2012, http://flashtrafficblog.wordpress.com/2012/09/26/exclusive-ahmadinejad-gives-most-detailed-explanation-of-twelfth-imam-to-date-says-mahdi-will-soon-reign-over-whole-world/ (accessed January 15, 2014).

3.   "670 Million Muslims Expect Mahdi in Their Lifetime." *World Net Daily*. August 12, 2012. Accessed at http://www.wnd.com/2012/08/670-million-muslims-expect-madhi-in-their-lifetime/ (November 21, 2013).

4.   Ayatullah Baqir Al-Sadr and Ayatullah Murtada Mutahhari, *The Awaited Savior* (Karachi: Islamic Seminary Publications, n.d.), 1; as quoted in Joel Richardson, *The Islamic Antichrist* (Los Angeles, CA: WND Books, 2009), 22.

5.   Al-Sadr and Mutahhari, *The Awaited Savior*, 3; as quoted in Joel Richardson, *The Islamic Antichrist*, 55.

6.   Mufti Mohammad Shafi and Mufti Mohammad Rafi Usmani, *Signs of the Qiyama and the Arrival of the Maseeh* (Karachi: Darul Ishat, 2000), 60; as quoted in Joel Richardson, *The Islamic Antichrist*, 54.

7.   Kenneth S. Wuest, *Wuest's Word Studies: In These Last Days* (Grand Rapids, MI: Wm. B. Eerdmans Publishing Company, 1954), 73.

8.   Thomas Newberry, *The Newberry Bible: The New Testament* (London: Hodder and Stoughton, MCMXLIX, printed in England).

9.   Joel Richardson, *Mideast Beast* (Washington D.C.: WND Books, 2012), 89–102.

10.   Richard Stengel, "Bibi's Choice," *Time*, May 28, 2012.

11.   Edmund Sanders, "Daystar, TBN Ready for Messiah in Jerusalem," *Los Angeles Times*, October 1, 2012.

12.   Recorded in Sahih Muslim Book 041, Number 7015; as quoted in Joel Richardson, *The Islamic Antichrist*, 52.

13.   Recorded in Sahih Muslim, Book 001, Number 0293, narrated by Jabir bin Abdullah and in Sais I-Nursi, "The Fifth Ray," in *The Rays*, 493, quoted in Ya hya, Jesus Will Return, 66. As quoted in Joel Richardson, *The Islamic Antichrist*, 53.

14.   Hakim Mustadrak (2:651) #4162 as related by Abu Harayra, as quoted in Muhammad Hisham Kabbani, *Approach of Armageddon?* (Washington D.C.: Islamic Supreme Council of America, 2003), 237; as quoted in Joel Richardson, *The Islamic Antichrist*, 53.

15. Shafi and Usmani, *Signs of the Qiyama and the Arrival of the Maseeh*, 60; as quoted in Joel Richardson, *The Islamic Antichrist*, 54.

16. James H. McConkey, as quoted in Mrs. Charles E. Cowman, *Springs in the Valley* (Grand Rapids, MI: Zondervan, 1968), 76.

17. Arthur Peake, with eds. Matthew Black and H.H. Rowley, *Peake's Commentary on the Bible* (Glasgow: Routledge Co. Ltd, 1962).

18. Leo Harris, "The Day Christ Returns," Crusade Publications, 1980.

19. Ruth Sachs, *Adolf Eichmann, Engineer of Death* (New York: The Rosen Publishing Group, 2001), 77.

20. National Park Service, U.S. Department of the Interior, "World War II Memorial: The Holocaust," http://www.nps.gov/wwii/historyculture/the-holocaust.htm (accessed January 14, 2014),

21. Joel Richardson, *Mideast Beast*, 155.

22. Sais I-Nursi, *The Rays*, "The Fifth Ray," 493, as quoted in Harun Yahya, *Jesus Will Return*, (London: Ta Ha, 2001), 66.

23. Al-Sadr and Mutahhari, *The Awaited Savior*, 3.

24. Sunan Abu-Dawud Book 37, Number 4310, narrated by AbuHurayrah; see also Sahih Bukhari Volume 3, Book 43, Number 656; as quoted in Joel Richardson, *The Islamic Antichrist*, 56.

25. Stephen Moore, "The National ID Card: It's Baaack!" *CATO Institute*, September 23, 1997, http://www.cato.org/publications/commentary/national-id-card-its-baaack (accessed January 14, 2014).

26. See http://forums.taleworlds.com/index.php?topic=226081.745;wap2 (accessed January 14, 2014).

27. "Turkey Cuts Euphrates Flow, Affecting Its Neighbors," *The New York Times*, January 14, 1990, http://www.nytimes.com/1990/01/14/world/turkey-cuts-euphrates-flow-affecting-its-neighbors.html (accessed January 13, 2014).

28. Tirmidhi as quoted in Ali Zubair and Mohammed Ali Ibn, *Signs of Qiyamah*, translated by M. Afzal Hoosein Elias (New Delhi: Abdul Naeem, 2004), 42; and Professor M. Abdullah, *Islam, Jesus, Medhi, Qadiyanis and Doomsday* (New Delhi: Adam, 2004), 54; as quoted in Joel Richardson, *The Islamic Antichrist*, 45.

29. William Smith, *Bible Dictionary* (Grand Rapids, MI: Zondervan, 1948, p.284); also 1884 copyright by Porter and Coates, in Great Britain.

30. Quoted from John Horsch, *The Hutterian Brethren*, as quoted in Charles P. Schmitt, *Floods Upon the Dry Ground* (Shippensburg, PA: Revival Press), 101.

31. Tim McHyde, "Malachy's Last Pope Identified—In Bible Prophecy," *Escape All These Things*, http://www.escapeallthesethings.com/last-pope-prophecy.htm (accessed January 13, 2014). See also "Uncanny! Popes' Coats of Arms Back Up Prophecy," *WND*, July 27, 2013, http://www.wnd.com/2013/07/uncanny-popes-coats-of-arms-back-up-prophecy/ (accessed January 13, 2014).

32. Barry Segal, "Syrian Insurgents Brutally Behead Catholic Priest and Two Others," *Jerusalem-on-the-Line*, July 7, 2013.

33.   Ashraf Sweillam, "Christian Killed in Egypt by Suspected Militants; Magdy Hibashi Decapitated in Sinai." Associated Press. *Huffington Post*, July 11, 2013. Accessed at http://www.huffingtonpost.com/2013/07/11/christian-killed-egypt-militants_n_3579741.html (November 23, 2013).

34.   Charles P. Schmitt, *Floods Upon the Dry Ground* (Shippensburg, PA: Revival Press), 68.

35.   Ibid., 86.

36.   Jason Mandryk, *Operation World*, 7th ed. (Colorado Springs, CO: Biblica, 2010), 864.

37.   St. Augustine, as quoted in *A Select Library of the Nicene and Post-Nicene Fathers of the Christian Church, Volume II*, edited by Philip Schaff (New York: Charles Scribner's Sons, 1887), 443.

38.   Gerhard Pfandi, "The Rapture: Why It Cannot Occur Before the Second Coming." *Ministry*, September 2001.

39.   *The Analytical Greek Lexicon*, (London: Samuel Bagster and Sons Limited, 1794, London), 219, s.v. "Katargeo." See also Joseph Henry Thayer, D.D., *A Greek-English Lexicon of the New Testament*, (Grand Rapids, MI: Zondervan, 1953), 336, s.v. "Katargeo."

40.   Arthur Peake, with eds. Matthew Black and H.H. Rowley, *Peake's Commentary on the Bible*, s.v. "1 Corinthians 5:20–28."

41.   Charles B. Williams, *The New Testament* (Chicago, IL: Moody Press, 1955).

42.   B.F. Westcott, *Saint Paul's Epistle to the Ephesians* (Ithaca, NY: Cornell University Library, 2009).

43.   Finis J. Dake, ed. *Dake Annotated Reference Bible: King James Version* (Lawrenceville, GA: Dake Publishing, Inc., 1963), 49.

44.   Watchman Nee, *God's Plan and the Overcomers* (Fort Washington, PA: Christian Literature Crusade, 1980).

45.   Erick Stakelbeck, *The Brotherhood: America's Next Great Enemy* (Washington, D.C.: Regnery Publishing, Inc., 2013).

46.   Ibid.

47.   Carl Medearis, *Muslims, Christians and Jesus* (Minneapolis, MN: Bethany House, 2008).

48.   Ibid.

49.   Ibid.

50.   Jerry Trousdale, *Miraculous Movements* (Nashville, TN: Thomas Nelson, 2012).

ABOUT THE AUTHOR

Charles P. Schmitt grew up in the Dutch Reformed Church in Brooklyn, New York. He was trained at Prairie Bible Institute in Alberta, Canada and then at Bethany College of Missions in Minneapolis, Minnesota. Charles also has four earned degrees, including a D. Min. and a Th. D., and a conferred Doctor of Divinity. Charles, with his wife of 50 years, Dotty, originally served in church leadership in Northern Minnesota, and now serve as lead pastors on the pastoral team of Immanuel's Church, a multicultural church of thousands in the Washington DC area, which began in their home. Both Charles and Dotty also travel extensively in world missions and in conference ministry in the United States. They have authored ten books between them, some of which have been translated into Russian, Spanish, Nepali and Telegu. The Schmitts have three married daughters and five wonderful grand-children. The passion of the Schmitt family is to see the ongoing out-pouring of the Holy Spirit in revival power across the United States and around the world right up to the return of Jesus.

CONTACT THE AUTHOR

You may reach Charles Schmitt by
visiting *www.immanuels.org.*